P9-CMK-610

Medieval Cultural Tradition in Dante's *Comedy*

Medieval Cultural Tradition in Dante's *Comedy*

By Joseph Anthony Mazzeo

CORNELL UNIVERSITY

GREENWOOD PRESS, PUBLISHERS
NEW YORK 1968

CORNELL UNIVERSITY PRESS

First published 1960

Reprinted with the permission of

CORNELL UNIVERSITY PRESS

First Greenwood reprinting, 1968

LIBRARY OF CONGRESS catalogue card number: 68-23313

PRINTED IN THE UNITED STATES OF AMERICA

TO

Dino Bigongiari

Preface

THE several chapters of this book are studies of some of the most important principles of structure of the *Divine Comedy* and their relation to characteristic ways of organizing experience in medieval intellectual culture. In the first chapter on hierarchy I have discussed the most important of such concepts and have attempted to give some indication of its place in medieval thought, of the way in which hierarchical models of organization were influential in unifying important areas of moral and intellectual experience as well as the way in which they set the stage for new conflicts, problems, and values.

The first chapter serves as an introduction to all the rest, since the hierarchical vision of the world is the guiding presupposition and, so to speak, contains all the other principles of structure treated in this book—light metaphysics, analogy, and even typology or figuralism to the extent that the *Comedy* involves a hierarchical ordering of such types. The second chapter introduces the reader to the fundamental conceptions of light metaphysics, the doctrine which makes the *Comedy*, and especially the *Paradiso*, a hierarchy of light. Chapter III applies the foregoing material to the works of Dante, and Chapters IV and V give examples of analogical and typological organization respectively. In my treatment of analogy I have tried to give some other uses of analogical principles of organization in literature, especially in seventeenth-century metaphysical poetry, in order to specify the precise and particular way that Dante uses this principle. Although my treatment involves a chronological reversal of order, it follows the order of greater familiarity of subject matter. In my last chapter I found it necessary to interpret Dante's self-corrections, especially those with regard to Epicurus, in order to unfold the process by which Epicurus becomes a type of heresy and comes to occupy a lower place in the hierarchy of evil moral states. As will be demonstrated, he might have been treated as simply one more pagan philosopher doomed to spend eternity in the melancholy pleasures of a perpetual colloquium with his colleagues. The Appendix is a further contribution to the study of Dante's derivation of symbolic values from norms given in the medieval cultural tradition.

Part of the research and writing of this book was done on a Guggenheim Fellowship, and I wish to express my gratitude to the John Simon Guggenheim Memorial Foundation for their generosity and the condition of perfect freedom with which they endow their fellows. Thanks also are due the staff of the library of Cornell University who have been helpful in many ways, especially in making the magnificent medieval and Dante collections as easy as possible to use in far from ideal circumstances. My gratitude goes as well to Professor Robert Martin Adams of Cornell University, who read the manuscript and made many happy suggestions. He, like all others who ever assisted me, receives the traditional absolution for whatever scholarly sins I have committed in this book.

Those chapters or portions of chapters previously published and covered by copyright are here reprinted, often with substantial changes, by permission of the original publishers. Chapter II and part of Chapter III originally appeared in *Traditio*, XIV (1958), 191–229, as "Light Metaphysics, Dante's *Convivio*" and the "Letter to Can Grande della Scala"; part of Chapter III in *Romance Philology*, XI (1957), 1–17, as "Light, Love and Beauty in the *Paradiso*"; parts of Chapter IV in *Modern Philology*, L (1952), 88–96, as "A Critique of Some Modern Theories of Metaphysical Poetry," in the *Journal of the History of Ideas*, XV (1954), 299–304, as "Universal Analogy in the Culture of the Renaissance," and in *Speculum*, XXXII (1957), 706–721, as "The Analogy of Creation in Dante"; parts of Chapter V in *Comparative Literature*, X (1958), 106–120, as "Dante and Epicurus," and in *Philological Quarterly*, XXXVIII (1959), 30–36, as "*Convivio* IV, xxi and *Paradiso* XIII: Another of Dante's Self-Corrections"; and the Appendix in *Studies in Philology*, LV (1958), 457–463, as "A Note on the 'Sirens' of *Purgatorio* XXXI, 45."

I would like to thank J. M. Dent and Sons, Ltd., for permission to quote from Philip Wicksteed's translation of the *Convivio* (1903); the Harvard University Press for permission to quote from H. Rackham's translation of Cicero's *De finibus* (Loeb Classical Library; 1914); John Lane, The Bodley Head,

Ltd., and the Oxford University Press for permission to quote from J. D. Sinclair's translation of the *Divine Comedy* (1948); the Oxford University Press for the use of Paget Toynbee's translation of the *Letters* (1920) and for permission to cite from A. C. Crombie's *Robert Grosseteste and the Origins of Experimental Science* (1953); Random House for permission to quote from Etienne Gilson's *The History of Christian Philosophy in the Middle Ages* (1955); and Mr. Austin Warren for permission to quote from his *Richard Crashaw: A Study in Baroque Sensibility* (1939).

J. A. M.

Ithaca, New York
May 1960

Contents

I

The Medieval Concept of Hierarchy

MODERN structural criticism of the *Divine Comedy* has turned for light on the organization of the poem to a deep and far-reaching study of medieval civilization and to a fresh application of what has been learned about the cultural context of the *Comedy*. For the most part the scholarly labors of the past were in the nature of "glosses." When Dante made reference to a philosophical or theological doctrine or to a scientific theory, this was explained in a note, and the reader was able to proceed to the next roadblock, which was again conveniently and more or less accurately removed.

The new approach considers the *Comedy* as a microcosm of the universe seen as the great medieval thinkers conceived it, a microcosm whose structural principles are the same as those of the macrocosm to which it is analogically related. Simultaneously, it is conceived to have a similar analogy to the book of Scripture so that its allegory demands an attitude in the reader different from what would otherwise be the case. It is important, too, to realize that both the structural and the literary principles of the *Divine Comedy* are conceived in a dynamic or organic way and not statically. For example, the structure of Dante's *Paradiso* is obviously Ptolemaic, and a clear idea is given of what it looks like. The problem is, rather, what are the principles or powers that propel the poet and his guides through the universe, and how do they operate? What convictions concerning history and personality guide the placement of the characters? In fine, the knowledge concerning medieval modes of thought is used to ask how we get from the beginning through the middle to the end of the *Comedy* and why we learn and meet those at each stage of the journey.

Hence, modern Dante scholarship has concerned itself with questions of allegory, figuralism, symbolism, figural realism, the concept of memory, and the notion of autobiography.

I would like to emphasize that although this approach to the study of the *Comedy* is rooted in scholarship it is really equally removed from the purely "aesthetic" criticism of De Sanctis or Croce and the scholarly studies of Bruno Nardi or Auguste Renaudet, the latter devoted to elucidating the doctrinal and philosophic passages of the poem or to interpreting Dante's thought on various questions. The *Comedy* is not written in the twofold allegory of the poets in which the literal meaning of the poem is conceived to be an envelope for a moral truth. As C. S. Singleton among others has shown, the model of allegory which the *Comedy* imitates is theological, a fourfold allegory in which things and events are signs. This knowledge calls attention to the peculiar status of the poem itself, removed from the category of fiction in the sense that Ovid wrote fictions, although not literally true in the sense that Livy is true. When the status of the poem is understood from the point of view established by a study of medieval exegetical theories, we come to know more clearly what are the appropriate critical questions. The antithesis "either-or" in connection with the allegorical significance of Beatrice or Virgil simply falls away when it is realized that we are to "believe" in these characters as both historical and figurative.[1]

Similarly a study of medieval rhetorical theory and its view of poetry as a branch of knowledge with species and subspecies, as *scientia*, can throw light on Dante's linguistic virtuosity and refinements of rhetorical techniques and permit us to see the *Comedy* as a poem which both rivals and completes the cardinal instances of the poetry of the past, classical as well as medieval. From this point of view the critic will discover in the texture of the poem not simply the history of the world but the history of poetry itself as that history looked to Dante.

Traditional Dante scholarship has, of course, been concerned with the structure of the poem, the outlines of the physical and moral cosmology. For the most part, however, the structure has been abstracted from the poem itself and studied in isolation from the unfolding dramatic progress. The true structure of the poem qua poem is not given by the moral system of *Hell* or *Purgatory*, or the theological system of *Paradise*, but by the interaction of character and event with the system which contains them. From this point of view the critic should be ever mindful that he must experience the poem from a double perspective, and simultaneously, as furnished by both poet and pilgrim, God and man, moral system and the dramatic response of the characters in the poem to each other as well as to the system itself.

The failure to see from a multiple perspective at once has led to some crude simplifications of Dante's moral vision. Thus romantic criticism was fascinated by the heroes in *Hell*, Ulysses or Farinata, or by an erotic heroine such as Francesca; these characters were taken from their context and presented as characters pure and simple, as if the reader of the poem were passing through a gallery of portraits. More theologically minded readers dwelt on the articulation of the structure of sin and the interrelationships between various specific sins, on the *Inferno*, for example, as a metaphor for the possibilities of human damnation. Yet the perspective which Dante demands is complex and somewhere between these two foci.

Dante, for example, places Ulysses in Hell because he is an example of the sin of *curiositas*, the thirst for knowledge unchecked by the demands of morality, the desire for mere experience, and it must be understood that the poet, if not the pilgrim, judges that sin worthy of damnation. So Dante the pilgrim (still a sinner in the Inferno) "glorifies" Ulysses in order that Dante the poet may condemn him. But it must not be concluded that we are asked to make a simple judgment on this figure or that the values clustered around the "event" Vanni Fucci or the "event" Ulysses are the same. They are neither the same nor reducible to the one category of damnation pure and simple. Sin is not only the dark negation of willful evil like thievery or treachery but is also a perversion of a good, its misuse or "misordering," and the good may shine through its own distortion.

A St. Augustine may see all mortal sin as finally, in the eyes of God, equally monstrous, but the very point of having a system of punishments in the *Inferno* is that we are thereby called upon to consider moral evil as something graded and hence understandable as a complex interweaving of worth and negation. Some admirable gifts of human nature may be employed in a sinful manner and be damnable, not in their origins or intrinsic nature, but in the goals to which they are applied. In the *Inferno* it is sometimes the function of the system as well as of the "action" to indicate the mode of disorder of some valuable human trait, presented to us as valuable at the same time that the context of its use subjects it to a negative judgment. Sin is thus for Dante not merely a matter of degree but also a matter of kind. Indeed, quantitative degree passes into difference of kind—a good altered and corrupted by being out of its hierarchical place loses its references to the final good.

It seems to me that the uses of theological and philosophical erudition in the study of the moral dimension of Dante's poem lie in giving us the structural system which provides us with the abstract judgments against which the pilgrim delineates the complex, paradoxical, and ironic judgments of concrete moral experience. Thus the philosophy and theology of the poem are as much poetry as anything else and serve not to simplify our moral judgments but to complicate them, by forcing us to relate the judgment of the system with the life, history, and action of the characters.

It is precisely this critical act which Croce and his followers failed to perform. Whatever the merits of Croce's aesthetic may be, his practical criticism presents us with a *Divine Comedy* which is little more than a number of passages of extreme lyrical intensity set in the matrix of "unpoetic" discourses on obsolete philosophy and theology. De Sanctis, on the other hand, powerfully renders the great episodes and characters of the poem, and few critics have been as sensitive to the way in which Dante can use a word or a phrase to bring his great creations to life. Yet he removes the characters from the context of the poem and inevitably simplifies them morally. They are presented to us as embodiments of passions and sentiments, and we forget that they inhabit one or another of the three great realms of the beyond. It must be acknowledged that De Sanctis, in spite of his great merits, finally gives us as much of an anthologist's *Comedy* as Croce, a poem of peaks and valleys, the peaks brilliantly illuminated and the valleys covered in darkness.

It is interesting to observe that the opposite, glossarial, approach to the *Comedy* arrives at a curiously similar critical result. The studies of Nardi, Reade, and other scholars who have approached Dante from the disciplines of intellectual and cultural history and placed him in relation to his time have given us many valuable glosses on the text. Although this is an indispensable propaedeutic for criticism, it is not criticism (or perhaps even intended to be criticism), and more remains to be done. Dante, after all, is a poet and handles ideas in a poet's way. They are part of the architecture and texture of the poem itself and, though they are not its flesh and substance, they are its nervous and circulatory system, the network of structure through which the poem functions. To study them as statements isolated from their function in the poem is finally to dismember the poem in as radical and unintelligible a manner as sectioning it into poetic and unpoetic passages.

Let me emphasize, however, that I am not objecting to the genuine achievements of Dante scholarship, but only to the limitations of a method which may discourage us from making the ultimately proper use of erudition. Thus modern Dante scholarship would agree that we must come to the poem with our awareness heightened by a study of medieval culture, for the true poetic of the *Comedy* is not, in the narrow sense of the word, literary. Its poetic is related to that larger "poetic" which makes the *Summa theologiae* and the cathedral of Chartres imitations of universal history and nature as they were interpreted in medieval culture. The poem is not governed by exclusively literary theories of allegory, but by principles of medieval scholastic realism which state a real analogy between God and His creatures. It is a work of *exempla*, *figurae*, and "epiphanies." The architecture of the poem is that of the real world of medieval thought, and, like that world, its events, characters, and landscape are not merely things but signs as well. Thus the characters of the poem are not only themselves but, like any "medieval" reality, representatives or signs of their spiritual condition.

In other words, the role of the cultural freight brought into our reading of the *Comedy* must be to establish a proper point of view and open our minds to forms of literary structure and statement which might otherwise be missed. Learning establishes the postulates of a poetic belief which is logically prior to the further poetic belief that the fiction of the poem is true. It must be related to the dynamics of the poem, the successive dramatic action, the changing moral states of the pilgrim, the statements of those who guide him in interpreting his various encounters. Thus the doctrinal content of the poem must be related to the fundamental distinction between Dante the pilgrim, the growing, changing character of the poet who goes from sin to salvation, and Dante the poet who constructs the world which the pilgrim is discovering. And if, in a sense, the poet has the last word and finally takes over from the pilgrim, we must nevertheless not veer too much to his side, the side of God or the divine judgment which distributes the inhabitants of the poem to their proper places.

In escaping from the sentimentalizing of De Sanctis and his followers we may run into the opposite extreme. If we see Brunetto as a mass of sin and error without redeeming traits, presumably because Dante would have seen him that way, we may be as false to the truth of the poem as the romantics.

In the first place I doubt that it is "medieval" to deny all worth to the damned. In fact, it seems like the Manichaean heresy to do so. Pure evil is nothing, so St. Augustine tells us, and even Lucifer himself, so far as he has any being whatever, is to that degree good. The power of the Brunetto episode lies, at least partly, in the very tension between the spontaneous impulse of the finite consciousness of the pilgrim and his shock at the working of divine judgment in this instance. We are, after all, sinners like the pilgrim and, perhaps, even like the poet, not in his role as theologian but in his role as author of the *Divine Comedy*. Dante's vision is a literary one. This means that it is precisely in the incommensurability between the divine and the human judgment that the complexity of his moral vision lies. It is the moral tension of the passage and not the judgment furnished by the divine *system* alone that moves us. There is a sense in which Dante always remained a poet and therefore a "sinner." The consciousness of a saint, insofar as he is saintly, is almost by definition unliterary, and the blessed in heaven have no more need of literature than of food and drink. Dante must have remained fascinated to the end by the very diversity of experience that the mystic ignores. I am trying to suggest that the procedure of transferring to Dante the perceptions of a St. Thomas or any other figure taken as some kind of medieval standard of culture and sensibility has its risks. Gravest among these is the simplification of the moral vision of the medieval period in order to imply that the men of that time were insensitive to moral paradox, to the antinomies present in any life of choice.

Another way of saying this is to say that the *Divine Comedy* is not exhausted in an analysis of its relation to its times, as if we could exclude the actualities of the work from our conception of the "time" and its "possibilities." The critic must also address himself to what the work says to our own time. Otherwise he may imprison the work in the categories of history and reduce it to a document, to something merely typical. One of the good things about historical reconstruction of the literature of the past is that it permits us to share more fully in a different set of values, to look at the world differently. But whether the locus of literary judgment and value is to be placed in this same act is another question entirely.

We need to know many things about medieval culture in order to read Dante's great poem with maximum understanding and pleasure and with full appreciation of Dante's poetic greatness. And much of what we know is "unliterary," as philosophy, cosmology, and history. In short, we must learn the systems of the poem, its principles of structure, so that we can understand how we get from the beginning, through the middle, to the end, and where we have been once we have made the journey. Its structure is also function, so that the "thought" of the poem is as much poetry as any other element we can abstract from it. Thus the moral or any other system of the poem cannot be isolated as its full truth. As sinner, as penitent, and as reconstituted natural man rising through the heavens, Dante never loses his wonder at the divine judgment. If Brunetto is unexpectedly in Hell, Manfred is surprisingly enough in Purgatory, and who could have imagined Ripheus in Paradise? Briefly, the poem imitates the ways of God even to imitating the ultimate inscrutability of his judgments, their apparent disproportion when considered from the ordinary view of the relations between guilt and retribution, merit and reward. Dante's characters are all unique instances; they call for a unique response in each case, and they live in that truly literary realm where moral values intersect and where competing judgments vie with each other in their unsuccessful attempts to absorb the particular wholly, for it is only to God that the moral universe is simple. The pilgrim who travels through the poem is really learning a very important lesson in how to be morally solvent, how to do business with all of reality including that aspect which is unredeemable, unchangeable, and incurable, with that part of the universe which declares that certain things are so whether we like them or not and whether we understand them or not.

In the last analysis, what I am discussing is the question of the uses of Dante scholarship, and, it seems to me, at the present time we can best contribute to our understanding of the poem if we consider medieval culture as furnishing Dante with "models" for organizing experience and for defining the characters he created, even though both experience and character are not exhausted by the perspective the model affords. Such a concept is not unfamiliar to modern philosophers and corresponds to Wittgenstein's concept of a "paradigm" or Whitehead's of the unconscious presuppositions of thought. Nor is it unfamiliar to the psychoanalyst, whose intent is to disclose to his patient the unconscious models or patterns which govern his behavior and through which he interprets the world. One modern philosopher defines the activity of the metaphysician by analogy with that of the psychoanalyst, as the bringing to light of established models which all men use to comprehend the character of certain classes of statements. The metaphysician's intent, however, is not to destroy or change the model but to become aware of both its power to illuminate and its limitations. Any complex pattern demands a model if we are to manage it, but we must always comprehend that the model can also distort as well as organize experience.[2]

Applied to literary criticism the concept of the model serves to clarify the problem of establishing the reader's point of view. If Dante demands that we read the *Divine Comedy* in a mode analogous to the way we ought to read Scripture, then we are asked to alter our point of view in a very significant way, for we view the poem through a different model. Similarly, if we understand the properties of light in the *Paradiso*, we will see what we were not previously able to see, for we understand the model for this part of the cosmic journey and can thus raise the proper critical questions.[3]

The essays in this book might now be defined as studies in the models of the *Divine Comedy*—the model of light, the analogical model, and the typological model—and, as such, preparations for and aids to a structural and holistic study of the poem. But before we turn to these problems, we ought first to examine another model which is even more fundamental than these, not only to the *Divine Comedy* but to the whole of medieval culture, the model of hierarchy.

The medieval concept of hierarchy in its philosophically most self-conscious form was by no means a simple metaphysical picture. An intimate part of it was the archetype-icon or exemplar-image analogy, for the hierarchy of reality ended in the divine archetype, and each grade or step up the ladder to the Absolute bore an analogical relationship to the final term in the series. Thus to grasp fully the nature of medieval hierarchism—and the subsequent studies in this book depend on an adequate comprehension of this principle of organization—we must first turn to analogical exemplarism, the concept on which hierarchical thought is based.

The point of departure for subsequent thought on the

analogy between God and creatures is a crucial passage from the *Timaeus* of Plato in which he tells us that the universe is a perceptible God made in the image of the intelligible (92C). There are thus, so to speak, two "Gods," one of the world of the senses and the other of the intelligible world, the world which is a paradigm (*paradeigma, eide*) or system of ideas.[4]

Plato tells us also that the cosmos perceptible to sense must be a copy of something else (*Timaeus* 29B). Man himself is such a copy, and this fact is merely the special case of a necessary principle. This special anthropological application of the principle of participation or imitation was not developed by Plato but was later elaborated by his followers. Thus by the time of Posidonius and the Stoic school, concepts such as *pneuma*, *logos*, *nous*, and *psyche*, which described the human spiritual or intellectual faculties, were held to be *eikona* or images of some more universal reality.[5]

Still later the Neoplatonists made the soul itself, in its unity, a divine image just as the statue of a god was a divine image (*agalma theion*) of an invisible reality. This development was important, for it clearly extended the concept of image from purely sensible realities to include purely intelligible realities, so that even the latter became in turn "images" of a still higher reality which is beyond predication. Such a result was inevitable after the Neoplatonists placed the Absolute beyond the realm of ideas, in the One, a reality which transcends the duality of thought and its object. The meaning of *eikon* was further enlarged when the term came to be applied to the mystic who was trying to assimilate (*homoiosis*) his soul to God and when, through Oriental influences, the king or emperor came to be regarded as a divine image.[6]

Further complexities in the meaning of the term were introduced with the rise of Christianity which brought the biblical doctrine of man as the image of God to the attention of philosophically trained Christians. In Genesis (1: 26 ff.) this term was meant to convey originally the idea of a physical likeness between God and man, although it later came to mean the supremacy of man over all other natural creatures (Cf. Psalm 8: 6 ff.). When, however, during the Hellenistic and patristic period Hebrew and Christian thought came into close interaction, the idea was intellectualized along Neoplatonic lines as in the work of Philo and Clement of Alexandria.[7]

Still another Platonic locus lies behind the tradition of hierarchical exemplarism, one which helps to explain the spiritual and moral uses which came to be made of such a view of the world. In the *Theaetetus* Plato tells us that there are really, from the moral point of view, only two patterns in the universe. One is the most blessed divine one, the other the most wretched godless one (176E). We must, of course, conform to the right pattern, and this is accomplished by escaping from the world. Such an escape is achieved by becoming as much like God as possible, and to become like God is to become righteous, holy, and wise (*Theaetetus* 176B). Thus exemplaristic thought was from the beginning bound to notions of escape from the world of illusion or imitations of the world of reality, and it is easy to see how these notions provided the rationale for Neoplatonic mysticism. The principles of exemplarism, of analogy within hierarchy, passed into the Christian tradition, and with further accretions from Neoplatonic sources became the keystone of the profoundly influential system of Pseudo-Dionysius the Areopagite.

The works of Pseudo-Dionysius the Areopagite enjoyed enormous prestige in the Middle Ages—and even thereafter—because they were believed to have been written by the same Dionysius the Areopagite whom St. Paul converted on his visit to Athens. The treatises attributed to him were probably written around A.D. 500 by a Syrian monk who was thoroughly acquainted with the works of Proclus, the last great pagan Neoplatonist. It would not be too exaggerated to say that whatever cultural unity medieval intellectual culture possessed was largely derived from the influence of Dionysius. Of course, no medievalist any longer believes, without some qualification, that the Middle Ages was a period of cultural unity. We know too much about medieval skeptics, rationalists, mystics, and heretics not to be fully aware of the great conflicts which arose within the unity of medieval culture. If we go outside the area of intellectual and philosophical culture, the diversity of medieval civilization becomes even more marked. Ecclesiastical and university ideals, the culture and ethic of the court, the values of the feudal military and political structure all seem to be fundamentally irreconcilable with one another. In spite of the attempts to spiritualize courtly love and to transform the fierceness of the feudal warriors by teaching them a code of religious chivalry, the flesh and war remained outside the control of the most exalted moral reforms. The romantic and adulterous ideal of love flourished in the very heart of a Christian civilization, and war remained for the most part as brutal and cruel as it had ever been.

Yet, at least in the realm of thought, there was a profound unity which overlaid most of the differences, wide as they were. As Ernst Cassirer has pointed out, there is perhaps no better way to grasp this unity than by studying the writings attributed to Dionysius the Areopagite, especially *On the Celestial Hierarchy* and *On the Ecclesiastical Hierarchy*.[8]

Although Dionysius accepts, as he must, the Christian principle of divine creation, his universe is constructed on the Plotinian principle of emanation. All things proceed from the first principle, the One, and all things are to be understood as derived from this first principle and as directly or indirectly related to it. Orthodox as he is in his theory of creation, Dionysius yet imagines this process in a pure Neoplatonic manner, as a diffusion of light from a primal source, a point of infinite intensity. As this ray descends, it creates all things —angels, men, animals, plants, matter, the lower forms of creation emerging as the ray becomes less and less intense. Beyond the ray is darkness, negation, the end of emanation and of being. Yet between the positive and negative infinities lies a system bound together in a "golden chain," for each rank in the resultant hierarchy strives to ascend and each one to transmit its divine light to the one below. The system is thus simultaneously a system of creation and of exaltation, an outgoing and a return.

The principle of order in this universe is hierarchy; the ray of light is a ladder of light, and light is the principle of being, goodness, beauty, each of the creations of the divine ray being a finite mirror image (*speculum*) of God, a theophany or manifestation of the divine, an image of the divine exemplar. The scale or hierarchy of existence is thus the scale of value whether ethical or aesthetic. Further, the hierarchical system is bound together by a system of analogical relations which obtain between the various levels of the ladder.

Let us now turn briefly to an examination of the doctrine of analogy in Pseudo-Dionysius and its relation to later scholastic doctrine. The term analogy in religious scholastic thought designates the kind of relationship which obtains between God and the creation. It defines this relationship as a kind of proportion between created and uncreated being. There cannot be identity between the two for this would mean pantheism, nor can there be an utter disparity between these two kinds of being or man would have no knowledge of God at all. It was in order to avoid these two dilemmas that Christian thinkers worked out the notion of the analogy of being, whereby the temporal perfections we attribute to God are seen to exist pre-eminently in Him.[9]

The source of the scholastic version of the doctrine of analogy is ultimately Aristotle, but it is abundantly clear that the whole universe of Dionysius is analogically constructed. If among other names God had the name of light, then the universe is made of mirrors. If God is the archetype, then the objects of the created world are really images (*eikona*, *agalmata*) in the sense that sculptured representations of the pagan gods were images of the invisible powers they represented. Finally, if God is the divine, then the created world is a system of theophanies or divine manifestations. All created things are more or less obscure images (*aenigmata*) of the divine.[10]

Thus the relationship between God and creature is not strictly something which exists at all. For St. Thomas and St. Bonaventura the things in the created world are signs which yield a dim but definite knowledge of the divine, whereas for Dionysius they are really symbols which point to a reality that they cannot even begin to define but can only somehow indicate. Creatures are primarily pointers, not "words" or true signs in the divine book of creatures.

So much for the ultimate status of creation. Yet Dionysius also tells us that the ideas or models of things (*paradeigmata*) do actually exist in God, although in some kind of unified way, as the principle which determines the order of the universe.[11] While the relationship of the divine cause to created effects is one of manifestation, the relationship of effects to cause is one of imitation (*mimesis*) or participation (*methexis*). The models are thus the causal principles (*aitiai archai*), but they are also the goals (*symperasmata*) toward which created things strive. Dionysius also conceives of these models as "predeterminations" (*proorismoi*) or "divine wills" (*theia thelemata*), so that the goal of every creature is the accomplishment of the divine will.[12]

The scholastic or Aristotelian-Thomistic theory of analogy is, in a sense, contained in Dionysius' system as a relative truth or as a special case within a larger whole which negates the ultimate validity of the doctrine. It would almost seem that Dionysius has a kind of modal view of ultimate reality, whereby the scholastic conception of analogy is seen as a relative mode for comprehending ultimate reality.

Thus analogy for Dionysius does not signify an actual correspondence between God and creatures but simply that which determines the possible imitation of the inimitable.[13] It is primarily a function of the capacity of creatures to participate in the divine virtues, and the capacity or "analogy" varies in creatures, determining the degree of being they possess and therefore their rank in the hierarchical structure of the universe. "Analogy" is not a passive faculty, however, for it is a function of the impulse that all creatures have to "love" their cause. In man this implanted natural love is a function of free will, and his goal, like that of all creatures conscious and unconscious, is assimilation (*aphomoiosis*) or union (*henosis*) with the divine.[14]

It is important for us to bear in mind that the idea of union or assimilation does not mean the disruption of the hierarchical principle. The universal ladder of creatures is not one that God intends to pull up after Him in some final age in which all things will become God or reach a state of uniform perfection. Some centuries before Dionysius, Origen had maintained such an evolutionary view of the universal process, but for Dionysius created beings will all achieve their supreme goal without breaking out of their proper hierarchical order.

God manifests Himself differently in each creature according to the analogy (capacity or proportion) it possesses. He confers His "vision" (*theoria*), participation (*koinonia*), and resemblance (*homoiosis*) according to the mode pre-established for each one. A perfect vision of God through theophanies will occur in some future time when all the blessed will have fully realized their pre-established analogies, their preordained goals, in which "His will is their peace." [15]

These "analogies" furnish the rules of the two great paths of divine love, one outgoing and the other returning, the one by which God proceeds from Himself creating all things in order to manifest Himself in all things and the other by which He inspires all things with love and draws them back to Him. Corresponding to this double process are two theologies, one apophatic or negative by which all predicates derived from the created world are denied of God who excels them all, which denial forces the soul upward, the other cataphatic or positive by which we grasp in creation the signs of Himself which the Creator pours down upon us.

The analogies which fix the stages in the universal process of creation-emanation and which set a limit on the upward ascent of creatures are ultimately nothing more than the divine ideas of all things (*proorismoi*, *paradeigmata*), for it is according to these ideas that God manifests Himself in theophanies. In a secondary sense "analogies" are creatures themselves, all of which embody the divine ideas to the extent that they are able.

Although the source of all being is unknowable, at least as source, God is knowable to the extent that the world reflects His ideas, if not Himself. The divine ideas are a set of limits on creation and thus are also divine "wills" (*theia thelemata*) in the sense that they determine the degree of love which any created object possesses for its creator and thereby reflect the divine intention concerning the order and destiny of creation.

Thus salvation is not dissolution of one's identity as a creature but the establishment of a perfect correspondence between the created world and the divine archetypes. The fall is a fall from the complete embodiment of an essence, so that redemption simply fulfills us in what we ought to be and establishes creation in its capacity as co-workers with God (*theou synergoi*). The possibility of the union or mutual assimilation of the divine analogies and the created analogies, of the realm of the divine ideas and their created imitations, was accomplished through the person of the God-man through whom all created beings arrive at their salvation in resembling him, in becoming Christ images (*Christoeidos*).[16] The whole universal process from this point of view is nothing less than the imitation of God (*theomimesis*), and every created thing whether visible (*horate*) or intelligible (*noete*) is only a theophany, now imperfect but in the fulfillment of time perfect in its order.

To summarize, the term analogy for Dionysius refers to the relationship of creatures to God, their capacity to love and their desire to be deified, if we understand the concept from the apophatic viewpoint. From the cataphatic perspective it refers to the relationship of God to creatures, the divine ideas and their manifestation in the created universe, the aspect of created beings as theophanies. In short, the term describes the place and role of all things in the hierarchy of reality, a hierarchy which is bound by love and which has an upward and downward dynamism.

Having considered the internal relations of the hierarchical system, we will turn to a more detailed consideration of Dionysius' conception of hierarchy proper.[17] The hierarchical construction of the universe or, as it has been called, "the Alexandrian vision of the world" was the last great result of ancient systematic thought and fused elements from all the philosophical schools of antiquity—with the exception of Epicureanism—into a new unity. From Plotinus to Proclus some of the most powerful minds of antiquity labored to construct this great ladder-cosmos, drawing freely on Platonism, Aristotelianism, the thought of Philo, the Gnostics, and the Neoplatonists. The result of this effort was a particular view of the universe and of intelligence and its place in it, a graduated representation of diverse orders of reality, sensible and intelligible, starting from a first principle from which all proceed either directly or through the mediation of higher orders. It was the work of Pseudo-Dionysius to adapt this great body of thought to Christian uses and to transmit it to the Middle Ages.

Dionysius defines hierarchy as a sacred order or ranking (*taxis*). The term is of military origin and denotes what we might call a cosmological chain of command. However, hierarchy is also a science (*episteme*) and an activity (*energeia*) by and through which creatures assimilate themselves as much as possible to the divine through the aid of divine illuminations which fulfill them in their powers of imitating God.[18]

Its goal or purpose is nothing less than such assimilation and union (the latter to be understood as involving retention of individual identity), for God is the master of each and every hierarchical order, the master of all knowing and activity, and the whole hierarchical order of the universe never ceases to receive his imprint to the degree that each creature is able, thus becoming a perfect image (*agalma*) of God, a spotless mirror of great efficacy, capable of receiving the ray of the primal fire and the divine principle. After having received this divine light in the plenitude of its splendor and in a most holy manner, each creature freely transmits this same light to creatures lower on the scale.[19]

Thus if hierarchy is considered from the point of view of its activity, it is the ordered transmission of divine radiation according to the orderings and dispositions of the Divinity. From a more static point of view, it is an image (*eikon*) of divine beauty.[20]

Dionysius used the imagery of light, as did the Neoplatonists, to describe the process of emanation of all things from the One. He accepts the doctrine of creation, however, no matter how incompatible these two cosmological principles may be. From a transcendent and absolute source, light pours down in the form of being, beauty, goodness, and, indeed, all value and existence. Citing St. James (1: 17), "every good and perfect gift is from above and cometh down from the Father of Lights," he adds that the gift of goodness from above has also the function of unifying us, raising us to a higher spiritual condition, and turning us to the divine unity. All things not only come from Him but go to Him. Thus hierarchy has the purpose of drawing its members toward the divine, providing them with a ladder, so to speak, as well as the function of distributing all divine powers through creation.[21]

This emanation of divine light on all the objects of its providence does not imply a loss on the part of divinity or a scattering of the divine unity and being into multiplicity. The divine light remains simple and, indeed, unifies what it touches.[22]

The concept of order is related to hierarchy in the sense both of arrangement and of commandment, for the structure of the universe and the beings in it, their relationship to each other, is the result of the divine will. Thus it is absolutely fixed by the divinely established laws of consecration that, for example, the second order should partake of divine illumination through the mediation of the first.[23]

This takes us to another notion in the idea of hierarchy, for each higher rank possesses the illumination and powers of the subordinates as well as attributes exclusively its own. Hierarchy is thus a "scale of forms," each higher form transcending but including the functions and powers of the forms below.[24] This notion is perhaps most familiar to us in Aristotle's biology in which each order of life has all the functions of the lower form in addition to functions proper to itself. Thus animals have all the vegetative functions but add sensibility, and man in turn adds reason. Dionysius, however, applies this same notion to the angelic intelligences and, as will be shown, to the ecclesiastical hierarchy.

Each higher order has more of the attributes of being and value, each imitates the divine with unswerving devotion in its order, and every function of each order has the only purpose of receiving and distributing that divine light and divine knowledge which perfects its recipients. The very first hierarchy is filled with primal light, and the celestial angelic beings who constitute it stand right around God. They need no mediatory images like the rest of creation to apprehend the divine, but circle round His eternal knowledge in a "stability which is perpetually moving." There—in an image reminiscent of Plato's *Phaedrus*—they are filled with divine food.[25]

The common name for the celestial hierarchy is angels, although there are nine species of these pure intelligences and they are endowed with different functions and powers. They are arranged in three triads, starting from the seraphim and descending through cherubim, thrones, dominations, virtues, powers, principalities, archangels, and angels.

The first triad has a perfecting function, the next lower an illuminating function, and the last purifies. Traditionally, the individual species have other tasks besides these. Angels are messengers to individuals, archangels are messengers to nations, principalities are the guides of princes, the powers are in a special sense subject to God, the virtues represent divine motion, dominations manifest dominion, thrones embody stability, the cherubim exercise knowledge, and the seraphim exercise love. Yet Dionysius dwells little on these particular functions and interprets the intelligences primarily as mediators and transmitters of light in its several meanings of grace, knowledge, being, and beauty.

In summary, the celestial hierarchy provided those intermediary beings between man and God which seemed necessary to a hierarchically minded civilization to provide degrees of continuity in the great ladder of creatures. They also served as spiritual and intellectual vassals of the Deity, performing various functions for Him, an aspect of angelology which tradition later developed. Tradition also identified these angels with the Aristotelian movers of the spheres so that the angels came to govern the processes of nature, by using the stars they governed as their instruments. They also represented degrees of knowledge and consciousness, a conception which is stressed in Dionysius' treatise, and thus helped radiate ultimate truth and grace down to the point where the celestial hierarchy meets the ecclesiastical hierarchy.[26]

Below the celestial hierarchy lies the ecclesiastical hierarchy, which picks up where the former leaves off. This particular subdivision of the universal hierarchical order will now be examined to see how Dionysius conceives of it.

The term hierarchy etymologically and historically refers primarily to an ecclesiastical order, a sacred order of priests in which authority is divided in an order of subordination for the determined end of fulfilling both religious and administrative duties. Hierarchy is, objectively speaking, the custody and administration of sacred things, but subjectively is the series of consecrated persons possessing the right and powers to undertake their tasks.

The ecclesiastical hierarchy is not multiple but one single hierarchy and, in modern Roman Catholic thought, has, from one point of view, three degrees: bishops, priests, and deacons or ministers. Both the bishops and the pope possess *plenitudo potestatis*, the power to sanctify, instruct, and govern. The power to confer holy orders is exclusive to a bishop, the only member of the hierarchy who possesses full priestly powers. Priests may by papal permission and in special cases confer minor orders and even confirmation, which is usually the prerogative of the bishop.

The sharp split between clergy and laity which this conception of hierarchy implies is derived by Roman Catholic theologians as a consequence of their Petrine doctrine, but they also acknowledge other historical influences in Jewish and Roman priestly and administrative divisions. Its structure is avowedly monarchical, with the pope as sole ruler of the whole structure, and although the Church has an aristocracy and populace, these play no part in the government of the Church.

The ecclesiastical hierarchy has undergone certain developments since its main outlines were fixed early in the Christian era, and they have been of two main kinds, episcopal and jurisdictional. The episcopal development involved the creation of new episcopal titles such as archbishop, patriarch, metropolitan, exarch, and coadjutor bishop to meet the needs of sees of different kinds or to facilitate the administration of large ones. These changes were essentially administrative like the jurisdictional development which created cardinals, legates, nuncios, apostolic vicars, and prefects to undertake special tasks of an administrative or diplomatic character.[27]

Dionysius, however, does not discuss the ecclesiastical hierarchy as it might be discussed by a modern theologian or even, in some respects, by a medieval theologian. As the celestial hierarchy is a purely intelligible reality and operates through purely spiritual principles, the ecclesiastical hierarchy differs only in that it is made up of incarnate intelligences and therefore must transmit spiritual truths and powers through sensible agencies, such as the sacraments, and its teachings. Each hierarchy, ecclesiastical and celestial, has its sacraments, its initiators of sacraments, and its recipients or the initiated. But, although the sacraments of the ecclesiastical hierarchy are partly sensible and partly intelligible, those of the celestial hierarchy involve immaterial and unmediated knowledge of God and divine things.

The knowledge of the ecclesiastical hierarchy is mediated through language, but the hierarchy possesses special knowledge of Scripture and also possesses and transmits an oral tradition "from mind to mind, through the medium of speech and so corporeal but nevertheless more immaterial for it is without writing." [28]

The very terms which Dionysius uses for the ecclesiastical hierarchy are highly metaphorical and mystical. The term for bishop is hierarch, but this also includes Christ, St. Paul, the apostles, popes, patriarchs, archbishops, metropolitans, and bishops. The hierarch is thus the name given to each of that succession of men who possess sacred powers, beginning with Christ, the God-Man from whom they received their sacred powers and knowledge. The esoteric manner in which Dionysius conceived this transmission will become clearer if we consider some of the synonyms he used for hierarch. A bishop is a perfecter or initiator (*telestes*, *telestikos*), words sometimes employed with the adjective sacred, and also the one who first initiates (*telestarchis*) and a mystagogue or a leader in the mysteries.

The ecclesiastical hierarchy is conceived in the last analysis as composed of consecrated and illuminated intelligences who are incarnate, and Dionysius prescinds them entirely from their administrative duties and largely from the routine religious duties of the bishops. Instead he imagines the long line of the apostolic succession as a procession of hierophants, the bearers of sacred and powerful symbols and functions which they semisecretly transmit to their successors. There is nothing that more suggests the spirit of this conception than the magnificent mosaic panels in Monreale, where the air of mystery surrounding the great Christ Pantocrator makes his bishops and saints seem more like the members of a heavenly imperial court than earthly figures.

The priests, the next lower order in the hierarchy, are less mysterious and hierophantic, and their functions, as Dionysius conceives them, are indicated in the variety of their names, such as illuminator (*photistikos*) or sanctifier (*hierourgos*). The last rank in the first of the two triads which make up the ecclesiastical hierarchy is that of the deacon (*diakonos*) who is also known as the minister of sacred things and a purifier (*leitourgos*, *kathartikos*). As can be seen from the various names of the first triad, the three different ranks of bishop, priest, and deacon have three different main functions. The deacons purify and discriminate among those who are ready for higher things, the priests illuminate and lead to light, the bishops perfect and complete.[29]

Each order subsumes the functions of the next lower order

in a higher synthesis composed of the lower powers plus its own. The three activities of purification, illumination, and making perfect are thus distributed among the various triads of both the celestial and ecclesiastical hierarchies and, although each order has its own proper function, all orders share in some degree in all three functions. This is so even though there is essentially one activity per order in the ecclesiastical hierarchy, whereas in the celestial hierarchy all three functions are more obviously shared. Thus each intelligence has a threefold power with one power more or less predominant, and each order has three degrees of power with again one power more or less predominant.[30]

The second and lower of the two triads in the ecclesiastical hierarchy begins with the subdeacon whom Dionysius calls a server of God (*therapeutes*) and who is followed by the solitary monk (*monachos eniaios*). Last come the Christian people themselves for whom in a sense this elaborate superstructure exists. Each order has the same two-way dynamic characteristic of the whole of hierarchism. Each order exercises its function on the next lower, and, as with the social classes in Plato's *Republic*, position and function go together, each order possessing knowledge appropriate to its function. The upward movement of the system is chaneled through the process of initiation into the additional knowledge that each higher order possesses. Each order initiates the one below it and is in turn initiated by the one above it.

It is obvious that Dionysius' system is one of the main Neoplatonic attempts to bring together the two worlds of being and becoming, thought and sense, into which Plato many centuries before had divided reality. Like Jamblichus, Dionysius multiplies the intermediaries necessary to do this and introduces the notion of theurgic powers. And like

Proclus he arranges all the intermediary beings in triads. What is essentially new is the adaptation of these traditions to the uses of Christianity.

An attempt should now be made to complete our picture of Dionysius' hierarchical structure of the universe and summarize the general characteristics of the system. In the last analysis all hierarchy is order, and its operations are performed in order, through the activity of primary, middle, and last powers. In addition to order, every subhierarchy, as well as the whole, possesses harmony, equilibrium, and joy. God is the principle of order, and the breaking of order and harmony is evil. Since the harmony of all creatures proceeds from the Good, the essence of evil for Dionysius resides in disorder. In this he manifests himself a Christian, for the pagan Neoplatonists had placed the essence of evil in the mere fact of the finitude of creatures. Of course, for St. Paul evil is located in a radical corruption of the will, and Dionysius arrives at his own position by trying to mediate between the Neoplatonic and the Pauline conceptions of evil. He is able to do this by interpreting the evildoer or breaker of order as a misuser of his will who does not seek unity with the infinite in the right way, breaking the proper order and measure with which all things are illuminated by grace and knowledge.

The harmony of hierarchy depends on the different capacities and functions of all its members. They are as members in the Divine Body, distinct and of varying value but all necessary and all contributing to the whole. Thus Dionysius' notion of hierarchy is not the systematic reduction of all things to identity, for each level does and must retain its own characteristics. All hierarchy is subject to laws, is divinely willed and ordained, is objective as well as interior. Indeed, his conception of hierarchy suggests nothing so much as a perfect monarchy, a spiritual Platonic Republic.

Far below the two glowing hierarchies of priests and angels there is a legal hierarchy which gives only obscure images of supersensible truth; it is an imitation far removed from its models and offers only obscure images (*aenigmata*) of truth, difficult to contemplate because of their very low degree of reality. The ecclesiastical hierarchy lies between the legal and celestial and thus brings us nearer to the divine, for it employs symbols of much greater value while the celestial hierarchy does not use sensible symbols at all but deals in purely intelligible truths.[31]

What all these hierarchies have in common is that they must use images to draw us up to God. Even though the celestial hierarchy in itself deals with the purely intelligible, insofar as the angels guide men they must transmit their truths in embodied form. Thus Dionysius believes, unlike the pagan Neoplatonists, that genuine knowledge is given in space and time although it is somewhat obscured by the intrusion of the sensible. Genuine knowledge is also contained in the events of the life of Christ, especially the Incarnation, and in the acts of the saints. In this view, we have a very unplatonic concession to Christian realism and to the importance of history.

Indeed, the deeds of the saints and martyrs are concrete examples of what all hierarchy aims to achieve, the progressive divination of all who are being saved, progressive unification with and assimilation to the divine through the instrumentality of love, a love which impels us upward and which is accompanied by the increase of knowledge and divine illumination.[32] God draws us upward through our amorous desire for the Beautiful which makes us tend toward Him, reducing our multiple diversities. He also perfects us by unifying and divinizing our life, our habits, and our dispositions, bestowing the sacred gift of holy sacerdotal powers.[33]

The divine principle thus works through love and is at the root of both the ascending activity and the descending activity of hierarchy, the descent of illumination and the ascent of intelligence to its source. All the activity of the members of hierarchy is merely an analogue of the divine activity, the mediated version of what in the Good is unmediated. Thus all the downgoing activity is really providence (*pronoia*), and all the upward activity is conversion (*epistrophe*). The mediatory and amorous activity of hierarchy is both a knowing and an ordering and has the single goal of divinization. All hierarchy purifies, illuminates, and perfects, and it does this with the double process of transmitting all value and existence from above and drawing everything below upward to knowledge of eternal things. Each rank simultaneously looks above to receive and looks below to transmit, yearning to ascend and draw its inferiors upward.

The universe is made of steppingstones of progressively more brilliant and divine beauties leading us upward, and it is the obligation of all who see more to assist others and to strike the divine sparks which lie dormant in humanity. The process of ascent ends when the sparks have burst into flame and when we achieve that incomparable immortality which is without grief and luminous with light.[34]

Here the reader's attention should be called to what Dionysius tells us about the importance of a guide in this process. The whole concept of hierarchy is of course one of mediation, and the notion of guidance is intrinsic to Christianity itself. The Deity does not reveal His will to all with clarity, and He reveals it to none completely. If revelation posits the general outline of the drama and machinery of salvation, the details are not clear, and the long line of prophets and saints are God's instruments for enlightening men in the darkness of sin. What is interesting in the conception of Dionysius is the individual twist he gives the notion, for the guide is not the transmitter of a divine message or a divine grace to a particular place and time but the guide who helps us out of the world of space and time. His framework for this concept is unhistorical and philosophical. He really defines the kind of guide Dante has and, indeed, is himself. Virgil and Beatrice lead the pilgrim up a cosmic, essentially timeless, ladder. Whatever Dante sees of particulars, historical or otherwise, is eternalized. So too Dante interrupts his narrative to address the reader as poet-prophet, as guide and not as guided, explaining his universe and helping us to experience its reality.[35]

It would be repetitive to trace the post-Dionysian developments of the concept of hierarchy. The next great figure in the tradition is Scotus Erigena, the translator and commentator of the Dionysian corpus, who is followed by some of the most important figures of medieval thought, such as Grosseteste and Hugh of St. Victor.[36] The system remains the same in all the essentials we have considered. There is simply a greater or less degree of metaphorical elaboration and of reinforcement of the doctrines of Dionysius with other texts such as the widely diffused *Liber de causis*. Next to the works of Dionysius this is perhaps the most important source for medieval Neoplatonism. The Latin translation of an Arabic adaptation of Proclus, it was long attributed to Aristotle. Since the author of the Dionysian corpus also drew heavily on Proclus, the doctrines of this "Aristotle" were in startling conformity to those of the presumed convert made by St. Paul.

Thus we find in the *Liber de causis* that the first cause is above all description, that it can be described only through those secondary causes which are illuminated by the light of the first cause, a pure light which has no light above it.[37] The first cause governs the universe without in any way departing of itself, and it pours out its goodness over all things which in turn manifest that goodness diversely. The diversification of the primal light, identical with being and goodness, which flows from the supreme goodness, constitutes a hierarchy. The rungs of this hierarchy are mediatory so that, between those substances which are eternal and those which are temporal and act in time, there must be substances which have their substance in eternity but which act in time. This reasoning, along typical Neoplatonic lines, establishes and presupposes the necessity of mean existences between any two major categories of existence. Every higher state in the ladder of being is more unified, exerts a wider range of power, has more of the infinite, and operates with more greatness, nobility, and marvelousness.[38]

With the presumed authority of Aristotle behind it, the doctrines of the *Liber de causis* did much to carry over Neoplatonic thought into the scholastic Aristotelianism of the later Middle Ages, creating that peculiar blend of Aristotelianized Neoplatonism so characteristic of the thought of Albertus Magnus and Dante.

One other tradition of hierarchical thought is of great significance for us, and this we can best examine in the work of St. Bernard.[39] Not only was the sensible and intelligible universe shaped into an objectively existing ladder to the Absolute, but there is also another tradition of internal or subjective ladders. In this tradition love is not appetition for external goods but the spiritual bond which unites man to God. This is the fundamental note in one major tradition of Western mysticism which reaches its culmination in St. Bernard. His ladder of love has really nothing to do with cosmology. It is exclusively tied to persons—self, neighbor, and God. *De diligendo Deo* explores how, beginning with the inborn and natural love of self, there is a gradual unfolding and transformation of self-love into love of neighbor and love of God.

All men begin by loving themselves for their own sake. This is inevitable and natural. But man learns early that he is not omnipotent, that he is a frail and brittle creature. Under the impact of this perception he turns to the love of God, but still for his own sake, seeking the safety that he knows he cannot provide for himself. This second phase is simultaneous with developing some degree of love for one's neighbor, since man learns that he is dependent on his fellows as well as on the Omnipotent.

In the third phase, the selfishness in this erotic investment in others and the "wholly other" disappears, and man begins to love God for His own sake, because He is intrinsically worthy of love. This phase too is accompanied by a different sense of the self and the neighbor. In the final phase, one loves oneself only for the sake of God and achieves the complete loss of selfhood, the apex of the inner dialectic of love. In modern terms this describes a complete doctrine of sublimation, not through external force, but through the inner necessity given by the erotic impulse itself and by the human situation wherein man finds himself forced to be unselfish in order to achieve his own best interests.

In the *Sermons on the Canticles* Bernard develops another scale, this time of feelings. In our relationship to God we begin with the feelings of a slave and then move to the feelings of a hireling and later of a disciple. This is followed by the feelings of a son and finally the feelings of a bride. Again the penetrating dialectic of Bernard traces out the steps in the growth of the psyche. Man first finds himself enslaved by the moral order and moral commands which surround him. He later gives a partial consent, like the man who works for hire because he must. Finally he sees the worth of what had appeared to be merely external constraint and proceeds to take up the position of the willing pupil. What had appeared external and harsh comes to seem more like the injunctions of a loving father, and he then feels like a son. The final union and assimilation of Reality are symbolized by the feelings of a bride.

Another anagogic path is expressed through an analysis of grace and free will. Man first has free choice. In this stage he is free but sinful. Later he acquires free counsel which is freedom from sin. The final phase is free enjoyment or freedom from misery. Humility too provides a very elaborate dialectic of twelve phases: (1) The person is ever mindful of God's commandments. (2) He has no concern for his own desires. (3) He submits to the superior for the love of God. (4) He bears all things. (5) He confesses truly. (6) He is content with what is mean and vile. (7) He confesses and believes his own lowliness. (8) He performs no action as an individual but fully lives a common life. (9) He is silent. (10) He is not easily moved to laughter. (11) He assumes a quiet behavior and a gravity of manner. (12) He achieves humility both in heart and in exterior actions.[40]

Humility achieved, it becomes in turn the first step of another ladder which has seven rungs. In the second step humility itself becomes free and voluntary. The third step is the achievement of the grief of repentance. This is followed by fervor for justice, compassion, purity, and, finally, contemplation.

All the steps on the various anagogic paths are the gifts of grace. Man's natural endowment, including the self-love which is the presupposition of the love of God, is the gift of creating grace. Humility, which is the first step up to contemplation, is the gift of preventing grace. Free counsel, or active charity, the second step in the threefold ladder of freedom, is the gift of saving or protecting grace, for man in his natural sinful constitution has only "free" choice in the sense that he is free to be sinful. Love, the capacity or nuclear endowment of growth, is the gift of vivifying grace. Contemplation is the gift of consummating grace.[41]

Bernard's ladders are psychological elaborations of the principle of the Benedictine rule in which St. Benedict advises the monks as follows: "If we would scale the summit of humility, and swiftly gain the heavenly height which is reached by our lowliness in this present life, we must set up a ladder of climbing ideals" (ch. vii). St. Bernard simply echoes this principle when he announces as the cornerstone of his thought: "Yet I have already erected a ladder reaching up to this with the aid of him who calls me." [42]

The two traditions of an objective and subjective ladder of love of course flow together, and the best example of this confluence is furnished by the thought of St. Bonaventura. St. Bonaventura presents perhaps the most complete and consistent synthesis of the various cosmological and psychological models we have been considering. The *Journey of the Mind to God* begins with a description of the universe as both a mirror and a ladder, a universe in which one may find both evidence of God and the means for reaching Him. More strictly, the universe is a set of mirrors or "footprints" (*vestigia*) of the Deity, and the subjective and objective sides of this concept are described as *speculatio,* which may be translated as "vision," "reflection," "speculation," or "consideration" according to context.[43]

These mirrors or *vestigia* are nothing less than all the realities which make up the universe, and they are arranged in a ladder or hierarchy.[44] Not only is the world a network of beautiful symbols, but it is itself the lowest in a ladder of beauty which rises to the spiritual beauty of the Church, to the beauty of Paradise, and to the beauty of the Trinity itself.

The mechanism of the world is very beautiful but the Church is adorned with the greater beauty of the holy charismata, and the holy Jerusalem with even greater beauty. Yet the very greatest beauty is that of the Trinity, most high and blessed.[45]

The familiar idea of theophanies—the elements of this ladder—is given a new turn by the time of St. Bonaventura, through the thought of the biblical exegetes and their theories of allegorical interpretation of Scripture. St. Bonaventura tells us, "God speaks not only through words but also through deeds, as in Him to say is to do, and to do is to say, and further, because all things created, as effects of God, point to their cause." [46] Indeed, the whole of the created universe is nothing but a system of mirrors reflecting their Cause (*Itinerarium* II, 7), and they initiate a process by which we enter into the internal mirror of our mind where the divine lights shine in the form of the light of intellect.[47]

Again, as for Dionysius, the ladders of existence and values are one and the same (*Breviloquium* I, 6, 3 and 4). The highest unity is first in the order of things (*summe unum est summe primum*) and is simultaneously the supremely true, beautiful, good, useful, and profitable (*summe verum, pulchrum, bonum, utile, proficuum*). The Supreme Being is conceived as light, and Bonaventura elaborates the light-mirror metaphors of the Dionysian tradition.

Divine wisdom is not only capable of knowing but also is the cause of our being able to know. It follows therefore that insofar as it is the cause of our knowing all things we call it light (*lux*), insofar as it is the cause for knowing things seen and judged we call it a mirror (*speculum*), insofar as it is the reason for knowing things predestined and reprobated we call it the book of life.[48] But it is also a ladder, Jacob's ladder, and its ascent is the Exodus of the Hebrews from Egypt to the promised land. Its lowest rung is all that part of the universe which is available to sense and which, like all of creation, mirrors the Deity.[49] All things are shadows, echoes, pictures, simulacra, reflections of the ultimate principles, the divine light, and fullness of all divine attributes. Indeed, God gave them to us expressly so that we may look upon Him and proceed from sensible things to invisible intelligible things in a manner analogous to that in which we proceed from signs to the things that they signify.[50] They are thus words, the words of God's book of nature which supplements His book of Scripture, the words of a God who manifests Himself in both books.[51] However, although every creature is naturally a picture and likeness of eternal wisdom, still those creatures mentioned in the book of Scripture are so especially, for the spirit of prophecy has elevated them to be prefigurations of eternal things.[52] It is thus that St. Bonaventura accommodates cosmic allegory, which is unhistorical and quite compatible with Philo's Judaism or with some varieties of Platonism, to the special claims of Christian revelation. Like all things, the realities mentioned in Scripture have a higher meaning, but it is clear that their meaning is higher, more specifically and importantly revelatory, than what the natural reason would find in them without the elevation of the spirit of prophecy.

This value of things as divine signs partly proceeds from purely philosophical grounds, such as the fact that God is the efficient, exemplaristic, and final cause of His creation. It also proceeds, however, from the fact that things may have their own proper representative value, partly in that they are divinely ordained to prophetic prefiguration, partly because of angelic operation, and partly because a given thing may be ordained to further purposes (*partim ex superaddita institutione*).[53]

Of all the images, the brightest and therefore most revealing is the angelic host, but even higher are those signs which are also sacraments.[54] Not only are the angels and sacraments generally images of God, but analogies go even farther and are even more explicit. Thus God's activity is divided, so to speak, among His angels so that He loves in the seraphim, knows in the cherubim, and manifests in the other orders of angels.[55] In addition, the seven sacraments correspond to the sevenfold form of grace which leads us through seven periods of history, completing a circular journey back to the rest of the eternal principle, and finally leads us into the eighth age of the universal resurrection.[56] Conveniently enough, there are also—and by no means accidentally—seven steps to orders: porter, reader, exorcist, acolyte, subdeacon, deacon, and priest. There are two preparatory stages in the clerical tonsure and elevation to reader of psalms, while above them are the bishop, patriarch, and pope from whom all others flow.[57]

All of this number symbolism and parallelism is based on the principle that number is the pre-eminent exemplar in the mind of the Divine Maker and that it is the outstanding vestige in things by which we are led to wisdom.[58] Of course, seven is not the only "sacred" number, since we find parallelisms based on the number six, with six stages of ascent in the journey to God, six wings of the cherub, six steps to the throne of Solomon, and the like.[59] The most important number symbolism is based on the number three. The creature, St. Bonaventura tells us, is directly created by the Trinity without any assistance from the angels as some medieval thinkers, including Dante, maintained. God's causality is triple, and from each mode the creature is stamped with a triad. From efficient causality it receives unity, mode, and measure (*unitas, modus, mensura*), from exemplary causality, truth, form, and number (*veritas, species, numerus*), and from final causality, goodness, order, and weight (*bonitas, ordo, pondus*).[60] These are no more than the familiar ontological triads of St. Augustine's *De Trinitate*. But again the analogies are pursued farther so that the branches of knowledge can be arranged as triads in analogy with the Trinity.[61] Thus there are three theologies, one symbolic, which makes use of the realities of sense, another which is literal and deals with "proper" or literal meanings and is purely intelligible, and a mystical theology which is above the level of both sense and thought. The task of the seeker is to make proper use of sensible and intelligible reality so that he may be carried up to supermental raptures (*supermentales excessus*).[62]

In addition to the hierarchical ladder of creatures, the ladder of cosmic allegory, there is another threefold hierarchy which we discover in Scripture. There we find a description of the hierarchies of revelation arranged in grades. They are the ecclesiastical, the angelical, and the divine, or the Church, the angels, and the Trinity, the last conceived as a hierarchy of persons.[63] These three categories in turn may be called the subcelestial, the celestial, and the supercelestial.[64]

The soul itself becomes hierarchical and capable of mounting upward, when it receives the triad of theological virtues. The ascent is through a series of nine steps:

Likewise the soul is stamped by the following nine steps when it is disposed in an orderly way: perception, deliberation, self-impulsion, ordination, strengthening, command, reception, divine illumination, union, which one by one correspond to the nine orders of angels, so that the first three stages correspond to nature in the human mind, the next three to industry, and the last three to grace.[65]

The supreme hierarch of all is Jesus Christ, and it is the Scripture which teaches how to become purified, illuminated, and perfected, a threefold process guided by a triple law, the law of nature, of Scripture, and of grace. From an entirely scriptural point of view it is the Mosaic law which purifies, prophetic revelation which illuminates, and evangelical teaching which perfects. This is primarily accomplished through the three spiritual senses of Scripture, for it is the tropological sense which purifies us for an honest life, the allegorical which illuminates and clarifies our understanding, and the anagogical which perfects us by elevating our minds and giving us the most delightful perceptions of wisdom.[66]

I have dwelt at length on these parallelisms simply to give the reader some idea of the ingenuity with which analogies and hierarchies were elaborated. Thus from three we go to the square of three, to the nine stages corresponding to the nine orders of angels which, as we recall, manifest nine activities of the divine. These in turn correspond to astronomical spheres, branches of knowledge, and virtues. We are in a bandbox universe where everything is neatly arranged like the objects in a curio cabinet. If a pattern of threes will not do, then four, six, seven, or nine might.

St. Bonaventura's cosmological and theological ladder-cosmos, which we have just considered, is the objective side of a psychological and spiritual process. For him there are three aspects or perspectives of a consciousness possible, and each one discovers another aspect of that universal ladder to God which is simultaneously His self-revelation. First the mind looks outward, exercising what St. Bonaventura calls *animalitas* or *sensualitas*, then inward in the exercise of *spiritus*, finally "upward" in the exercise of *mens*.[67] These three perspectives disclose in the creation three kinds of analogy to God. The first is the perception of the *vestigia Dei* in the created universe, the *specula* which make up the whole of the created universe and the evidence of God available to all men. Turning within, we find an *imago*, which is the divine image in man and which he alone of created things possesses. Looking upward, we discover a *similitudo* to God. As the *imago* is found in the triadic aspect of the love of the mind of itself, its knowledge of itself, and its memory of itself (each of these also triadic, consisting of two terms and a relation between them), so we find a *similitudo* in the light of the eternal truth stamped in our minds.[68] To contemplate the *imago* and the *similitudo* demands grace, since both have been deformed by sin. The first is a seeing of God as in a mirror whereas the second is a seeing of God as light. Thus we rise from a reflection to the source. *Vestigia* too are mirrors, but the *imago* is an evidently brighter one, and in the *similitudo* we discover the divine light itself because of which the mirrors shine.[69]

Further, the three prespectives all have a twofold aspect, as when in one mode we may see God "through" a mirror (*per speculum*) or "in" a mirror (*in speculo*). The second mode of vision is higher than the first, for the first sees God as a trace in His creation whereas the second sees God insofar as He is actually in His creation through His essence, potency, and presence.[70]

We have thus six stages of illumination which lead to contemplation, and they are actually levels or faculties of mind: *sensus*, *imaginatio*, *ratio*, *intellectus*, *intelligentia*, and *apex mentis* or *synderesis scintilla*, the spark or point of the mind which is transcended in supermental ecstasy.[71] This procedure is therefore all to be classified as "speculation" in the broad sense of the term, the indirect vision of God which can only be completed in the life hereafter. It is speculation which begins in the senses but travels to the imagination, reason, intellect, and understanding and finally to wisdom which is the highest perception but which can merely just begin in this life. Contemplation, strictly speaking, is a direct vision of heavenly things or even of God. This sixfold procedure beginning with the senses was not needed by the prophets, who possessed contemplation through revelation according to a threefold vision, of the body, of the imagination, and of the intellect.[72]

From the one point of view we may consider the *Divine Comedy* as a representation of the three major kinds of reflection of God. The whole universe of the poem and especially of the *Paradiso* can be seen as *vestigia*, which specifically appear as *specula* in the manifestations of substantial light that make up the landscape of the *Paradiso*. The whole of Purgatory is an attempt on the part of the pilgrims to reconstitute the *imago*, the specifically human reflection of the Deity through the continual self-confrontations and corrections of the errant will. The *Paradiso* with its continual upward aspiration is the process of the creation of a *similitudo* to God by a continually growing illumination. Dante's final vision of God as pure Being, Trinity, and Incarnation or Good suggests the content of the last degree of contemplation as expounded by St. Bonaventura.[73]

It was not only the weight of philosophy and theology which lay behind the elaborate hierarchical ordering of the universe that we have been considering but also the weight of science, Aristotelian science. Aristotle's unmoved mover, the divine thought that thinks itself and causes motion as the object of universal desire, needed the assistance of subordinate intelligences to move the celestial spheres. They, moved by their desire for the first cause, moved eternally in the perfect circular motion of the fifth essence and in turn determined the processes of nature, the combinations and transformations of the four sublunary essences or elements, earth, air, fire, and water.

The great dividing line in Aristotle's physical universe was the sphere of the moon. The world above the moon was made of an incorruptible, unchanging "fifth essence" or *ether*, something radically different from the other four essences which compose our own sublunary world. The motion of the superlunary world is perfect, uniform, and abiding, a circular motion, whereas our world is a world of linear motion, with air and fire going up and earth and water down. Ours is a world of change, of things coming to be and passing away; and the principle of change is the desire of all things to seek their proper place, of fire to go up and of water to go down. There is something analogous to love in things which bids them seek the place where they will be at rest. The world of Aristotle's *On the Heavens* is a world in which everything has not *a place* but *its place* and in which the various places are distinguished as more or less real and more or less good.

Thus history and culture both conspired to express and reinforce what had deeply penetrated the hearts and minds of men, including men of little or no philosophical training, all of whom would have agreed that chaos would follow the removal of degree. All experience, intellectual, political, and social, was bound to the notion of upper and lower, better or worse, and all measured on a universal scale. It was hierarchy that made experience intelligible. The processes of history had created social and political hierarchies which found their ultimate rationale in what we have called the "Alexandrian" vision of the world, a conception of things which served, ideologically speaking, to turn a result of historical processes into a "natural" and "divine" order of things.

Recent studies of medieval architecture indicate the extent to which the picture of the universe as a ladder of light penetrated to the aesthetic ideals of the Middle Ages. The function of light in the Dionysian and Augustinian traditions was both form-creating and space-constituting. It was the principle of intelligibility but also, as we have seen, the principle of value, for the hierarchy of values of being, good, and beauty is also a hierarchy of light. As the principle of beauty, light is also the principle of desire, because any desire is for what is good and beautiful. It is this conception of light which the designers of the great Romanesque and Gothic structures of the Middle Ages had in mind and which they sought to imitate in the microcosms of their structures. While light in Romanesque architecture is conceived of as space-creating, Gothic architecture treats space as environment and thus represents a shift within the complex of ideas constituting the light-metaphysics tradition. Nevertheless, both create a hierarchy of light and space, and the two reflect the same cosmology. Gothic as well as Romanesque preserves "the mystic symbolism of divine illumination, the worship of light in architecture—the preservation of a mystic religious symbol in spite of the contradictions of a new technique, a new and quasi-materialistic naturalism." [74]

The same principle of hierarchical order which permeated theology, philosophy, architecture, and science provided a comprehensive image of the political and social order and served to reinforce the implicit values of a social and political order which had evolved out of the revolutionary processes marking the end of classical antiquity. Pope and emperor, ideally regarded, stood at the summit of the ecclesiastical and political hierarchies, whatever the vicissitudes of the two offices in fact were. In the case of the emperor, he kept his role in theory and in the imagination of some long after he had lost it in fact. From this point of view Dante's *De monarchia* is a curiously anachronistic work which expresses the ideal of universal empire at a time when practical political business had long been given over to the vigorous independent monarchies such as England and France.

Again from an ideal view and regardless of heresies, conciliar movements, and practical monarchical politics, spiritual and secular powers were seen to flow from exalted sources to inferior recipients, as from bishops to priests or from dukes to lower vassals. The social and ecclesiastical order which we would see as conventional, as one way of meeting social and institutional needs, was regarded by its contemporaries as the embodiment of an eternal divine order which was discoverable wherever one looked.

It is not enough, and it would be misleading, to point out the obvious similarity between all these hierarchies and thereby argue for the unity of medieval civilization. Each of these hierarchies embodied different values, values which were not always compatible with one another. In the case of the divine and cosmological hierarchy, the bond which united the whole system was love, whether the lowest analogue of love such as impels a stone to descend to its proper place or the naturally implanted love of God in the human soul which, as St. Augustine said, "makes my heart restless until it rest in Thee." [75]

The bond of the ecclesiastical hierarchy was the sacramental powers invested in its members and the authority to administer them, to teach, and to discipline which its leaders possessed. The feudal hierarchy, too, had its governing value which functioned as its bond—the loyalty of feudal inferior to his superior lord. We ought also to bear in mind that, from the political and ecclesiastical point of view, hierarchical organization is fundamentally the manner in which authority is distributed from the top down, whereas from the philosophical and theological point of view it is essentially the way that multiplicity is reduced to unity or man led back to God. Thus the hierarchies have a different dynamic context in each case.

There are further differences between the values embodied in the various hierarchical structures. The feudal hierarchy was *particularistic* and personal. Homage and fealty were given to another person in a higher rank, not to the rank itself alone. The particularity which is a characteristic of courtly and romantic love was also, in the phenomenon of courtly love, conceived on the feudal analogy, in that the beloved occupied a higher rank in the relationship and received *loyal* devotion. Loyalty was the value of both chivalric love and feudal chivalry, unshakable loyalty to a superior and to one's lady, at least ideally. I would like to stress again that we are here discussing political, cultural, and moral ideals and the institutions that embody them. The daily life, passions, and ambitions of men are far more similar in any age than the ideals after which men live, love, and strive, the values which attach to these activities and with which they are measured. Thus the fact that feudal ties were frequently broken, that adultery was often severely punished even if courtly love theoretically countenanced it, and that other ideal codes were commonly fractured is only of historical consequence. Roland and Lancelot still remained heroes, and Ganelon and Mordred villains.[76] The history of culture and of sensibility is more the history of what men revere and hope to see than of what they actually do.

The ecclesiastical hierarchy, on the other hand, was *universalistic* in its essential nature. Of course, to the extent that ecclesiastical administration was feudalized or that jurisdictional powers were delegated by eccleciastical authorities, it was particularistic. The principle behind the ecclesiastical hierarchy, however, was a distribution of sacramental powers, necessary for all mankind in the achievement of salvation. These powers were held and exercised in an essentially impersonal manner, and their efficacy, as St. Augustine definitively established during the Donatist controversy, did not depend on the character and personality of the man exercising them. Each rank in the hierarchy had powers and obligations which extended to the whole of mankind and which were exercised not out of his particular identity but solely out of his rank.

Feudal particularism found its philosophical correlate in the scholastic-Aristotelian emphasis on the primacy of each individual substance in the structure of reality. Interestingly enough, this emphasis on particularism in medieval thought, an emphasis expressed politically by the notion that the group exists for its members and not vice versa, did not lead to individualism in the modern sense of the word.[77] Indeed, medieval culture—the higher culture—is characterized by its impersonality. If the individual thing is primarily real, nevertheless he or it exists in the universal. The anonymity of so much medieval literature, combined with the fact that this literature at its best is so sensitive to descriptive detail, is some witness of this interesting combination of particularism with impersonality.

Medieval realism has provided many arguments for those who would invalidate the concept of the Renaissance, and indeed there are many realistic, vivid, and accurate descriptions of persons in medieval literature. The very grotesqueness of some medieval art often derives from the abundance and juxtaposition of many minute details. Yet it is hard to find examples of detail subordinated and eliminated in the interest of the presentation of a complete and individualized character. And it is precisely this interest in detail for its own sake that precludes obtaining a complete and reliable estimate of a personality as a whole.[78] Dante, I think, is the first writer in the medieval period consistently and systematically to use the realistic description of outward detail to make a unitary moral portrait of an individual man, to use such detail in the interest of a general moral evaluation of a personality.

The values of the various medieval hierarchies we have been discussing did not exist in separate compartments no matter how incompatible some of them may have been, and there were not only interactions between them but some deliberate attempts to fuse or relate the various orders. Thus feudalism and the Church were bound together, since, whatever the spiritual claims of the Church, it held its land according to feudal principles. Ecclesiastics gradually began to develop a conception of religious chivalry until they finally created an ideal in which the loyalty of the feudal vassal to his lord was extended to include the Church. Again, this was not entirely true in practice, although most feudal nobles were at least loyal to the faith if not always to the institution and its representatives.[79]

When the feudal hierarchy first began to develop in the tenth century, it was strictly military, and its political functions were inseparable from its military ones. Its values were typically those of the soldier: prowess, loyalty, trustworthiness. Perhaps the best example of feudal chivalry is a *chanson de geste* such as *Raoul de Cambrai*, with its brutal battle scenes and its reflection of very coarse manners. To be *preux* was to be a good rough soldier, more like a marine sergeant than the fairy-book version of St. George. Feudal "largesse" did not mean indiscriminate kindliness to the vanquished but referred to what we would call military courtesy, a generosity motivated by the class solidarity which united both sides in any battle. Glory, the aim of the true knight, could and did involve battlefield brutalities, at least to the "villains" who were commonly scornful of the knightly code anyway.

Religious chivalry, anticipated by the ideals reflected in the *Chanson de Roland*, flourished in the twelfth century, when it found two great spokesmen in St. Bernard and John of Salisbury. They introduced, practically speaking, the idea that the feudal lord had to live up to certain inherent and special obligations to Church and society and thus attempted to bind the feudal hierarchy to the service of the ecclesiastical. Using the same Pauline metaphor of members and body that they used in political and religious theory, they worked out the delegation of special functions to each special rank of the feudal hierarchy. Further, they allegorized and made symbols of the knights' gear and of the ceremony in which knights were created. The clergy thus attempted to tame the nobles and to give them, in addition to their sense of personal obligation, a sense of communal obligations. For a sense of communal obligations as we understand it today, men had to wait for the growth of the towns and that urban civilization in which capitalism and the culture of the Renaissance were coming to birth. We may note in passing that the prose fabliau is the only literary form which the burghers produced in the Middle Ages, an indication of their lack of a self-consciously held ideal of life.

Another blending of values is furnished by courtly chivalry, which we might well call the attempt of women to tame the feudal nobles, to give them higher values. It started in Provence where, although involved with love, it was generally unconnected with sex and the development of those good manners necessary to attract the ladies. It was the forceful introduction of sex into the pattern of courtly love in northern

France that made it incumbent on the knight to look and act in a manner more pleasing to the ladies. Thus courtly love, which in Provence usually meant the one-sided love of a troubadour for a lady who might well be utterly indifferent, took on in the north of France the character of mutuality and drastically changed the quality of the feudal hierarchy's ideal of life.

The quintessential instance of this development in chivalry is Lancelot, as Chrétien de Troyes depicts him, the knightly lover so motivated by the single emotion of love that he will break the knightly code itself in order, paradoxically, to be the perfect knightly lover and obey his lady even when she commands something shameful. This is perhaps the most interesting case of the dilemmas possible when erotic and feudal loyalties blend and both press absolute claims.

Pervasive hierarchical thinking also lies behind many of the cultural dilemmas and debates in the medieval period as well as the social ones just considered. The literature of debate includes some subjects which are mere rhetorical exercises, such as the debate between water and wine or between the lily and the rose. But many such works also treat important issues, as the active versus the contemplative life, man versus woman, medicine versus law, sculpture versus painting, the mixed versus the single constitution, the vernacular versus Latin, and so on. All this literature is based on the assumption that to know what a thing is, is to know its place in a ladder of values and that values are absolute and hierarchical rather than functional and relative. Any purely functional theory of society would not lead to a serious attempt to rank values in this way. Some indication of the persistence of this debate literature is offered in the seventeenth- and eighteenth-century battle of the books the remote ancestry of which goes back to the medieval battle between the *artes* and *auctores*. And we may well recall Don Quixote's eloquent defense of the soldier as against the scholar.

Thus hierarchical thinking, a principle of harmony, came to be a source of conflict and created the structure for medieval tragedies and for conflict between feudal and amorous loyalties. It was thereby the vehicle for the expression of the pessimistic dimension of experience and this in spite of the fact that such an ordering of experience was also conducive to optimism. Hierarchy implies a well-defined conception of duties and ranks, simplifies choices, and reduces, at least in appearance, the irrationality of life itself. Yet the conflict between hierarchical values and between various hierarchical commitments engendered the most tragic episodes of medieval literature. In the *Nibelungenlied*, Rüdiger is torn between his obligation to two conflicting objects of feudal loyalty, Gunther and Etzel, and the claims of both are absolute. His only choice is finally death, a heroic death which in turn creates the fresh values of tragic suffering. So too Tristan is torn between the absolute loyalties of love and fealty, and again the solution is death. This is not surprising, for in a hierarchical system change and correction can occur only under external pressure or internal disruption.[80] This concept is implicit in the medieval notion of tragedy although, of course, it does not define it. Such a concept of tragedy perhaps best describes medieval tragic literature simply because the conflict is set in so patently hierarchical a structure and because most conflicts involve the one value of loyalty. This, the supreme value of an aristocratic warrior class, is so strongly and unquestioningly held that the outlines of the conflict are delineated with a majestic simplicity. Hagen, Roland, and Rüdiger have none of the subtleties of Antigone or Hamlet and offer only the most simple rationalizations, if any, of their actions.[81]

The concept of hierarchy, although much of its working appears arbitrary, was ultimately bound to an important philosophical and psychological principle, which has by no means lost its validity for some contemporary philosophers. In contemporary philosophical thought it appears as the concept of a philosophical scale of forms. Such a scale of forms combines differences of degree with differences of kind. Thus the moral virtues, although they differ in kind, also differ in degree, for they can be arranged on a scale of increasing value. This mode of thought received its greatest expression in modern times in Leibnitz' formulation of the principle of continuity as the central methodological concept in philosophy, and he first clearly stated its character. In the philosophical scale of forms the variable is identified with the generic essence so that the lower forms of the scale are simply imperfect specifications of the generic essence, an essence realized with more and more adequacy as we go up the scale.[82]

From the psychological point of view, travel along such a scale will be, to use the terminology of the Gestalt psychologists, both gradual and "saltatory"—it will be continual but with sudden leaps as the quantitative scale reaches a qualitative point. The *Divine Comedy* is the most perfect artistic and imaginative representation of such a journey and thus exploits the resources of the hierarchical organization of experience to its utmost. The pilgrim must be carried down to the lower Hell, from which he makes mysterious transitions upward during the nights in Purgatory, whereas every transition to a higher sphere in the *Paradiso* takes place in the luminous blindness of ecstatic raptures.[83]

Between these transitions Dante has been in a section of the universe which is in some sense uniform and in which the distinctions are more of degree than of kind, so that the transitions signal the entry into a new dimension of moral experience. The miraculous or ecstatic character of these transitions is really the representation of the charismatic nature of the journey. They are of the type of divine intervention through grace and remain essentially mysterious, requiring the help of supernatural agents or special gifts of divine illumination.

Yet the gradualistic nature of the journey is indicated in Dante's careful preparation of events, whether through imagery, dream, or vision. Questions are introduced and increasingly clarified at intervals through the poem in conformity with the expansion of the pilgrim's consciousness, and everywhere the universal vision is filtered through the gradually altering consciousness of the pilgrim. Not only is the progress of the pilgrim through the whole hierarchy thus a dramatic one, but he also dramatically reveals his altering character by his interaction with his guides and the souls he encounters. At each level of the poem there is a variety of tone and event which permits the pilgrim to react variously *within* each level of the ladder as well as *on* each level.

Dante's whole revaluation of the doctrines of love of his predecessors depended on shifting the seat of love from lower to higher levels of the psychological faculties, from the vegetative and sensitive souls to the rational soul itself. The failure to understand this has been a source of some confusion in Dante scholarship, a confusion which may be said to have its point of origin in reading too much explicit philosophical content into the erotic doctrines of the troubadours, Andreas Capellanus, and the early Sicilian poets. Dante does of course draw on the traditions, but the great work of conceptualizing, adapting, and systematizing an inherited cluster of values and attitudes on love is largely his own. However, Dante did not follow Avicenna and Cavalcanti in placing the seat of love in the mortal, interior sense called the *vis estimativa* or *cogita-*

tiva. Man shared this sense with the animals, and it was, as St. Thomas tells us, a "particular reason," in that it could judge of dangers and pleasures but could not abstract universals. It was therefore not a spiritual function like reason. To say that Dante locates love in this faculty is to make the pursuit of Beatrice through the *intelligible* universe beyond the grave philosophically and psychologically untenable, and for obvious reasons. Indeed, it is the burden of the *Vita nuova* to tell us how Dante transcended this point of view, shared by so many of his predecessors, and how Beatrice became the glorious lady of his mind (*la gloriosa donna della mia mente*). Certainly the first encounter with Beatrice was experienced in the sensitive soul, with all the clamor of vital spirits and agitation of their organic seats, but this love became transformed into a love of the mind, *amor mentis*, both transcending and incorporating the lower form.

This is the message of the great lyrics "Amor che nella mente mi ragiona" (Love which reasons with me in my mind) and especially "Donne ch'avete intelletto d'amore," which is perhaps more accurately translated as "Ladies who have loving intellects" rather than "Ladies who have intelligence of love." As I have tried to show elsewhere, Dante in the *Purgatorio* even coped with the problem of why the love of the mind can seize on a particular as well as a universal good by adapting the scholastic doctrine of *complacentia* or *connaturalitas*, terms which he renders by the Italian *piacere*. In transcending the doctrine which located love in the *sensitiva* or *cogitativa* Dante was forced to explain what had previously needed no explanation at all, for the *cogitativa* turned by nature to a particular and to no other. The new problem was how the volitional faculty of mind will turn to a particular, bind itself there, and then pursue it. *Piacere*, a certain affinity or "complacency" between the mind and a particular, is the answer. We recognize in this problem the kind of question which led Duns Scotus to his concept of *haeceitas*.

The *Vita nuova* is the record of the transformation of love from the bewildering first experiences felt in the lower vegetative and sensitive souls to the realization of the presence and efficacy of the love of the glorious lady of his mind.[84] It encloses as personal experiences, and in the hierarchical framework, the moments of troubadour love, the experiences of love of the so-called poets of the *dolce stil nuovo*, transforming love into a power that can reach through the whole of reality including those rungs of the universal hierarchy which lie beyond the grave.

II

The Light-Metaphysics Tradition

FROM the beginning of the *Divine Comedy*—"where the sun is silent"—to the final vision of light, the poem is a carefully ordered hierarchy of lights and shadows. Not only are we asked to see clearly, we are asked to see qualitatively, to distinguish degrees of light and kinds of vision. It is in the last canto of the *Paradiso* that the degree of light is most intense and that our attention is called to a unique kind of seeing. With extraordinary insistence, Dante repeats some form of the verb *vedere* (to see) or a derivative thereof every few lines. The transition from time to eternity and from the finite to the infinite makes all the more sophisticated resources of language inadequate, and one must revert to a childlike form of emphasis, mere repetition. This simplest of rhetorical devices is, by some miracle of art, adequate for the expression of an almost unimaginable human experience. In every line we feel something of Dante's joy in the possession of a *novella vista* and his rapture in the divine vision, an effect conveyed by the very struggle to express the inexpressible. The struggles are, of course, those of Dante the pilgrim; Dante the poet is in perfect control of his artistic resources, and it is through the masterly rendering of inadequacy that the whole presentation becomes—paradoxically—adequate.

With mounting intensity we are brought face to face with that light which is God, the supreme, pure, true, and eternal light. We see Him both as *luce*, the source of light, and as *lume*, His reflected splendor in the universe of thought, the radiance which beautifies the angels and the blessed. We see Him as the simple light, the unity wherein Dante saw the reduction of all the multiplicity of the universe, substance and accidents, the scattered pages of the universe bound together.

The question for us here is whether the metaphors of light and vision are simply figures expressive of what is a purely intellectual comprehension of the ultimate reality, or are they literally used? Is light for Dante an ontological principle, as it was for many in his day, a principle which runs through the whole of reality, ordering it in a hierarchy of graded intensity and purity of light leading to a light which is both supersensuous and supernatural? Was there for him a ladder of light leading to the same ultimate reality which thought reached as it worked its way up through the structure of the intelligible universe? An examination of what we now call the "metaphysics of light" will show that Dante's imagery of light was not conceived as more or less adequate representation of a reality whose real nature is conceptual and imageless, but as a literal description of that reality.

Light from the most ancient times has been symbolic of divinity. Man's natural revulsion before the darkness of the grave expressed itself as a striving toward the sun, toward the source of light and warmth, the very principle of life. The divinization of the sun and of light finds expression in many of the religions of the East, especially Zoroastrianism, and even the Greek Olympians shone in a blazing splendor.[1] There is, of course, a great difference between the early mythological thinking which raises the sun or visible light to the status of a divinity and the biblical expression of God as light, which is rather an attempt to express a purely spiritual divinity through light symbolism, although the appearance of God as a burning bush or as a pillar of fire is evidence of a residue of sun mythology. The image of ultimate reality as light appears in the earliest period of Greek thought in Heraclitus' conception of the first principle of fire, a fire which is Zeus, the world order, and universal reason at the same time.

The ultimate sources of the metaphysics of light go back, therefore, to the very beginnings of religious and philosophical speculation, to what we would call today a universal and archetypal image for the interpretation of experience. For the more sophisticated forms of the metaphysics and theology of light, which were so important in the history of Christian thought and which were especially developed in the thirteenth century, there are three principal sources.[2] The first is Greek and goes back to Plato's famous analogy in the *Republic* between Good and the sun (508B, C; 509B).

Plato begins his argument by maintaining that the artificer who made the senses was especially lavish with the sense of sight. All the other senses have only two aspects, the active sense itself and the object of sense. Sight stands in need of a third factor, light, which is par excellence the property of the sun. Likewise there is a third factor needed between truth and the intellect—the Good, the sun of the realm of ideas. The sun of the sensible world stands in the same relation to vision and visible things as the Good of the intelligible world does to intelligence and intelligible things. Indeed, the sensible sun is an offspring which the Good created in the visible world to fulfill a function of mediation analogous to its own. The Good is the cause of knowledge, of truth itself, and is of still higher worth than both of these. Just as light and vision are like the sun but not identical with it, so knowledge and truth are like the Good, different from and lower than it. There are thus two powers, the Good which reigns over the intelligible world and the sun which rules over the visible world. The one confers being on its world, the other is the principle of generation in its world.

The question soon arose whether Plato literally meant that the source of physical light was derivative from the source of intellectual light or that there was merely a relationship of simple analogy between them. The subsequent development of this doctrine of an intellectual light by the Alexandrians, Stoics, Gnostics, and especially the Neoplatonists tended to emphasize a relationship of real filiation between intellectual and material light. The Neoplatonists made light rather than the sun the highest principle of the visible world and affirmed that light, in the most proper sense of the word, referred to an intellectual and immaterial light of which sensible light was a lowly derivative. It was in this form that the doctrine was known to the Middle Ages through the works of Pseudo-Dionysius, the *Liber de causis*, and, most of all, through the works of St. Augustine who constitutes a second and Latin source for this doctrine.[3]

In St. Augustine we find these Neoplatonic influences used to elucidate the numerous biblical allusions to God as light. Christ is called light in the true sense of the word, not in the figurative sense in which He is called a stone: "Neque enim et Christus sic dicitur lux, quomodo dicitur lapis: sed illud proprie, hoc utique figurate." [4]

St. Augustine adopted the famous Platonic metaphor of the Good as sun of the intelligible world, which had been widely used by both pagan Neoplatonists and Christian fathers, and made it the cornerstone of his doctrine of illumination as a substitute for abstraction in the process of understanding.[5] In the operation of the intelligible sun there are three factors analogous to three factors in the sensible sun: that which is, that which is understood, and that which makes something capable of being understood. Similarly the physical sun is, makes something glow, and shines upon it.[6] Indeed, God is nothing other than intelligible light itself, by which all intelligible things shine in their intelligibility.[7]

God—light in the true sense, which is spiritual rather than corporeal—is the uncreated light who creates an incorporeal light by which we understand and a corporeal light by which we see.[8] In his attack on Manichaean materialism St. Augustine sharply distinguished between an intelligible light which is created, an uncreated light which is God Himself, and a created material light which is needed by the physical sense of sight.[9] These are not the only kinds of light, for besides the light of reason, the God of light, and physical light, the angelic host is made of some kind of substantial light.[10]

In the sensible universe light is the finest, noblest, most active, and least gross of substances and holds the first place: "In corporibus autem lux primum tenet locum." [11] The relationship between the various kinds of created and uncreated material and immaterial lights in St. Augustine is not always consistent, but it is abundantly clear his epistemology and, to a lesser degree, his ontology depend on some such kind of *sui generis* light which the Neoplatonists postulated.[12]

The third source of the philosophy of light is directly Judaeo-Arabic. Among the Arabs in the twelfth and thirteenth centuries there was a great development of the philosophy of light, and this was preceded and accompanied by considerable work in optics and in the psychology of vision. The ideas of leading Arabic and Jewish thinkers on light such as Algazel, Avicenna, Avencebrol, and Isaac Israeli were transmitted to Christian Europe by means of Latin translations.[13]

As a result of these translations, a strongly Neoplatonic doctrine of light penetrated the whole intellectual atmosphere of thirteenth-century Europe. Sometimes the emphasis was on a mystical theory of light, sometimes on the metaphysical theory, and sometimes on a scientific theory. St. Bonaventura and the author of the *De intelligentiis* synthesize the various forms of speculation about light, and these represent the most comprehensive attempts to see the whole universe *sub specie lucis*.[14]

St. Thomas Aquinas, however, whose writings are often used as "source books" for the study of the *Divine Comedy*, was aware of the speculation on light going on in his time and decided against the existence of a *sui generis* light. He calls attention to the difference of opinion among the fathers on this question and ranges St. Augustine against St. Ambrose and St. John Damascenus. Citing an Augustinian passage that light is literally and properly predicated of spiritual substances, he decides against Augustine[15] and attributes Augustine's notion that corporeal light is the noblest and first of corporeal things to the philosophy which was prevalent in his time and which he naturally learned. His authority in these matters was therefore not compelling.[16]

St. Thomas' most comprehensive treatment of the question of light metaphysics is in lectio XIV of Book II of his commentary on Aristotle's *De anima*. He takes up in turn the various theories on corporeal and immaterial forms of light and rejects them, deciding that light is a quality or "accident" of body. Although he rejects the various theories of a substantial light, no matter how it was conceived, St. Thomas also offers to explain why these errors came about. In the first place, the metaphysicians of light mistook metaphorical for literal expressions, an understandable error because sight is the noblest and most spiritual of the senses. The primacy of sight was also most important for the metaphysicians of light who, as will be shown, made it a central doctrine in their speculations on the relationship between beauty and truth. St. Thomas also accepts the idea of a scale of luminosity, the nobler elements being more luminous than the inferior ones; but light is merely a quality for him, an accidental sign for a higher grade of actuality in corporeal things, not the key to the structure of the universe. St. Thomas rejects the view that light is a body and maintains that the proponents of this theory have been misled by metaphors of light such as "a ray goes through the air," it is "thrown back," "rays intersect." The use of metaphors drawn from corporeal phenomena applies no more to light than to heat (nn. 413–414).

St. Thomas also rejects the view that light is spiritual. The proponents of this view have been deceived by the metaphorical language applied to light, as when the term light is used in speaking of intellectual matters. Their position is untenable because anything spiritual or intelligible cannot be an object of sensation. St. Thomas adds, however, that if anyone wants to maintain that there is a spiritual light other than the light which appears to the senses, he will not argue with him so long as he admits that the sensible light is not spiritual. He concludes, with a slight touch of irony, that there is no reason why two entirely different things should not have the same name, thus rejecting any conception of filiation or analogy between various so-called kinds of light. He seems in this instance to have St. Bonaventura in mind (nn. 415–416).

He continues explaining why light and terms drawn from seeing are used in reference to intellectual matters. This is done because of the special dignity of the sense of sight. It is the most spiritual and subtlest of the senses. One reason for this conclusion is that the objects of sight are visible in virtue of properties which the inferior, that is, sublunary, bodies possess in common with celestial bodies. Touch, on the other hand, senses properties such as heat and cold, which are properties of the four sublunary elements; taste and smell sense the properties of compound bodies in various ways corresponding to the proportions of the four primary qualities, hot, cold, wet, and dry, or fire, earth, water, and air, that they possess. Sound, which is a result of motion through space, is, like light, also sensed in terms of properties shared with the celestial regions, but the kinds of motion are different, celestial motion being circular, whereas sublunary motion is linear. In virtue of this, hearing is next to sight in dignity (n. 417).

St. Thomas maintains that the dignity of sight is also manifested if we consider the way in which sight operates. With all the other senses a material or "natural" change takes place along with whatever is spiritual in their operation. What St. Thomas means here is that in taste, smell, touch, and hearing the sense organ suffers material change. They all, in various degrees, receive sensible forms without which we could not have knowledge, but the organ itself is modified in the process. With the sense of sight, however, the organ does not change. There is only a spiritual change. When something is tasted or touched, the organ itself grows hot or cold by contact with a similar object. There is not merely some spiritual alteration, but a change in the natural or physical order as well. This does not happen with the sense of sight, since it is exclusively spiritual in its operation. It is therefore the noblest of the senses (n. 418).

St. Thomas then rejects the opinion of those who maintain that light is simply the manifestation of color (n. 419) and of those who think that light is the substantial form of the sun (n. 420). He rejects the first opinion on the obvious grounds that objects are sometimes visible without their color being also visible, at night, for instance, and the second on the same grounds that he rejected the notion that light is spiritual or intelligible, namely, that such a light would not be an object of sensation.

The same people who maintained that light was the substantial form of the sun also maintained that it had the kind of being that belongs to objects causing knowledge as such (*esse intentionale*). This idea he rejects on the ground that whatever has this kind of being cannot cause material change, whereas it is apparent that the light radiating from the heavenly bodies does cause change. He concludes that, just as corporeal elements possess certain active qualities by means of which they effect material changes, light emanating from the heavens affects material things on earth, thereby revealing itself to be the active quality of the heavenly bodies. Thus the latter are active through their light (n. 420).

If light is not either a corporeal or spiritual substance or a substantial form, what is it? St. Thomas answers that it is a quality of the first among those bodies which effect changes and that, unlike heat, it has no contrary ("qualitas primi corporis alterantis, quod non habet contrarium"). The first among those bodies which produce change is the kind of body which constitutes the celestial realms. The fact that it has no contrary is important, for St. Thomas uses this property of the quality or "accident" of light to explain the instantaneous diffusion of light which Grosseteste and his followers explained by conceiving light as the first substantial form of body as such. Since light has no contrary, there is no "resistance" in its recipient or in the matter for its act. St. Thomas also accepts Aristotle's view that light is a kind of color of the transparent or diaphanous (n. 405). A transparent body is thus always immediately disposed to receive its form, and this is why illumination takes place immediately, whereas heating takes place by degrees. This effect, the spreading of light (*lux*) through the diaphanous or transparent, is called luminosity (*lumen*). It is a ray (*radius*) when it takes place in a straight line from the source to what is illumined, and it is *splendor* when it is reflected. But *lumen* is also the generic name for every effect of light in the transparent or *diaphanum* (n. 421).

Because light possesses these characteristics, St. Thomas continues, we can understand why certain bodies are opaque, others diaphanous, and others lucent. Since light is primarily an accident, a quality inhering in corporeal celestial substances, the closer a nature is to these same substances the more luminous it will be. The various corporeal substances are arranged in order from earth, through air, water, and fire, to the most perfect and least material of bodies, and this same series also constitutes a scale of greater actualization, greater possession of form, and greater luminousness (n. 422). Light is thus a quality that the bodies with more form, being, and act possess more fully than lesser bodies, but it is not their very essence or substance.[17]

In this passage St. Thomas does not name his opponents, although, as we have noted, he elsewhere rather circumspectly rejected the authority of St. Augustine. In *Quaestiones quodlibetales* VI, q. 11 a. 19, on the question whether or not the empyrean heaven influences inferior bodies, he explicitly rejects the authority of the *Liber de intelligentiis* on light as the actualizing principle, although he agrees with the author that the empyrean does influence lower bodies. St. Thomas, incidentally, refers in this instance to having changed his own opinion on the matter. He maintains that the author of the *De intelligentiis* was right about the influence but wrong in maintaining that light is basically the actualizing principle. The latter is rather "being, in act" (*ens actu*).

We note again St. Thomas' mistrust of metaphor and the implication that the light metaphysicians are misled by them. He continues that light can be predicated properly only of bodies, directly contradicting the authority of St. Augustine who had, as shown, maintained that it is properly predicated only of God. It is for St. Thomas a form of the first among those bodies which act as agents, that is, the celestial bodies, a quality which they possess.[18]

That Dante was profoundly influenced by the metaphysics of light will become apparent in the course of this study, and in view of this influence the prevalent and popular view that Dante was a thoroughgoing Thomist needs considerable revision. The speculations of St. Bonaventura, for example, provide a better key to some elements of great importance in the actual architecture of Dante's universe, especially the *Paradiso*, than does the work of Aquinas. Dante seems in this instance to have accepted a philosophical position which St. Thomas found untenable. As a true artist he instinctively chose the viewpoint which gave the symbol and image a higher status than St. Thomas was willing to grant them. Some further examples from St. Thomas will serve to make his distrust of poetry and poetic method clearer. In the *Summa theologiae* St. Thomas takes up the question of the difference between metaphor in Scripture and theology and in poetry. St. Thomas grants that theology needs images, but only to transcend them as much as possible. Sacred Scripture uses metaphor to accommodate divine truth to our finite intellects, to lead the mind to true comprehension. Metaphorical expression also serves to stimulate the mind to a quest for a true comprehension of divine truths and, in the case of the ignorant, to explain these truths to people who are not capable of rising to the realm of the "intelligible."

Poetry, on the other hand, is merely the lowest of the kinds of knowledge (*est infima inter omnes doctrinas*). Its function is to make pleasing pictures or representations, since man, by nature, is pleased by such pictures.[19] St. Thomas thus maintains that the use of metaphor is common to both poetry and theology, but in the former it obscures a lower truth whereas in the latter it discloses a truth which would not otherwise be known. This particular emphasis is made clear in a passage on metaphor from his commentary on Peter Lombard's "Sentences," where he argues that the methods of branches of knowledge which are entirely different cannot be the same. Although poetry which contains the least portion of truth uses metaphor in common with theology, the science of poetry concerns things which cannot be comprehended by reason because of their lack of truth, and the reason must therefore be deluded by similarities; but in theology the symbolical method is used to lead the mind to the suprarational.[20]

Thus St. Thomas accepts metaphor in theology as the only way to a suprarational truth, but not, as we have seen, in philosophy where discourse must be proportionate to reason. Metaphor in poetry lures the mind into some kind of pseudo-understanding by "seducing" it with mere similitudes. However, similitudes have an important psychological power: they can persuade a person to vary his estimate of a thing so that the notion of food, for example, may inspire loathing if it is described in terms of something loathsome. It is the function of the poet to use this power responsibly and to draw his reader to virtue.[21]

Dante was able to find a suitable cosmology within the light-metaphysics tradition, a tradition which rendered reality in a richly metaphorical way and which reduced all substantiality to analogous forms of light. We must first examine the main doctrine of the metaphysics of light in the final elaboration of the doctrine that took place in the thirteenth century. In the *Liber de intelligentiis*, erroneously ascribed to Witelo, an older contemporary of Dante who was famous for his work in optics, but now dated earlier, we find the derivation of material from spiritual light repeatedly affirmed. The author begins by citing an Augustinian passage that St. Thomas had attacked in support of his own views. "God," he says, "is called light in the literal and not the metaphorical sense of the word." Light is the first of substances, and it is indeed God Himself of whom light is actually predicated. This is a literal predication and is not "translated" or metaphorical, as when God is called a lamb.[22] All other substances besides God, the first of substances, merely participate in light in varying degrees of intensity and *per prius et posterius*, according to their nearness to the primary light, either immediately or through varying degrees of mediation.[23] The most divine, noble, and beautiful aspect of things is their light, a light which all things have in varying degrees and which thus constitutes a hierarchy of luminous beauty leading to God. Every substance that exerts any influence on another either is light or possesses the nature of light. All causality is therefore reduced to the efficacy of light and is conceived in terms of an emanation of light as causal power from the first of substances Himself.[24]

Bartholomew of Bologna, the author of another important

treatise on light, the *Tractatus de luce*, expounds the idea of the causal power of light at greater length than does any other light metaphysician. Superior bodies act upon lower bodies through the agency of light and motion which flows down from them. Since the greater the extent of concentration of causal power, the greater the activity, it follows that the earth is the most capable of producing things, and in greater diversity than any other element, since the efficacy of the heavens is concentrated upon it from every direction.[25] The power of light is in direct proportion to the unity of the body which emits it. The more unified such a body, the more it is capable of multiplying its own rays and consequently its own power.[26] Since the earth is at the center of the universe, it receives the multiplied energies of all the more unified bodies and that power which is light. This is the reason why there is more activity on earth than in the celestial regions. Light as the causal principle also conciliates the elements so that they may form stable mixtures. The processes of nature thus depend on the agency of light. It is the light radiating from the luminous heavenly bodies which provides the "act" of this conciliation.[27]

Unlike the author of the *De intelligentiis*, Bartholomew makes a rather careful distinction between the divine light and the light radiating from the heavenly bodies. He finds in the operation of material light suggestions as to the properties and workings of the divine or spiritual light. But the relationship between the two kinds of light is purely analogical and is never described as substantial or essential derivation. Thus as the light of corporeal bodies conciliates the elements, the divine light conciliates body and soul. As the natural hostility between the elements of the "greater world" of the created universe, the macrocosm, is overcome by light and changed to a certain "friendliness," so the divine light, by conferring grace, overcomes the natural hostility of body and soul in the "lesser world" of man, the microcosm.[28]

Corporeal light is first in the order of sensible things, and the immaterial light which is God is first in the higher order of spiritual or intelligible things. Material light is highest in its order because not only is it visible in itself but is is the cause of other things being seen. Similarly, God is both the perfect intelligible and the reason whereby all things are intelligible. God and light are respectively first in their own genus, and all things ordered beneath these two categories are more or less visible or more or less intelligible to the degree that they are "close" to the very principle of intelligibility or visibility.[29] The closer a thing is to what is supreme in its own genus, the more it participates in its condition. We might note that Bartholomew does not use participation to mean a sharing of the same essence, nor does he derive sensible light from the divine or intelligible light.[30]

Unlike Bartholomew, who keeps the intelligible and sensible realms distinct and carefully distinguishes the divine from sensible light, the author of the *De intelligentiis* states that to the extent that a thing participates in the nature of light—and as we shall see below, all things do—to that extent it participates in the divine being itself: "Unumquodque quantum habet de luce, tantum retinet de esse divini . . . si lux est ens divinum per essentiam, sicut ostensum est, participatio lucis est participatio esse divini."[31] It follows from this that the hierarchy of light and the hierarchy of being are one. It is to the degree that its nature is luminous that a thing finds its place in the hierarchical order of beings which extends from the lowest of finite beings to the infinite being which is God. For the author of *De intelligentiis* this hierarchy seems to be constituted throughout by a diffusion of the divine being itself, a pantheistic, or truly monistic, version of light metaphysics which Bartholomew avoids. Both would agree that the degree of being of a thing as well as its causal efficacy is a function of its luminousness, but Bartholomew carefully breaks the universal ladder of light in two, keeping the Creator distinct from His creation and establishing a purely analogical relationship between the two kinds of light, whereas the author of the *De intelligentiis* unifies the universe with the divine being itself.

Albertus Magnus also finds in light the principle of continuity in the universe and calls the first cause pure light, adding, however, that in this pure light alone are existence and essence one, thus radically distinguishing the self-subsistent nature of the divine light from other kinds of light: "Causa enim prima lumen purum est, super quod non est aliud lumen, propter quod in ipsa idem est esse et quod est." [32] Yet the whole ladder of being results from the "downward" radiation or fall of this primal light of being and is described in language strongly suggestive of emanationistic pantheism: "Ordinem in gradibus entium non facit nisi casus et occubitus a lumine primi entis." [33] We have here a kind of halfway position between Bartholomew and the *De intelligentiis*. The philosopher in Albert pushes toward the unified conception while the Christian forces him toward orthodox dualism in his ontology.

Light is also the measure of nobility in that the divine being is communicated to the lower beings in the form of light, so that the more luminous a thing appears the nobler it is. Indeed, *nobilis* is virtually a transcendental predicate corresponding to *lux*.[34] Light thus not only constituted a hierarchy of being and causality but a hierarchy of value, of good, "nobility," and beauty.[35] From this notion the author of *De intelligentiis* draws the conclusion that light is the principle of life. All things have the nature of light, but light does not confer life and motion to all things, not because of any defect in its power, but because of a defect in the "matter" receiving it, the passive principle which is, in the lowest beings, too inert to receive or manifest the gifts of light.[36]

Light is the source of all activity and has peculiar properties which reveal its essentially active nature. The behavior of light which elicited the most curiosity and speculation was the manner in which it diffused itself in all directions from a center, forming a sphere. This diffusion was not conceived as either a material change or a change in place but as an instantaneous multiplication of light itself in three dimensions (*multiplicatio*). Grosseteste provides us with one of the earliest descriptions of this process in the Western literature on light, and he is echoed by others later. We might observe that his conception is different from that of St. Thomas, who thought of the spreading of light as the instantaneous diffusion of a quality, a quality which can so operate because it has no contrary. Grosseteste, on the other hand, thinks of light as actually and substantially multiplying itself, a conception properly belonging to light metaphysics rather than to the more general currents of light speculation.[37]

This capability of self-multiplication suggested to the author of the *De intelligentiis* the manner in which light was the principle of motion and life. It is the first operation of light in things of the sensible order to confer life: "Est autem prima lucis operatio in sensibilibus quod motum et vitam operatur in viventibus." [38] The reader will recall the Platonic and Aristotelian notion of the soul as essentially motion or activity, not the passive recipient of activity but an originating source of it. The *multiplicatio* of light was obviously analogous to the notion of soul as essentially motion, for both conceptions imply the concept of autonomous activity. Light was therefore conceived as a kind of creative force similar to soul. But God is creative activity par excellence and therefore light in the true sense of the word.[39]

Corporeal light was thought to have another peculiar characteristic which gave it a unique status among corporeal things. It was not pure form because it was something material and not spiritual, nor could it be pure matter because it could not then be the active energetic substance that it is. It was therefore the form of corporeity itself (*forma corporeitatis*) or the principle of extension itself. Since light possesses of its very nature the power to multiply itself in every direction, it introduces dimension in every direction into matter and extends matter in its own self-diffusion. If light were either form or matter alone, it would lack dimensions, but light is a form with the power of creating dimensions through its capacity of self-diffusion.[40] As such a corporeal form it is the most exalted and noblest of all corporeal forms and bears the closest resemblance to the forms which exist apart from matter, the intelligences or angels themselves.[41]

St. Bonaventura repeats this notion and calls light the fundamental form of body as such.[42] Therefore, wherever there is body there is light.[43] He also agrees with the author of the *De intelligentiis* that light is the principle of being of all corporeal objects. Things are constituted in their order in the hierarchy of being to the degree that they have light in its role as the substantial form of bodies. Whence it follows that the most noble of corporeal substances, the empyrean, is the most luminous and that the lowest, earth, is opaque. All things between are more or less noble according to their luminousness.[44] Light itself is therefore the noblest of corporeal things: "Lux cum sit form nobilissima inter corporalia, sicut dicunt philosophi et sancti." [45] Even the lowest of corporeal objects are not entirely without light as may be proved if we polish some opaque object or make glass from "cinder." [46] In all corporeal substances, light is not only their principle of being and nobility, dignity and excellence, but the form which conserves them in their being and is their principle of activity.[47]

The metaphysicians of light not only agree in reducing all the positive principles of the universe to light, but conceive of the corporeal universe as a hierarchy of gradations of light whose luminosity is the measure (*mensura*) of the place they occupy in the order of things. Between heaven and earth are ranged the elements in mounting degree of being, efficacy, nobility, and splendor.[48] The Empyrean, which is the most luminous, noble, and efficacious of bodies, controls the processes of generation that take place in the sublunary world by transmitting its light down through the hierarchy.[49] It is the cause of life by transmitting that light whose effect is to "vivify" by actualizing the vegetative and sensitive functions of living things.[50] It is the very form of the first sphere, and through this instrument it controls the processes of generation in all that the first sphere encloses.[51] For Bonaventura, light was not only the hierarchical principle and the principle of continuity in the corporeal universe; he also accepted the Augustinian view that light is that by which the body is united to the soul and by which the soul rules the body.[52] Its status as the corporeal substance most like spirit made it a kind of connecting link between the spiritual and corporeal orders.[53]

Bartholomew, with evident reference to the Augustinian doctrine of the intellectual light, maintains that the ladder of intelligibility as well as the ladders of light and being are ordered in relation to their distance from the first or uncreated light. The higher levels of the ladder of being and light are in themselves more intelligible, although the subject of knowledge knows them only to the extent that the subject is near to the Primal Light itself. Light is both the principle of being and the principle of intelligibility, and the understanding of the "outer light" requires proportional increase of the "inner light" *pari passu.*[54]

In summary, the essentials of this *doctrina communis* of light were the following:

(1) Light is the principle of being, activity, extension, causal efficacy, life, motion, nobility, and excellence; indeed, everything positive is somehow light or of the nature of light, the opposite of which would be the sheer negation of darkness.[55]

(2) As the fundamental form of body as such, light is the substantial form of the universe and provides the universe with its principle of continuity.

(3) It is the noblest of corporeal things and has an intermediate place between body and soul, matter and spirit.

(4) It is not only the principle which constitutes the universe but, as spiritual light, the principle by which the intellect understands.

(5) All these notions were set in the framework of a hierarchically ordered universe.

Light was truly a kind of Proteus, appearing in many shapes and forms, as uncreated spiritual light, as created spiritual light, as intellectual light, as corporeal light. One way or another, the whole of reality turned out, upon examination, to be light in various disguises, and the various forms of light were not always carefully distinguished from each other. In some cases the distinctions did not matter too much, but one related problem had the most important implications for Christian orthodoxy: What is the relation between the corporeal light which is the principle of continuity in nature and the immaterial light which is God? Are these two lights ultimately one? If so, there is one explanation for the totality of things, and the intellect can rest. Or are the two "lights" radically different and irreducible to one principle? The danger in this problem for Christian thinkers is the danger of pantheism, for if light is predicated of God and His creatures in a univocal sense, then God and nature are of one essence. We have seen that there were three typical answers concerning this relationship:

(1) Emanation, whereby the corporeal light was derived from the uncreated light and participated in the Divine Being, for example, the doctrine of *De intelligentiis*.

(2) Analogy, wherein the two kinds of light bore a purely analogical relationship to each other, having no community of being, for example, the doctrine of Bartholomew of Bologna and St. Bonaventura.

(3) A mixture of the two in which the relationship was *imagined* as emanation but *conceived* in terms which kept the Creator quite distinct from His creation, for example, the doctrine of Albertus Magnus.

The various treatises on light do not, of course, fit perfectly into these categories. The *De intelligentiis* distinguishes, as do all the "light metaphysicians," between the corporeal and incorporeal light while affirming that both partake of the Divine Being.[56] On the other hand, St. Bonaventura and Bartholomew affirm an analogical and metaphorical relationship between the two kinds of light, yet color their accounts in some degree with the language of emanationistic Neoplatonism.[57]

St. Bonaventura provides us with a classic orthodox solution to the problem. He begins by citing the same Augustinian text cited in the *De intelligentiis*, that God is the true light and that light is more properly to be predicated of spiritual than corporeal things.[58] The predicate, light, is only "literally" true of spiritual substances and therefore only metaphorically true of corporeal things. But even in the spiritual realm there remained a problem, for God, who is pure intellectual light, and the light which is the substance of the intelligences were both spiritual light.

The answer resided in the concept of analogy. As the problem of pantheism was solved in the predication of being by the notion of a purely analogical relationship between God and His creatures, so the pantheistic tendencies of a doctrine which made light the substantial form of the universe, its principle of continuity, were avoided by an equivalent analogy of light: "Lux spiritualis est communis creatori et creaturae secundum analogiam."[59] Corporeal light is simply that which in its active, energetic nature most closely resembles the eternal light, Bonventura maintains, referring to the authority of Dionysius.[60]

Bartholomew of Bologna is even more detailed about the analogical nature of the resemblance between the immaterial and material light. His method is to draw rather elaborate parallels between the properties of the two kinds of light. For example, there are three modes in which mental illuminations descend upon us from the First Light (*Prima Lux*) who is Christ: (1) by drawing close to the source of light Himself (*per illuminabilis ad lucem approximationem*); (2) by a concentration or focusing of the emanating rays upon us (*per radiorum emanatium aggregationem*); (3) by a direct linear procession of the rays to their object (*per rectitudinalem processionem*). For each one of the modes of spiritual illumination an *exemplum* is to be found in the properties of material light.[61] Clearly, there was an exemplarism of light as well as an exemplarism of creatures. The widespread doctrine that the world constituted a set of images of a spiritual reality, that things were not merely things but signs and lessons as well, was applied to light.

The first source and principle of all light, created and uncreated, is the Eternal Father, from whom there directly proceeds the principal ray, Christ. The source of light, the Father (*luminis fontale principium*), through the chief ray, Jesus Christ (*per ipsum principlem radium*), produces three secondary lights (*tria secondaria lumina*) which in their various ways illuminate the mind: the book of creatures, the book of Scriptures, and the book of internal inspiration. If anyone should turn to these secondary lights and thereby desire to see with the mind the Father or fount of all these lights Himself (*horum omnium luminum fontem*), he must pass beyond the limits of these secondary lights to the principal ray, Jesus Christ, in seeing whom he will also see the Father. The divine light, in a manner similar to corporeal light, reveals its source. That is to say, it is necessary to pass from the secondary lights to the principal ray to the source of light. We discover the divine light in a manner similar to that in which scattered light leads to a ray which in turn leads to a source.[62]

This passage is striking in the curious transitions from a literal to a purely metaphorical discourse on light. The light of internal contemplation clearly suggests the intellectual light, and the light of creatures suggests light as the principle of being, but the light of the book of creatures is obviously metaphorical and dictated by the need to establish perfect parallelisms and analogies. Bartholomew, here as everywhere, distinguishes carefully between the created and the uncreated light, yet the vocabulary is suggestive of emanationism; the Father is *fontale luminis*, Christ is the principal ray proceeding from the Father; Himself light, He produces three secondary lights, and so on.[63]

The same paradox which manifests itself in the principle of continuity as applied to the great chain of being manifests itself in the continuity of the great chain of light. Light in its various senses is found everywhere in the natural order and in the supernatural order. It is found among angels who are spiritual and created beings and in God Himself who is infinite and uncreated. No matter how the relationship between the various kinds of light was conceived, the transition from the natural to the supernatural order or from the finite to the infinite remained conceptually unbridgeable. No matter how many ideal rungs were placed in the ladder to God, the gap between the last finite rung and God Himself still remained an abyss which thought could not bridge. But if metaphysics of light could not satisfy the intellect, it could feed the imagination which found in the imagery of light a bridge over otherwise impassable gulfs.

We have seen that the ladder of light was also a ladder of nobility, excellence, and dignity, terms suggestive of aesthetic values. Indeed, nobility is virtually a synonym for beauty. Grosseteste is among those who explicitly make light the principle of beauty. He says that light, inasmuch as it is the principle of color, is the beauty and ornament of everything visible. As the principle of extension it creates the proportion and symmetry also necessary for beauty.[64] St. Bonaventura calls light the most beautiful and delightful of all corporeal things: "Lux est pulcherrimum et delectabilissimum et optimum inter corporalia."[65]

Bartholomew considers in some detail how the degrees of light correspond *pari passu* with the degrees of being, truth, actuality, and intelligibility. He concludes that those things are more noble to the sight of the intellect which are more similar to the Primal Light ("patet quod illa essent intellectui, quantum in se est, ad videndum nobiliora, quae primae luci erunt similiora").[66] In discussing the manner in which the divine light perfects and beautifies the soul (*perficit et decorat animum*), he draws an analogy with the way material light beautifies objects. All things being equal, the closer a recipient of light is brought to the heavens, the more it is beautified by light (*lucis natura decorat ipsum*). Therefore the empyrean is more beautified by light than the crystalline sphere, and the crystalline sphere more than the starry sphere. A thing is also made more beautiful by possessing a greater concentration of light (*per maiorem . . . lucis aggregationem*): witness the greater beauty of the sun in respect to the other planets and the greater beauty of the planets themselves when compared to their own transparent spheres.[67]

The author of the *De intelligentiis* affords a more interesting bit of speculation about light as beauty and connects it to a conception of light as the principle and power of cognition or knowledge, an idea which in turn is related to light as the principle of life.[68] The purer and more simple the light in a knowing subject, the more fully is form or species expressed in it. In light the form of things is made manifest, and form is the principle of both being and cognition. The light which is the power of cognition receives the forms of things, that is, knows, with increasing clarity as its light is simpler and purer; but as a more highly polished mirror it will capture images better.[69] The process of knowing, conceived as the union of subject and object, is reduced to a union between the exterior light of the universe and the interior light of the soul, between the light which is the principle of being and the light which is the principle of knowledge. Light therefore brings to our apprehending faculty the highest degree of joy because joy always arises from the harmonious unification of a thing with an object that fits this thing. No relationship can be more harmoniously unifying than that which binds the light of the soul with the light of the universe, the "outer" with the "inner" light. It is as the most pleasing of the objects of apprehension that light reveals itself as beauty, for beauty, in the phrase which was a commonplace of the schools, was that which pleased immediately upon apprehension.[70]

In this same connection the author calls our attention to the unique status of the sense of sight as the most "knowing" sense and quotes Plato's *Timaeus* in the partial translation of Chalcidius.[71] It is important to bear in mind that the joy which light brings to the apprehending faculties is experienced in both sensible and intellectual apprehension. The proper object of the sense of sight is light (*operatio autem visus fit mediante luce*), and the proper object of the inner light of cognition is the outer light which is the principle of being of the universe. In either case apprehension brings both knowledge and that immediate joy which is the experience of beauty. Thus the perception of beauty is inseparable from the process of knowing. Light as the principle which constitutes things in their bodily aspect also "translates" their form, reveals their inner essence, transferring it to the inner light of cognition. The process of knowing which accompanies the perception of beauty takes place on both the corporeal and incorporeal levels. The operation of the sense of sight brings greatest joy, but it also brings knowledge; the operation of the intellect brings knowledge, but it also brings greatest joy. This is so because light is both the principle of cognition and the principle of vision, the principle of being and the principle of "being-known," the principle of beauty (*maximum delectabile*) and the principle of knowledge.

Although the author of the *De intelligentiis* did not follow all the implications of this analysis, they are profound, and the common doctrine of light metaphysics taken as a whole does work them all out. Light as beauty initiates a process of knowing which can rise from the corporeal to the incorporeal level along the continuous hierarchy of light in all its protean identities, through levels of spiritual beauty and truth to the source of all beauty and truth. It was common scholastic doctrine that sight shares knowing with the intellect and that thought has, when dealing with first principles, something of the immediacy of sight. What is important here, however, is that vision and thought have been assimilated to each other through positing some form of light as the basis of both activities. The senses are, in effect, not merely gateways to the intellect, but lower forms in a continuous hierarchy of faculties of knowing, unified by light.

St. Thomas is even more explicit than the author of the *De intelligentiis* in correlating sight and beauty. The eyes desire beauty in the same way that all things seek the possession of a good in which their striving will cease. The appetite for beauty, however, is quieted by the sight or cognition of its object. The function of the eyesight is virtually to be lured by beauty, and this is so because it is a knowing sense and possesses revealing powers. Of all the other senses, only hearing comes close to sight as an avenue of knowledge. For this reason St. Thomas reserves the beautiful as adjective for the object of sight and secondarily for the object of hearing. Things seen and heard may be beautiful, but something tasted or smelled is good.[72]

This discussion by St. Thomas of the good and the beautiful naturally leads to a consideration of love, the correlate of these two. The good is the cause of love from the point of view of the object loved, but a good cannot become the object of appetition unless it is first apprehended. It is for this reason that Aristotle says that corporeal vision is the beginning of love in the order of sensible things (*amor sensitivus*); similarly the contemplation of spiritual beauty or goodness is the principle of spiritual love.[73] Love takes precedence over knowledge only as the principle of motion; knowledge goes before love in attaining. Citing St. Augustine, St. Thomas says that nothing is loved but what is known. Therefore the intelligible which is the goal of understanding is first attained by action of the intellect, as the sensible object is first attained by the action of the sense. There is thus an internal principle of motion directing objects toward their goals, but man will never get there without the use of the faculty of knowledge. He may be automatically impelled, but he can never attain without having conscious knowledge of where he is going.[74] Thus, for St. Thomas, love follows cognition.

The author of the *De intelligentiis* does not share this view. For him love precedes cognition, although it is perfected by cognition. *Delectatio*—the joy which corporeal light brought to the eyes and which light as the principle of being brought to the knower—is finally equated with love. Light, *maxime delectabile*, is thus clearly *maxime amabile*. The ladder of light as the principle of being, beauty, and knowledge is, in effect, the ladder of love.[75] The voluntarism of this view is in disharmony with the dominating intellectualism of St. Thomas, and we find ourselves in a truly Platonic world of thought. Cognition is subordinated to emotional elements of the soul as a means ("ad delectationem enim et amorem ordinatur cognitio"), and it is through cognition that love perfects itself and is increased. This is the true Platonic eros, the power which initiates a striving of the soul for understanding, "an itching and burning as of sprouting wings," eros not as the consequence but as the presupposition of the dialectical process. The renewal of the doctrine is found at least two centuries before the Renaissance and the tractates on love.[76] Cognition helps direct the course of eros, but is clearly ancillary to it. Of course we do not have here the further Platonic conception of love as recollection in the incarnate state of the pure universal forms seen by the soul when it was unencumbered by the body, although the common scholastic doctrine of the natural love implanted in all creatures could serve to account for the existence of eros and thus provide a substitute for *anamnesis*.

The author of *De intelligentiis* further explains that love arises from the union of a thing with something that fits it (*ex coniunctione convenientis cum convenienti*). This union takes place in creatures without understanding through the natural appetite whereby they seek their "ends." In creatures possessing sensation it occurs through the agency of amorous desire, whereas in rational creatures it is a function of the will. Hence natural appetite, desire, and will are themselves means whereby union is achieved with the exemplar, God, or, alternately, the means by which proper subordination to Him in the hierarchy of things is obtained. Thus cognition is a means for love which is in turn a means for ordering the universe and achieving union with God.[77] But we have seen that love was released by the perception of light on both the sensible and intellectual levels, light as beauty and knowledge calling forth the love which, with the help of cognition, orders us and leads us to God. We may thus rise through an amorous vision of "knowing-amorousness" along the ladder of light from levels of corporeal light to levels of spiritual light.

Other metaphysicians of light emphasized this theme and made it central. Commenting upon the creation St. Bonaventura says that the creation of corporeal lights serves as an avenue to the spiritual light.[78] Indeed, they were made to make known the spiritual light.[79] Rupertus Tuitens (Rupert of Deutz) affirms that spiritual light is light in the true sense and that the stars were created in the pattern of spiritual light so that men might rise in their knowledge from material to spiritual things. He also uses the Platonic metaphor of the sun of the intelligible world, important to Augustine as well, to affirm that, although angels are the true light if we compare them to sensible light, compared to God they are not the true light. God is the true light.[80]

This same notion is found in Dante when on the ledge of envy in Purgatory the poets hear the voices of Cain and Aglauros, warning of the penalty the envious must pay. Virgil explains:

> That was the hard bit which should hold a man within his bounds; but you take the bait, so that the hook of the old adversary draws you to him, and then little avails curb or lure [lit., "recall"]. The heavens call you and wheel about you, showing you their eternal beauties, and your eyes gaze only on the earth; therefore He smites you who sees all.[81]

In this passage Dante refers to two "lures" or "calls," the lure of Satan which is a baited hook and the lure of the eternal beauties of the heavens. It is the purpose of the stars which are the beauties of the heavens to "recall" the sinner to God, but this is not possible when he is hardened in his sin and has become, by his own failure to turn his eyes upward, a child of Satan. The lights which are the stars (Dante calls them "luci") are beautiful, and their function is to "call" by their beauty. We see that light in its aspect as the principle of beauty exists in the universe to direct us heavenward. We must use creatures to ascend to the Creator, a process which is actually nothing else than a description of love, the lure of beauty calling the soul.

As St. Bonaventura explains in a striking passage, the beauty of the Creator shines through His creation, and we must climb to the invisible things of God by means of this creation, using it as a ladder. He cites St. Bernard to the effect that the magnitude and beauty (*pulchritudo*) of the creation proclaim the magnitude and beauty (*species*) of the Creator (*De consideratione*, V, 1, 1). So also the Psalmist for whom the heavens proclaim the glory of God; and so also John Damascenus who, commenting on this statement, explains that the proclamation of God's glory takes place through the beauty of the universe from which we infer the beauty of the Artificer and glorify Him. St. Bonaventura adds that for this reason no one should remain in the stage of considering just the beauty of creation, but should use this beauty to rise to the highest beauty—otherwise he would take what should be a means (*via*) and use it as an end, the lowest form of misuse and perversion. The function of beauty is to lead us to the Supremely Beautiful and, as is clear from the authorities, this created beauty is eminently manifested in the heavens and is light, for the Wisdom of the Supreme Artificer is not only manifested in His work but shines through or is "reflected back" through it (*relucet in effectu*).[82]

This theory of a corporeal light necessarily implying the existence of incorporeal light is also a phase of a general doctrine made popular in the thirteenth century by the Neoplatonic *Liber de causis,* a work to which Dante frequently refers. The proposition in question states that a power present in matter is but a weaker manifestation of the same power as it exists apart from matter. Every higher cause in the chain of causes includes every positive quality of the lower, and at the same time it transcends the lower cause.[83] In proposition five of this work we find the same idea applied to the conception of the first cause as the purest and highest light, a light so exalted that it is beyond the power of language to describe.[84]

The presupposition of thought is now clear by which it was possible to infer from the power, beauty, and nobility of corporeal light the true beauty of the spiritual light. Corporeal light exists for the sake of the incorporeal light; the power of the former is simply a reflex or a mirror image, finite but faithful, of the power of the latter. The works of Pseudo-Dionysius the Areopagite were often cited as authority for the doctrine that the created world is constituted by a kind of analogous light, a light analogous to the Father of Light who is essential light. Any created object therefore gives us a means by which we may return to our creator.[85]

It is the function of any hierarchy, and especially the celestial hierarchy, to transmit this essential light to the inferior orders to the extent that the latter are capable of receiving it and to constitute them spotless mirrors (*specula*) of the divine light.[86] They in turn, by receiving the essential light, are rendered capable of further transmitting this light which is beauty. Beauty and light are synonymous terms, and indeed the traces of Dionysius are everywhere evident in medieval speculation on the nature of beauty.[87] The heavenly hierarchy are the first recipients of this divine ray and, by transmitting it to the rest of the universe, constitute the hierarchy of light-beauty, numberless mirror images of the infinite, each one reflecting the infinite in some finite mode, numberless incarnations of beauty arranged in their degrees.[88]

It is in the striking fourth chapter of the *Divine Names* that Dionysius most fully works out the equivalences of the names Light, Beauty, Good. The supreme divine existence, the Good under the aspect of Good-Being, extends its goodness by the very fact of its existence to all things in a manner analogous to the sun shedding its beneficent rays (par. 1).[89] Beginning with the Platonic conception of the Good as the sun of the intelligible world, Dionysius works out in great detail the parallelism between this immaterial sun and the corporeal sun. Both radiate light, spiritual in the one case and material in the other, and both kinds of light are the principle of measure, order, being, life, efficient and final causality, and unity in their respective realms. The two "beams" draw to themselves all things, animate and inanimate, material and spiritual, but their spheres are delimited, the sun operating in the sensible world and dimly imitating the analogous operation of the Good in the intelligible world. The Good is the creator of the visible sun, and its properties are derived from this relationship of filiation. The sun is preeminent among those things by which we may proceed *per visibilia ad invisibilium* (par. 4).[90]

The Good is, under another aspect, the Spiritual or Intelligible Light, the transcendent archetype of light and therefore light in a truer sense than any other light we know (par. 5).[91] It is also the Beautiful, the very principle of Beauty itself, and all things are Beautiful only to the extent that the Beautiful radiates its beautifying rays upon them like light. All beauty is thus a reflex of Divine Beauty, a ray of the Absolute Beauty itself. It is because of this radiation that anything that is beautiful is so in its degree (par. 7).[92]

Light, Beauty, Good are thus interchangeable terms and belong to the same class of terms predicable of the divine. Dionysius blends these Neoplatonic speculations with the Aristotelian principle that God causes as the object of desire, moving, and changing all things through their love for Him. He makes an interesting modification of this doctrine, however, by emphasizing that it is as the Beautiful that all things desire Him. The Good summons all things by its beauty. As the beautiful, it is the object of desire, luring and drawing all things to it. In addition to being itself beautiful, light also confers beauty by being the principle of proportion and measure. Light is thereby the means for unifying two separate ideas of beauty: (1) that beauty is a harmony of parts and (2) that beauty occurs in simple objects (e.g., as color) in which it is a reflection of the Beautiful itself, a participation in the divine essence.[93] The result of the illumination by the

Beautiful and Good of the divine intelligences is union, and when so united they are spoken of as moving in a circular motion.[94] The reader of the *Paradiso* will recall that this is the very same image that ends the poem, signifying the change from rectilinear to circular motion, from the motion of time to the "motion" of eternity.

In addition to being one of the prime medieval authorities for beauty and light, Dionysius was especially important to mystics, for whom the symbolism of light and beauty is a natural language for the inexpressible vision of the absolute. The Cistercian mystic Thomas Gallus of Vercelli at the beginning of the thirteenth century gave particular expression to the union of light metaphysics with mysticism and accorded exclusive importance to light as a path to the divine.[95] Appealing to the authority of Dionysius, he calls God Essential Beauty and Love and identifies divine beauty with pure light. God draws us to Him by means of the luminous beauty of created things, and the end of life is union with that God who is light and in the contemplation of whom there is no difference between vision and love. We must—paradoxically—ascend to that ocean of inaccessible light (*in pelago lucis inaccessibilis*).[96]

The ascent to God along the road of light-beauty culminates in the acquisition of a unique state of being. On the one hand, there is "vision" of the ultimate spiritual reality, direct apprehension of what had previously been an object of thought. The spiritual senses, the "eyes of the soul," begin to operate, and the duality of sense and thought is overcome; the new vision is immediate in its mode of operation and has a spiritual world for its object. On the other hand, this new vision is synonymous with loving; the faculties of apprehension and of appetition are also one. Will, sense, and thought have all been fused into an indivisible unity. In this state, sense does not oppose thought, desire does not outstrip possession, to know is to love, and to love is to know.

Bartholomew of Bologna, elaborating Dionysian ideas in a sermon on the Nativity, distinguishes three ways in which man can see or has seen God. The first, the direct vision of God in heaven, involves the acquisition of a new kind of sight. The "pupils of the eyes" of the saints are made transparent, and they can then see the uncreated light directly and with a sight which reveals its essence (*per nudam et revelativam inspectionem*). The second way is the vision of the incarnate deity in Christ. The third way is through the things of the created world that constitute mirrors in which the uncreated light reveals or expresses Itself.[97]

It is interesting to note that Dante unfolds the vision of God in the *Paradiso* in these three modes. There is a final vision of the primal simple light which is also a vision of totality, all ideas, forms and beings, substance and accidents bound together in one book. The figure of the God-Man also appears in the uncreated light Itself, God in His assumed humanity. The pilgrim reaches these final visions after having seen Paradise as it manifests itself in space and time, in the created world. This manifestation is a kind of "speculation," the primal light reflected in *specula* of ever-increasing luminousness and beauty. Light metaphysics is the controlling conception in the architecture of the *Paradiso*, to such an extent that it requires detailed analysis to show the great degree to which Dante made use of this body of doctrine. Dante's earlier works, however, give abundant evidence of this interest, and the famous letter to Can Grande della Scala is itself a treatise in the light-metaphysics tradition.

III

Light Metaphysics in the Works of Dante

DANTE had been interested in light speculation from the time of the *Convivio* and makes frequent reference to the doctrines. In *Convivio* III, vii, 2–3, Dante describes the manner in which the divine goodness descends upon all things, conferring and maintaining them in their existence. This goodness is at its source most simple and unified, but it is received by all things in various degrees. Citing the *Liber de causis*, he compares it to an outpouring or overflowing of the primal goodness and gives the light of the sun as an example, light which is one in its source but is received diversely by different bodies.[1] The passage he refers to from the *Liber de causis* is section 19 and is an Aristotelianized description of the Neoplatonic conception of emanation. The first cause or Good, remaining one, rules all things. Nor does its essential unity, which differentiates it from all things, prevent it from governing them. This is so because, while remaining one, it is yet able to radiate its power of life and its excellences on all things which receive its gifts to the extent that they are able. This Good which pours itself out is the first cause, and Being as well, an interesting deviation from the main stream of Neoplatonism which places the Good above Being, but in closer harmony with both Christian and Mohammedan theism. The first cause is truly active because there is no relation of continuity between it and what it makes. It is thus a true agent and governor, making things through its beauty and making their final cause a beauty which is supreme.

This inconsistent blend of Neoplatonism with Aristotelianism—which fuses emanationism with a notion of creation; which describes the Good as overflowing in one great outpouring, and yet identifies it with Being and a first cause that remains transcendent over what it produces; which makes the first cause the supremely beautiful acting as final cause through its beauty, yet describes it as the ruler of all things—is far more characteristic of medieval Platonism than any consistently worked-out position.[2]

We have already noted that this blending is best typified by Albertus Magnus among the major medieval thinkers, and, indeed, Dante follows this reference to the *Liber de causis* by a reference to Albertus' *De intellectu et intelligibile* which he cites as an authority for the parallel between the various degrees of illumination and coloring of things and their degree of immateriality. It is essentially the same doctrine St. Thomas propounded in the commentary on the *De anima* but far more elaborately worked out in Albert.[3] Following Albertus, Dante makes the following classifications:

(1) There are earthy substances mixed with one of the more diaphanous elements such as air or water so that they shine in the light, for example, gold or precious stones which "multiply" the light they receive.

(2) There are completely transparent substances which transmit light and color it as does a piece of colored glass.

(3) There are completely opaque substances which can be polished to reflect light as mirrors.

(4) There are completely opaque substances almost void of a diaphanous quality, such as earth.

The brightest of these substances can even overcome the power of sight as a mirror can do.[4] Analogously the angels, men, animals, plants, and minerals share in various degrees in the divine goodness to the degree that they are diaphanous or immaterial.[5] Creatures thus share in their different degrees of the divine goodness, from the pure "luminousness" or transparency of the angels down to man, who is, metaphorically speaking, partially visible, like a man standing in water, and, further, down to the lower and more opaque orders.

This gradation or hierarchy of light, immateriality, nobility, and being proceeds not only by genus and species but by particular individuals. Within each species there is a further hierarchy of individuals so that, for example, the highest of the individuals in the human species would be virtually an angel.[6] Both the sensible and the intelligible orders display this continuous gradation. Between the highest forms of animals and the lowest forms of men and between the highest forms of men and the lowest forms of angels there is really no intermediate grade, so that we see some men who are virtually nothing but beasts. Likewise we must posit a human individual so noble that he would be virtually an angel; otherwise the human species would not be continuous in both directions.[7] This best individual of the human species, virtually an angel, stands on the very pinnacle of the graded ladder of luminousness and immateriality which constitutes the universe. To use Dante's own metaphor about man being half in the water of materiality and half in the air of materiality, such an individual would barely have his feet wet. Dante adds that Aristotle calls such people divine.[8]

The compassionate lady, the perfect individual of the human species, receives the divine virtue as an angel does,[9] and this Dante proves by the behavior of the lady in those operations of the rational soul—speaking and general deportment—proper to a rational person. This external activity is thus an expression or translation of that faculty, the rational soul, which especially receives the divine light. Her behavior, carriage, and speaking, her beauty and grace are external manifestations of the inner "light." [10] The beautiful woman is thus on the very highest point of the earthly ladder of light-immateriality-being. It is because the divine light or goodness most manifests itself in her that she is beautiful. Dante develops at some length this doctrine of external beauty as a kind of translation of the inner light.[11] Indeed, Dante means to speak of such a creature only insofar as the goodness of her soul is revealed in the beauty of her body, in sensible beauty. The soul reveals itself as color through glass—and what is smiling but a scintillation of the soul's delight, the visible outward light of the light which exists within? [12] The mouth and the eyes are the two parts through which the rational soul most fully translates this inner light into an outer light expressed in terms of sensible particulars. It is there that the rational soul is most operative in its role of beautifying its instrument, the body.[13] The most beautiful parts of the body will thus be precisely those parts which are closest to the soul, the eyes and lips, balconies looking out of the edifice which the soul inhabits. The soul is, as it were, a woman who inhabits a palace, the body, and the eyes and lips are her balconies. We might observe in passing that the importance of laughter or smiling was well buttressed by the authority of Aristotle, who said that man is a laughing animal.[14] Laughter is his *proprium*, a property not of his essence but one which he shares with no other animal. Hence it is not mere preference that Dante shows in emphasizing the mouth as the most "spiritual" and beautiful organ along with the eyes, all of them in the face, the most beautiful part of the body. We have already discussed the importance of the sense of sight in medieval philosophical speculation as the most spiritual and "aesthetic" of the senses, and it is only natural that the organ of this sense should share in the dignity of its function.

Dante frequently refers to other doctrines of light metaphysics in the *Convivio*. In III, xii, 6–8, he mentions the analogy between the corporeal and spiritual sun which corresponds to corporeal and intellectual light. The spiritual sun is God. God first illuminates Himself with intellectual light, then illuminates the celestial creatures and all other things in the intelligible realm. As the sun gives heat, the principle of life, and if anything is injured by it, it is not part of the sun's purpose, so God in His Goodness gives life, but if any living thing is evil, it is not part of His intention but an accident.[15]

The two kinds of light are again described, but as material and spiritual instead of corporeal and intellectual. As white is the color most filled with corporeal light, so contemplation is most filled with spiritual light of anything in this world.[16] Dante also draws the conventional distinction in light speculation between *lux*, *lumen*, *radius*, and *splendor* or the source of light and the various forms of luminosity around it. The first agent, God, colors some things by His power in the manner of a ray directly shining upon them and other things by a kind of reflected splendor. The angels receive the direct ray immediately, and other things receive it as reflected from them. *Luce* is the source of *lume*, the ray is a linear radiation from the *luce*, and the *splendor* is the light reflected from the first things which the ray emanating from the source may strike.[17]

Dante also conceives of the principle of efficacy as a divine ray. The rays of light descending from each star or planet are the means through which they exert their effects on the world below. These rays are nothing more than a light (*lume*) which comes from a source of light (*luce*). The stars emit light and therefore exert influence; the diaphanous spheres in which they are fixed, being transparent, have no influence on the world below.[18]

The Catholics, Dante tells us, place the empyrean heaven, the luminous heaven or the heaven of flame, outside of all the heavens. It is immovable because it is fully actual, that is, "it has in itself, in every part that which its matter desires." The *primum mobile* has the swiftest movement because of its intense desire to unite itself to the heaven above it, a desire so intense that it spins with enormous velocity. All motion, as in the Aristotelian universe, is a symptom of incompleteness, of the "desire" to become fully actual and to be assimilated to the Pure Act which moves the world as an object of desire. This heaven is the still and quiet light in which the Deity dwells who alone completely beholds Himself; it is the abode also of the blessed, as the Holy Church "who cannot lie" maintains.[19]

Dante continues by telling us that the divine light shines in and through the soul as it shines in the angels. The human soul possesses all the virtues of the lower forms of soul as well as the ultimate perfection of reason. By virtue of reason it participates in the divine nature as well as in the lower natures in the scale of creatures. By virtue of possessing reason the human soul is so noble and immaterial that the divine light shines on it as it does on the angels.[20] Philosophy itself is that most virtuous light whose rays make the flowers bloom, the analogy here being to the generative powers of the sun.[21]

To the two main kinds of light correspond two organs of vision, the sensible eye and the rational eye. The sensitive part of the soul has its eyes by which it discerns the difference between things according to their external coloration. Similarly, the eyes of the rational part of the soul—judgment, or discernment—estimate things according to the ends for which they were ordained. The man who lacks this faculty will follow the popular clamor whether right or wrong.[22]

It is, however, in the letter to Can Grande that the light-metaphysics doctrine is more fully worked out. Citing the *De causis*, Dante presents the chain of causality descending from God in terms of an emanation of light.

Inasmuch as the second cause has its effect from the first, its influence on what it acts upon is like that of a body which receives and reflects a ray; since the first cause is the more effective cause. And this is stated in the book *Of Causes*, namely, that "every primary cause has influence in a greater degree on what it acts upon than any second cause." So much with regard to being.[23]

Dante continues with an exposition of the "proceeding of every essence and virtue" from the "primal one" through the mediation of the intelligences or angels. In this connection he cites both the *De causis* and Dionysius.

Whence it is evident that every essence and every virtue proceeds from a primal one; and that the lower intelligences have their effect as it were from a radiating body, and, after the fashion of mirrors, reflect the rays of the higher to the one below them. Which matter appears to be discussed clearly enough by Dionysius in his work *On the Celestial Hierarchy*. And therefore it is stated in the book *On Causes* that "every intelligence is full of forms." Reason, then, as we have seen, demonstrates that the divine light, that is to say the divine goodness, wisdom, and virtue, shines in every part.[24]

The creation is thus derived from God in its being and in its essence, from God who is omnipresent, His glory shining throughout the universe although this omnipresence involves degrees.

He says well, then, when he says that the divine ray, or divine glory, "penetrates and shines through the universe"; penetrates, as to essence; shines forth, as to being. And what he adds as to "more and less" is manifestly true, since we see that one essence exists in a more excellent degree, and another in a less; as is clearly the case with regard to heaven and the elements, the former being incorruptible, while the latter are corruptible.[25]

Thus Dante explains the opening lines of the *Paradiso* that the glory of the First Mover shines forth in every part of the universe and why it shines forth in one part more and in another part less. Causality, being, essence, and power radiate down from the highest Reality as light, and all the universe reflects this light in varying degrees according to the capacity of its parts. The divine ray or glory penetrates everywhere as to its essence, that is to say that the light is a manifestation of God Himself, revealing what He is everywhere that it is present. It shines forth as to being because the divine light constitutes things in their being, the light conferring forms as the principle of both knowledge and being to the intelligences, who transmit them to the lower orders and control them. We may recall that the light which constitutes both the principle of knowledge and the principle of being translates the inner essence of what it constitutes. A thing is known because the same light that constitutes its being radiates out as the form or species through which it is known. The light is ultimately no more than a reflection of the glory and beauty of the Creator shining back to Him from His creation as the splendor or reflection of His light.

The radiation of the Primal Light creates a hierarchy of light, goodness, power, being, and glory; all are but splendor or reflected light of the Primal Light. The imagery here is clearly that of emanationism with all its monistic, or rather pantheistic, implications. However, like Albertus Magnus, Dante does maintain that every essence except the primary one is caused (21, l. 385—*Omnis essentia, praeter primam, est causata*). There is thus in this document an inconsistent mixture of the imagery and concepts of emanationism with Aristotelian conceptions of the transcendence of the divine and the orthodox conception of creation *ex nihilo*. Here and in the *Paradiso* Dante imagined the relation of the universe to God as one of emanation, although he never seems to have inferred any of the more heterodox implications of this conception of the universe.[26]

He continues:

And having premised this truth, he next goes on to indicate Paradise by a circumlocution; and says that he was in that heaven which receives the glory of God, or his light, in most bountiful measure. As to which it must be understood that heaven is the highest heaven, which contains all the bodies of the universe, and is contained by none, within which all bodies move (itself remaining everlastingly at rest), and which receives virtue from no corporeal substance. And it is called the Empyrean, which is as much as to say, the heaven glowing with fire or heat; not that there is material fire or heat therein, but spiritual, which is holy love, or charity.[27]

The empyrean is the heaven which stands "closest to the divine light and therefore receives the most of its glory or light (*lux*)." This is glory conceived as the light itself, not as the reflected glory which shines forth or shines back. It is the supreme heaven which encloses the whole of the corporeal universe and is itself circumscribed only by the love which moves all things, itself unmoved, the love which is a spiritual fire or heat as well as a spiritual light. It is a "quiet light," everlastingly at rest.

That this empyrean receives most of the divine light can be proved in two ways: it contains all things, without itself being contained by any, and therefore stands closest, in some sense, to the Primal Light. As the containing body it stands in the same relationship to what it contains as does that which confers form to that which receives it or, in the more usual vocabulary of the schools, as does act to potency. As such it also stands in relation to what is contained as a cause to its effect, and since all causality is of the nature of a ray emanating from the first cause, and the empyrean is the highest of causes in the corporeal universe, it is clear that the empyrean must receive the most of the divine light. It thus follows from the fact that the empyrean is the most powerful of causes that it is the most luminous, for causal power or efficaciousness is a function of the light that radiates from the divine light or first cause, which is God.

Now that this heaven receives more of the divine light than any other can be proved by two things. Firstly, by its containing all things, and being contained by none; secondly, by its state of everlasting rest or peace. As to the first the proof is as follows: The containing body stands in the same relation to the content in natural position as the formative does to the formable, as we are told in the fourth book of the *Physics*. But in the natural position of the whole universe the first heaven is the heaven which contains all things; consequently it is related to all things as the formative to the formable, which is to be in the relation of cause to effect. And since every causative force is in the nature of a ray emanating from the first cause, which is God, it is manifest that heaven which is in the highest degree causative receives most of the divine light.[28]

Here again we find a curious blending of Neoplatonism with Aristotelianism. There is on the one hand the distinctive light speculation of the Neoplatonic tradition, but it is coupled with the Aristotelian doctrine of natural place, the inherent source of motion or natural tendency which impels all things to seek their place in the universe. Once anything arrives in its place, assuming it had been displaced, the same nature which was the cause of motion is the cause of its quiescence.[29] When a thing is in its natural position, it is most fully actual and therefore most fully causal. At the same time it is quiescent in the sense that it does not undergo motion. Motion, in the Aristotelian universe, is a sign of lack of realization of a thing's essence. Anything which changes in the Aristotelian universe is, in a sense, very busy becoming itself, finding its place, or, finally, being resolved into its elements.

Light is thus the principle of being, efficacy, actuality, and causality. Previously (20, ll. 349 ff.) Dante had, in discussing the opening lines of the *Paradiso*, explained how by the glory of the First Mover shining forth or reflecting back in all parts of the universe in different degrees he had meant that, after the fashion of mirrors (21, l. 405), the divine light, excellence, wisdom, and virtue reglowed or shone forth everywhere (21, ll. 410 ff.). This glory, excellence, and splendor which the whole of creation reflects back on the Creator is not only beauty as light, but also perfection proceeding from the Primal Perfection as a ray. Dante argues that nothing in motion or change can be perfect. The empyrean is, however, in a state of rest. It must therefore receive most of the perfection of the light emanating from the Primal One and therefore receive more light than any other heaven.

As to the second the proof is this: Everything which has motion moves because of something which it has not, and which is the terminus of its motion. The heaven of the moon, for instance, moves because of some part of itself which has not attained the station towards which it is moving; and because no part whatsoever of it has attained any terminus whatsoever (as indeed it never can), it moves to another station, and thus is always in motion, and is never at rest, which is what it desires. And what I say of the heaven of the moon applies to all the other heavens, except the first. Everything, then, which has motion is in some respect defective, and has not its whole being complete. That heaven, therefore, which is subject to no movement, in itself and in every part whatsoever of itself has whatever it is capable of having in perfect measure, so that it has no need of motion for its perfection. And since every perfection is a ray of the Primal One, inasmuch as He is perfection in the highest degree, it is manifest that the first heaven receives more than any other of the light of the Primal One, which is God. . . . Hence it is clear that when the author says "in that heaven which receives more of the light of God," he intends by a circumlocution to indicate Paradise, or the heaven of the Empyrean.[30]

He continues to strengthen this argument by citing Aristotle that the nobility or "honor" of a heaven is in direct proportion to its distance from the terrestrial. This is the heaven above the heaven to which Christ ascended that He might fill all things. It is the heaven of the delights of the Lord, the heaven from which Lucifer fell "full of wisdom and perfect in beauty."

And in agreement with the foregoing is what the Philosopher says in the first book on Heaven, namely that "a heaven has so much the more honourable material than those below it as it is further removed from terrestrial things." In addition to which might be adduced what the Apostle says to the Ephesians of Christ: "Who ascended up far above all heavens, that He might fill all things." This is the heaven of the delights of the Lord; of which delights it is said by Ezekiel against Lucifer: "Thou, the seal of similitude, full of wisdom, beautiful in perfection, wast in the delights of the Paradise of God." [31]

Thus the hierarchies of being, truth, beauty, perfection, indeed of all value, are reduced to a hierarchy of light ascending to the very Primal Light itself, spiritual, uncreated, divine, the vision of which is the vision of all. The doctrines we have considered are the bare bones of the most important part of Dante's universe. The flesh and substance are the *Paradiso*, to which we now turn.

While the *Inferno* and *Purgatorio*, in their respective ways, are concerned with the correction of moral error, the *Paradiso* as a journey through the intelligible universe celebrates truth and involves the correction of intellectual error. Here Dante rectifies his mistakes of thought and knowledge on such questions as the ordering of the celestial hierarchy, the origin of the spots on the moon, and the language of Adam. The *Paradiso* is thus philosophical poetry, both in the obvious meaning and in the most exact sense of this term. It solves the problem of rendering a systematically ordered world of pure thought in terms of images. To the extent that the *Inferno* and *Purgatorio* deal with virtue, they bear on the ethical realm and are dramatic and psychological. Readers of the *Paradiso* are sometimes disappointed because it lacks those dramatic qualities which dominate the previous *cantiche* and which, we generally assume, are central to literature.

For Dante, however, the ethical realm and the life of conflict and choice prepare the way for a life of ideal emotional and intellectual activities. The ultimate objects of desire are not actions but states of mind and spirit—understanding, love, joy. The *Paradiso*, so to speak, evokes "a life beyond life," pure spontaneity which transcends morality and the ordinary forms of human experience. Hence comes its lyrical and evocative character, the subjective mode in which Dante describes this part of the universe. He is, in a way, the single character here, the only one still capable of surprise. What we feel about his experience at this stage of the journey we feel through the effect his various experiences have on him.

If the problem of the *Paradiso* was the reduction of objects of thought to objects of vision, how was this accomplished? First, the ladder of light constituted an ontological principle which ran through the whole of reality, from the sensible to the intelligible to God. Light metaphysics also unified and made continuous these two orders of reality, by positing light, in its various analogical forms, as the single strand running through the whole universe. To the various forms of light corresponded various forms of apperception, both sense and thought being explained by the union of "inner and outer lights." There was thus no truly sharp cleavage in light metaphysics—at least for the imagination—between the realms of matter and spirit, sense and thought. Thought was not a world of pure colorless concepts, but one of even brighter light than the world of senses. Thus the intelligible world was supersensuous both in a privative and in a positive sense. Clearly, the solution to Dante's problem lay at hand in the concepts and images of the light-metaphysics tradition. He could shape the ladder of light—the ultimate principle of all value in the universe—to render his own universal vision in terms of shapes, grades, and kinds of light.[32]

The second mode of rendering the celestial universe was

to make the heavenly host *manifest* itself in space and time during the journey through the spheres. The *Paradiso's* imagery thus functions as symbolism since it refers to a higher reality than language can formulate. Dante's images, however, far from being arbitrary are drawn from the world of knowledge and observation; they mean what they say and simultaneously point to a reality which transcends them. Dante shapes light to build the universe of the *Paradiso*, but this light has the same properties and obeys the same laws as the light of the universe according to the knowledge of his time. His universe is thus simultaneously an imaginative creation and a world about which one might ask the same questions as one asks about the real world.

The eyes whose function it is to be lured by beauty discern it through its garment of light, the latter a reflection or incarnation of the immaterial, uncreated light that is God. Luminosity in matter is simply a defective manifestation of the same power as it exists detached from matter. Thus in canto XXX a ray of immaterial light from the immaterial tenth heaven or Empyrean materializes itself at a point in the concave surface of the ninth sphere "which derives from this ray light and power." At this point time and space begin, as well as causality and natural law, for in the Empyrean "where God rules directly, natural law is of no effect." This light is the "lume" or "splendor of God" (XXX, 97–123). This power communicates existence and activity to the entire universe through the agency of the *primum mobile*, which, spinning within the Empyrean, transmits its *virtù* to all the lower spheres that it encloses and through them to all other beings (II, 112–123). Thus the unitary power and efficacy of the heaven of light are diffracted through the stars and planets, constituting a graded ladder of light as causal power.[33]

The visible light of the stars is constantly affected by the immaterial light of the intellect that moves it—"the heaven which is beautified by so many lights takes its image from the profound mind that turns it and itself becomes the stamp of that seal." Material light reveals itself as a reflection or "copy" of the immaterial light, the "profound mind." We are thus prepared early for the assimilation of thought to light and of thinking to vision by the conception of material light as the "stamp" and image of God (II, 124–148).

God's power is therefore a function of light, distributed and differentiated through the heavenly bodies by the process of "multiplication" peculiar to light alone. Dante carefully uses the medieval term *multiplicatio* to describe the manner in which light diffuses itself (II, 137).[34] This light, the principle which beautifies the heavens, shines in various degrees in different places because "diverse power makes a diverse alliance with the precious body which it quickens" (140). As the vital principle manifests itself differently in various parts of the body, so God's power shines differently in the various parts of the heavens. Thus the physical light of the stars proceeds directly or indirectly from the immaterial qualities of the moving intellect, for "the mingled virtue shines through the body" (144). The gleam of the heavenly bodies is a reflection of God's joy in His creation, as joy in humans is evidenced by light spreading through the pupil of the eye. Recall the passages in *Convivio* III, viii, about sensible beauty as the translation of an inner immaterial quality, an external light reflecting an internal light: Dante is saying here that the sensible beauty and light of the heavens is the "translation" of the immaterial light and beauty which is God. In human beings this translation of the internal into the external light was most manifest in the eyes and the smile. Thus the stars are, metaphorically, the eyes of God: they most reveal

His beauty and His joy, they gleam through a kind of rejoicing.

In *Paradiso* XIII, 52–81, light is described as the actualizing principle descending from its source, the Father, through the living Light, the Son, coequal to the source and to the Love that binds them. It shines first upon the nine subsistences that form the heavenly hierarchy, descending down to the "last potencies," and thus constitutes the ladder of actuality or being. The light from the "living Light," the Word in whose mind are the archetypal forms, operates on the natural world through the agency of the light streaming from the heavenly bodies and their motions. But the potencies awaiting actualization, the "wax," and the actualizing agent, the luminous heavenly bodies, are not invariably in the most suitable relationship, so that the "idea" is not always fully realized in the matter. Thus the light of being and of beauty fails to shine through creatures in the same degree. This resistance of "matter" accounts for the inability of some individuals to embody fully the essence or idea.

Here Dante is primarily concerned with light as the principle of being; but the notion of spiritual light shining through the form which actualizes and dominates "matter" is light viewed as beauty. Note further that the relationship between the Persons of the Trinity is described as a relationship between "Light," the Source, the living Light which it begets, and the Holy Spirit as the love between the two (XIII, 55–57). That Dante is simultaneously describing the ladder of beauty follows also from his personification of nature as the craftsman whose hand trembles. Nature sees the perfection of the archetypal forms but cannot perfectly produce them (76–78). Only twice did she achieve perfection, with Adam and in Christ, and then only because of the direct operation of the burning Love which is the Holy Spirit, alone capable of perfectly realizing the idea in matter (82–87).

These ideas are mere elaborations and applications of the principle announced at the very start (I, 1–6) when the luminous beauty of God was described as shining in different degrees throughout the universe. Thus light functions as the principle of actuality, being, efficacy, and beauty. The glory, power, and creativity of the Creator operate in and through light, a protean light whose ultimate source is God Himself. Intellectual vision itself is a ray of the Mind which fills all things. This ray has its origin beyond all that appears to it and is its own witness to its dependent and derivative nature. The principle of knowledge is thus described as light whose ultimate source is the divine mind (XIX, 51–56).[35]

The light which is the principle of being, beauty, efficaciousness, and knowledge emanates, we know, from the immaterial qualities of the moving intellect. This radiation of the divine power is affected by the spiritual splendor of the blessed souls and of Beatrice. This is most beautifully exemplified in Dante's and Beatrice's passage from the Moon's sphere to Mercury's (V, 94–99). Here Beatrice's joy is so great that Mercury turned brighter for it and "smiled" through its luminosity.

Let us return to the point of material light which Dante saw on the concave surface of the ninth sphere (XXX, 11) and consider some of the other functions of light. He had previously seen this point from below, a sight which so impressed him that he literally quoted a line (canto XXVIII) from Aristotle's *Metaphysics*, Book XII. The staggering significance of that point of light is best expressed by a short simple statement of philosophical truth from its discoverer. What Aristotle thought, Dante now sees: "From that point hangs heaven and all nature" (41). The point is surrounded by nine concentric circles, of which the closest circle is the *primum mobile*. It spins with maximum speed because of its great "desire," as all bodies spin faster in proportion to proximity to that point. The light emanating from here is the source of all natural things and the substantial form of the universe and, as such, is the form and nature that preserves every corporeal form and gives it power to act.

Dante next questions Beatrice about the angelic circles he sees revolving about the point. He notices that the noblest and most divine orbits, the fastest and brightest, are closest to the point, whereas in the world of sense the orbits are more divine in proportion to their increasing distance from the center. Dante, puzzled by this apparent reversal of ideal pattern and physical copy, looks to Beatrice for an answer (XXVIII, 52–57). She explains that the magnitude of the material spheres depends on the amount of power (*virtù*) diffused through their parts. Greater excellence makes greater blessedness, which in turn demands a greater body when its parts are uniformly and equally perfect. Thus the point of material light is the source of the degree of excellence and blessedness that anything possesses. The heavens and nature depend on it for their being and for their order of excellence (64–72). Dante is here elaborating the concept of light as the substantial form of the universe, one that constitutes things in their power and their being.

Beatrice concludes that Dante should interpret the spirits that appear to him as circles in relation to their power and not in terms of magnitude. Thus the outermost circle, the *primum mobile* or crystalline sphere, corresponds to the innermost circle in the "manifestation" or "appearance" of the angelic hierarchy. What the material and the angelic orbit have in common is speed of motion and intensity of light, functions of their worth and desire (73–78).[36] The relationship between the two systems of circles might also be described in terms of the scholastic doctrine of intensive and extensive quantity, the former corporeal and apparent, the latter incorporeal and unapparent.

As Dante, gazing on the point of material light in the ninth heaven, looks upon the one principle on which the whole corporeal universe depends, the light which is the substantial form of the physical order, so in the Empyrean, beyond space and time, he looks upon the "living ray" (*vivo raggio*, XXXIII, 77), that source of spiritual uncreated light which connects the categories in their transcendental being and so fuses them as to make them a "simple light" (*semplice lume*, 90). This universal form of all the categories of reality is analogous to the luminous point which, in the material order, is the source of the substantial form of the heavens and nature.

In the final vision, a purified sight penetrates more and more the ray of the "high" light which is essential truth (52–54). Here Dante insistently calls our attention not only to a new kind of sight but to an utterly different kind of light which is its object. The object is, of course, God; God is the Eternal Light (*etterno lume*, 43) as *lume* or radiated light. He is Supreme Light (*somma luce*, 67) and Eternal Light (*luce etterna*, 83 and 124) as *luce* or the source of light. The love and knowledge relating the Persons of the Trinity are a kind of circling of reflected light (127–128). As material light is the highest principle of the corporeal universe, spiritual light is the highest principle of the immaterial universe and ultimately of all reality. The one functions as the substantial form of the universe and of nature, conferring actuality, being, and excellence. The other, God as Light, is the universal form of the categories and relations which exhaust reality. Material light is seen with the eyes of the flesh; Eternal Light, with a purified vision.

The relation of multiplicity to this unitary Primal Light (*prima luce*, XXIX, 136) is one of creation and of "emanation." The higher cause remains in itself while producing that which is next below it in the order of things. It diffracts itself into many mirrors, remaining a unity nevertheless, but it also makes the mirrors into which it is broken (142–145). The mirrors in this instance are the angels, previously described as constituting a ninefold mirroring of the divine goodness (XIII, 58–59). The nine mirrors of the celestial hierarchy also constitute a hierarchy of forms of knowledge or "vision" of God.

The relation between the various orders of being including the angels is one of an "outflowing" or "downpouring"; Dante frequently describes it as a "raying" (*raggiare*, VII, 75). God pours out, without stint, His goodness, beauty, love, and light—irradiating all things and conforming them to Himself in their degree (cf. XIII, 52 ff.).[37] The pure forms of angelic intelligence, the heavenly bodies, composites of form and matter which are their instruments, and the prime matter which holds the potentiality of created things and upon which the angelic intelligences operate through the heavenly bodies —all these came into existence in the same way that light instantaneously diffuses itself through a transparent medium. The sequential creation recorded in Genesis took place after this creation, through the instrumentality of the angels (XXIX, 25–30). The primal light that irradiates (*raia*) the numberless angelic mirrors and the rest of creation is received by them—Dante calls them "splendors" or reflected lights of the primal light—in varying degrees. Hence the love which this light arouses in the angels is uneven. Note that light is defined as beauty and good, being the correlate of love (136–141).[38]

In this cosmology Dante inconsistently mingles the ideas

and images of emanationism with Aristotelian doctrines as adopted and modified by Christian theism. The literature on the degree and kind of Dante's Neoplatonism tends to push him too far into either the Thomistic or Neoplatonic camp. His universe is startingly Neoplatonic, but also colored by Aristotelianism and governed by the doctrines of Christian theism. His speculation is reminiscent of the Aristotelianized Neoplatonism of treatises like the *Liber de causis* and the *Liber de intelligentiis*. After all, Dante was a poet, not a philosopher, and the Thomistic universe was too abstract and colorless, too poor in imagery to feed the poetic imagination in any direct way. The grand and beautiful cosmic metaphors of the Neoplatonic tradition which Dante could find in the greatest of the Church fathers and in the writings of many of his contemporaries were far more stimulating. The thought and learning of this true artist were at the service of his imagination.

As we follow Dante on his journey, the spheres which increase in size, excellence, and blessedness also become more luminous. A further clue to the role of luminosity is found in cantos XIV and XXI, where we meet Solomon and Peter Damian, in this order. Solomon, the fifth and most beautiful light of his sphere, radiates light as the vesture of his love. Peter Damian shines so brightly as he comes to greet Dante that the poet says to himself: "I see well the love with which you signal to me" (45).

Solomon explains his luminosity thus: the love for God of the disembodied spirits shall radiate its vesture of light until the final resurrection of the body. The brightness of their light is in proportion to the intensity of their love, which in turn is directly proportional to the clarity and depth of each soul's vision. Finally, vision itself, or knowledge of God, is proportioned to the degree of grace each spirit receives over and above its deserts. After the resurrection, God will grant more of the light of grace which makes their vision adequate to Him. The transformed body will be even more luminous than the light the spirits now radiate; it will then possess "physical" eyes capable of direct vision of God. Even greater love will follow upon this greater vision. The physical eye and the "eye of the soul" will be fused into one organ, thought and vision will merge into one "supersense," and the very substance of the state of the resurrected saints will be a light more luminous than that which now constitutes them (XIV, 37–60).

Clearly, light is here a function and correlate of love and therefore functions as beauty—indeed, it is the principle of beauty itself. The circular operation of the triad light-love-vision, or beauty-love-knowledge, is made clearer by St. Peter Damian. A divine light centers upon him, penetrating the light of which he is made. Its power, joined to his sight, so uplifts him that he is able to see the divine essence from which it comes. This light produces the joy with which he is aflame; the clearness of the flame matches the clarity of his sight (XX, 83–90). The union of the "inner" lights of the faculties of apprehension with the "outer lights" constituting reality releases joy (*delectatio*), in the tradition of light metaphysics—a special application of the general scholastic principle that joy attends the union of a thing with that which befits it (*coniunctio convenientis cum convenienti*). Thus the wisest of men and the great contemplative expound a complementary doctrine. Increase of vision-knowledge results in an increase of love which in turn demands more and higher light. This circular process is characteristic of the ascent from heaven to heaven and ends only when the infinite eternal Light is reached.

The circularity of vision-love-light is adumbrated early

(IV, 140–143) when Dante asks Beatrice whether unfulfilled vows can be compensated for by other means besides fulfillment, such as good works. Before answering, she increases in luminous beauty, a beauty which overpowers him. At the very start of canto V she explains her beauty, which blinded him, as a function of love and vision or truth. It is the flame of love, an "exterior light" which derives from the perfect and immediate vision of the Eternal Light, a vision which kindles love or, more precisely, is an amorous vision. Beatrice observes that she can already see in Dante's mind the implied "interior light," a shining of the eternal light of truth (V, 7–9).

Dante here explains the activity of the beatified consciousness partly in terms of his own, partly in terms of Beatrice's, but (witness the souls of Solomon and Peter Damian) the process also takes place in each consciousness separately. Beatrice in effect tells us that Dante now shares more fully in the eternal light and is thus prepared for the reception of the truth she is about to divulge. As Nardi demonstrated, Dante's epistemology is Augustinian and posits some form of divine illumination as the actualizing principle in the process of knowledge.[39] Beatrice concludes by explaining that the eternal light of truth is the true object of love and that any other becomes such only because the Eternal Light shines through it in its beauty (V, 1–12).

Happiness also manifests itself as light, and the brightness of a soul grows with increase of joy. Beatrice shines with greater splendor when she sees the Eternal Light of truth shining in Dante's mind (V, 7–8); Justinian glows with joy when ready to impart a new truth to Dante (130–132). As Beatrice's joy rises while she leads Dante closer and closer to ultimate reality, her beauty and luminosity increase with each ascent. But light here as everywhere in the *Paradiso* is no simple external sign of an inner state but is functional as the principle of truth, beauty, and being.

This circularity is, then, both a convenient metaphor and a structural rhythm permeating the *Paradiso*, at once the pattern of expanding consciousness and of ascent through the intelligible universe. The expanding spiral of growing awareness has a triadic structure, being constituted of moments of increasing light-beauty, followed by growth of love and knowledge and of a fresh desire which demands greater beauty. Each ascent is accompanied by an increase in knowledge and so leads toward God through the intelligible universe. We journey simultaneously through the ladder of love, the scale of being, and the hierarchy of all value rendered as light.

The virtuous triadic circularity of the *Paradiso* describes the way in which consciousness extends its range both *qualitatively* and quantitatively. It describes the progress of consciousness as the development of perception already known and as the successive introduction of new dimensions of insight not derivable from the preceding state. Each moment of Dante's "blindness" as he ascends from sphere to sphere is really the moment of superrational ecstasy which precedes conscious awareness of a new and higher level of reality; this sort of "blindness" comes from an excess of light.

But the *Paradiso* actually has a linear as well as a circular rhythm: these correspond to two simultaneous journeys, one through the sensible, the other through the intelligible, world. As the spirits of the blessed only manifest themselves in the universe of space and time but reside in the Empyrean, so the architecture of the intelligible universe is gradually revealed through its sensible analogue. Finally, with the acquisition of a new sense of vision, once the limits of the universe of space and time have been passed, all reality is simultaneously grasped in one flash. Dante's linear ascent frequently comes to life through the imagery of wings and of the arrow seeking its mark. It is interrupted as Dante, upon entering each sphere, is carried along for a time by its diurnal motion. Circularity—a "motion" proper to spiritual and incorruptible substances—manifests itself in the moment of transition from sphere to sphere primarily in Dante the pilgrim's consciousness and, upon completion of the journey, as the "motion" of his desire and will after they are "revolved by the Love that moves the sun and the other stars" (XXXIII, 145).

The state of blessedness, in the very presence of God, is not identical with the activity of consciousness on the road to God. It is rather the activity at the journey's term. This state begins with grace which rectifies and makes good the will. A good will and grace constitute merit which determines the degree of vision or "sight" of God's essence. This sight, in its own right, awakens love (XXVIII, 109–114). The circularity which Solomon and Peter Damian describe, also ultimately a gift of grace, may be said to have a fourth phase as the presupposition of its triadic movement. However, the state, as distinct from the attainment of blessedness ends with the love which follows vision, for the angels and the blessed are completely filled with beatitude, and their vision is as complete as it can be. In the process of ascent, the emphasis is placed on love's demand for more light as beauty and knowledge, since vision is not yet complete and love must therefore demand and obtain more of the light which is beauty (XII, 31–32).

This light is a reflection of the infinite, eternal light. It is divine goodness which reveals its beauty through its burning and sparkling (VII, 64 ff.) and the Primal Light irradiating the angels and eliciting their love (XXIX, 136). Every lesser good is as a light from its ray, and more than any other it moves the mind to love (XXVI, 31 ff.). It operates through all the lesser lights and beauties of creation, including Beatrice.

Beatrice's blinding supernatural beauty is but the light in which, like Peter Damian and the other saints, she is "embosomed," the light of which she is now made. Now that Beatrice has put off the corruptible body, that inner splendor shines in all its power. The incorruptible body she, along with Solomon and the other saints, will put on after the resurrection will be even more beautiful because it will have still more vision and its inner flame of love will shine yet brighter.

From the two sources of light, material and immaterial, there radiate being, actuality, excellence, blessedness, and the luminosity which is beauty itself. All, *pari passu*, constitute various hierarchical orders and are reducible to properties of the analogical forms of light. The ladders of light, being, love, knowledge, and beauty are all actually fused; this fusion permits Dante to ascend to God as poet, lover, philosopher, and mystic seer all at once. For each step in the ladder includes and transcends the qualities and perfections of the one below it until Perfection and Reality themselves are reached and found to be a "simple light," from whose virtuous radiation the entire universe is ultimately derived. The ladder of light and beauty is thus, in one way, the *scala Dei* par excellence, for if all the distinctions in reality are traceable to light, so Dante's distinctions in forms and modes of apprehension and appetition are reduced to a kind of *sui generis* unitary faculty which transcends and unifies sense and thought, love and knowledge, and is the faculty for perceiving this supersensuous immaterial light. Paradise contains no object of thought which is not at the same time an object of "sense," no object of love which is not fully an object of knowledge. To light, as the principle of All, corresponds this faculty as power of simultaneously grasping all (*totum simul*).

The light that is beauty motivates the ascent to "simple light" by engendering the desire which drives the soul to God. The light is ultimately the radiated light (*lume*) of God, His grace (I, 73–79). But light as motive power resides mediately in Beatrice's beautiful eyes which have lifted Dante from planet to planet through the heavens (XVII, 113–121). The beauty of her eyes comes into play especially as the poet mounts from sphere to sphere. The surge from the earthly paradise to the heavens begins when Beatrice fixes her eyes on the heavens and Dante fixes his own upon hers. They had previously both been looking at the sun together, she first and he imitating her.

Dante, in his reconstituted unfallen nature, can bear to contemplate the sun in all its splendor, along with Beatrice. Suddenly the sky is doubly bright, as if two suns were shining in it; Dante then fixes his eyes on Beatrice's; she, in turn, is looking heavenward (I, 49–63). Her aspect transforms, divinizes him, an indescribable experience the nature of which he suggests only by analogy with the story of Glaucus and allusion to St. Paul's experience (64–75). Only after gazing on her eyes is he transhumanized and he hears the music of the spheres. Simultaneously he sees a further increase in light which arouses his desire to know the cause of his experience (76–93).

The pattern here described repeats itself at every stage of the journey through the spheres: Beatrice looks toward a higher reality, Dante gazes into her eyes and, as light increases, reaches another sphere. At first she has to tell him that he is ascending; later, from any increase of light he gathers that he has reached a higher sphere. Such an increase of light is always accompanied by a growing desire or love and by a change in the "spiritual gravity" or natural love of the soul, which, free from sin, shoots off like a bolt of lightning toward its natural place. In the explanation which follows, Beatrice describes the doctrine of the *pondus amoris*, the internal principle of all things, corporeal and intellectual, prompting them to seek their proper place, moving to different ports over the great sea of being, each with a guiding instinct of its own (112–114). As Glaucus became a sea-god, Dante, extending the image, intimates that he has become a god in the sea of being. Beatrice concludes by explaining that his natural motion upward is no miracle. It is as natural for him to rise as it is for fire to ascend to its sphere (139–142).

The process of ascent is thus a version of the same virtuous circularity of Peter Damian's and Solomon's light-love-vision. Dante "sinks" himself in Beatrice's eyes which themselves are "sunk" in the vision of the Eternal Light. An increase of light is accompanied by an increase of love, which in turn demands more light. To clarify this process, let us examine the various moments of transition from star to star.

In ascending to the moon, Dante simply describes some aspects of the process later stated more emphatically. He fixes his eyes on Beatrice's and in an instant is carried to the lunar sphere by the "inborn and perpetual thirst for the god-like kingdom." He recalls her happiness and beauty and describes his entry into the body of the moon, still uncertain whether *he* is in his body. Weighing the possibility of the miraculous interpenetration of bodies, he likens the physical process of ascent to a ray of light passing through water without breaking it. The light of this sphere calls to mind a pearl and a diamond sparkling in the sun (II, 19–49).

Dante concludes this episode by announcing an important principle. Paradise is the direct vision of that reality which is in this world the object of thought and belief and which will not be discursively and mediately "demonstrated," but will be known with the immediacy of sight and the directness with which we know axiomatic truths (43–45). Here the theme of the developing power of vision begins, the powers of sense and thought gradually fusing until a "new sight" is acquired.

The second ascent is to the sphere of Mercury. Beatrice turns to the brightest part of the universe, the *primum mobile*. Dante, gazing upon her face, notices a changed look, and he shoots up like an arrow to the second sphere. The increase of light takes place explicitly in the planet itself and implicitly in Beatrice whose extreme joy makes the planet turn brighter, the joy and happiness of the blessed, the poet proclaims after the ascent, being signaled by their shining (V, 85–99).

Dante tells the first spirit he encounters, Justinian, that he understands his smiling because the light which constitutes him sparkles when he does so. What Dante so describes is the smile as a sparking of the soul's joy, an outer light reflecting an inner one. Here it refers to a disembodied spirit who draws the "outer light" of heaven through the eyes of the soul and whose subsequent increased love and joy it expresses through an increase of light (124–126). Finally, Justinian is so filled with joy that the light he radiates conceals his shape (133–138).

In the ascent to Venus, the increase of light and joy which accompanies every transition is depicted as an increase in Beatrice's beauty. Indeed, Dante, never aware exactly how he goes from sphere to sphere, gathers from her heightened beauty that he has arrived. The motif of her increasingly luminous beauty henceforth becomes progressively emphatic (VIII, 13–21).

In the ascent to the sun, Dante expressly emphasizes the bewildering and "unconscious" nature of the process: Beatrice, we learn, is leading him so instantaneously that the movement cannot be measured in time (X, 34–39). After Solomon's discourse on the resurrection of the body an overwhelming brightness, the "very sparkling of the Holy Ghost" (XIV, 76), blinds him. At the same time, Beatrice appears so beautiful and smiling that his memory cannot retain her beauty. The simultaneous and blinding increase of light and beauty is the "moment" of ascent to the sphere of Mars, which "smiles" with more than its accustomed brightness (76–88).

As she climbs to Jupiter, Beatrice gains more than before in beauty, especially in the luminous beauty of her eyes. Dante notes that he has ascended to Jupiter at the moment when he observes Beatrice's heightened beauty and immediately afterward senses that his circling movement in the spheres has a wider arc (XVIII, 55–69).

On the way to Saturn, the light-beauty which functions as the final cause of the ascent, turning desire into the motor power of the flight through the spheres, appears ever more strongly in Beatrice's countenance. She here explicitly mentions what we have gradually come to realize: her intensified beauty is nothing less than her "light." She increases in light-beauty as she ascends the ladder of ever-higher grades of light which lead to the uncreated light. Like Aristotle's first cause, she is the cause of Dante's motion as the object of desire. If Beatrice were to add the "second" beauty of her smile to the first beauty of her eyes, Dante would be consumed. Her "inner light" externally translated as beauty in these two regions of the "body" has become too great for him to bear (XXI, 1–18).

The ascent to the starry sphere is briefly described. Beatrice, with a sign alone, impels him up the ladder, Jacob's ladder, which leads from Saturn upward (XXII, 100–106). Ascent to the crystalline sphere, the *primum mobile*, again clarifies the process. Dante's is an enamored mind, a knowing faculty which at the same time loves. All human beauty, natural or portrayed, is a bait, serving to capture and fix the *eyes so as to possess the mind.* Beatrice's now surpasses all forms of temporal beauty; to the beauty of her eyes is added that of her smile. Dante has now the strength to bear this addition, which, at the previous ascent, Beatrice withheld lest it destroy him (XXVII, 88–99).

Human beauty, incarnate or depicted, thus has a purpose. It lures the eyes in order to possess the mind, forcing it toward a higher reality of which it is the manifestation. Through its revealing power, it initiates a process of loving and, at the same time, of knowing. The experience of beauty is self-transcending in that it arouses a love which can finally be satisfied only in the Good and a desire for understanding, to be fulfilled only in Truth (X, 1–12).

The ascent to the Empyrean follows upon the vision of the angelic circles revolving around the point of immaterial light analogous to the point of material light from which nature "hangs." The increasing brightness of the central point obliterates the spinning circles, as the brightness of the rising sun outshines the stars. The blinding light and Dante's desire make him turn to Beatrice, so beautiful now that only God can see her beauty in its fulness (XXX, 7–21), a beauty no artist can describe. His whole life has been the poetic pursuit of her beauty, but now the lover-poet must be transcended and included in something higher (22–33). The task is done, and Dante is ready to see Paradise as it really is, not as it has hitherto been manifested to him (34–45).

Dante will see both the angel and the saints, the latter as they will appear at the last judgment, that is, in the resurrected flesh. He has left time and space, the "greatest body," has gone from material to immaterial light, pursuing it as beauty through the whole universe, and is now in eternity. Passing from time to eternity, the lover and poet become the saint, endowed with new sight so strong that it can bear to look upon ultimate reality. This faculty is a fusion of sense and thought, of will and intellect (46–69).

This vision of light arouses Dante's desire to know, and Beatrice, the sun of his eyes, she who, like the sun of the intelligible world, was a light for him between truth and intellect, explains that what he has seen is symbolic of ultimate reality. His new sight is not yet fully developed (70–81). Dante then "drinks" with his eyes of the river of light as a child sucks its mother's breasts; the light reveals itself as the yellow rose of Paradise. Canto XXX is filled with sensual imagery; the flowers of light intoxicate the "saintly sparks" by their odors, Dante greedily "tastes" the river of light, and the verb "to see" recurs insistently. More significantly, the senses seemed fused, for he drinks light and sees odors: mystical synesthesia which accompanies the superhuman unification of consciousness. Dante has also been reborn, having become a child once more, a conception he adumbrated by describing himself shortly before (50) as swathed in the effulgent veil of the vivid or living light (82–90).

Before this moment Dante suffered a spell of blindness, when at the end of canto XXV he was blinded by St. John's spirit prior to his examination on love. St. John, we recall, assures him that his loss of sight is temporary and that Beatrice can restore it, possessing the same power in her glance as resided in the hand of Ananias, who restored the sight of St. Paul (4–12). Dante submits, likening his eyes to doors through which passed the fire of love that Beatrice infused in him along with her image. At the moment of his examination on love, Dante points back to the beginning, the first moment of erotic possession, and begins to tell St. John all that he learned of love in his journey up the ladder: that it is both a cosmic and a supernatural principle, one which comprehends both his first experience of it with Beatrice and his last with God. When Beatrice finally restores his sight, upon this blindness, as upon all the others suffered in Paradise, there follows a higher and stronger vision.

Dante is blinded again in passing from the *primum mobile* to the empyrean; this moment of blindness precedes the acquisition of a "new sight"; indeed, it proleptically defines all its precursors. It is the blindness which prepares the candle for the flame, the moment in which the final change—qualitative and not simply one of degree—endows him with a new sight (XXX, 46–60).

Dante's previous spells of blindness had all involved the acquisition of stronger sight, but the poet, we remember, now describes a special kind of vision, not only sharper, but different. He does so by frequently repeating the word "to see," especially in a triple rhyme on *vidi* (95–99). The eaves of Dante's eyelids drink of the river of light which then becomes round in shape (85–90). There follows a description of the universe of light. The material universe is a spherical body whose outermost circumference is the *primum mobile.* A ray of divine light is projected on the sphere, conferring on it life and power, motion and efficacy. The reflection of this ray is transformed into a circular disklike shape of light which is the floor of Paradise (100–114).

The same light which swathes him and which he sees is also the light by which he sees. The splendor of God, an emanation of His light, reveals a clearer vision of the empyrean; we have returned to the same ray of immaterial light with which Dante began and which he described as materializing itself on the surface of the *primum mobile.* Above the girdle or plane of light formed by this ray there rise, tier on tier in an ever-expanding circular pattern, the souls of the blessed who constitute the petals of the heavenly rose. Beatrice's final act of "attraction" is to draw Dante into the yellow of the eternal rose (124–128).

So far we have focused our attention on Beatrice, the final cause, starting with the point at which her mission ends, considering the nature of the light to which she leads him, then going back to the beginning of the ascent and working our way forward to the goal of their joint journey. The idea of desire as the motive of the flight, a desire aroused by beauty-light and proportioned to it, finds its concrete expression in the imagery of wings, often in language so strikingly reminiscent of Plato's dialogues of love that it almost seems as if Dante had the actual texts at hand.

Let us now explicitly state the nature and function of "wings." In canto XV Beatrice is described as having made Dante grow the wings for this heavenly flight and as the person whose beauty, specifically her smile, strengthens the wings of his will or desire (49–54, 70–72). Again, in XXV, during St. James's examination of Dante on hope, Beatrice is described as the compassionate one who directs the feathers of his wings to this high flight (49–54). In the final stages of the journey, it is not desire which must strengthen Dante's wings but grace coming from the Virgin, who thus replaces Beatrice as the immediate final cause which motivates the journey. The restored original goodness of human nature which permitted Dante's wings to respond directly and immediately to the urgings of desire and to pursue Beatrice's beauty through the spheres has reached its limit. The journey so far has been natural in the sense of something possible not to fallen nature but only to restored nature—it has conformed to the cosmological principles of spiritual gravity. Henceforth the highest grace, the supreme gift of divine love, must operate, a gift which, if granted at all, is granted to prayer. As the poet and lover yield to the saint, so eros, a natural cosmological principle, gives way to *agape*, a purely divine and supernatural principle (XXXII, 145–147).

Desire for the final vision is not enough. As justice and mercy were necessary for the flight from the earthly Paradise through the spheres, so supreme grace is necessary for the vision of the divine essence—"the supernatural journey." As St. Bernard says to the Virgin, whoever does not seek this grace from her is like one whose desire would fly without wings (XXXIII, 13–15). For the ultimate inexpressible vision of God even wings strengthened by Mary's intercession are not strong enough. Dante is passive, totally dependent, he is not "flying" toward his goal but is poised in the air. He need not, rather cannot, use his wings. Dante again refers to a "new sight" (*vista nova*), both the object of his apprehension and the faculty by which he apprehends it. As he seeks to understand this "strange sight" which his new unified and transcendent consciousness can see, he is struck as by a bolt of lightning, his mind is filled, and his desire is satisfied. The ambiguity of the term *vista nova*, the objective and subjective aspects of this final vision, is deliberate, for the end of the journey is union. The two aspects of the experience are now indistinguishable, and Dante is one with the love that moves the sun and the other stars. He takes on the "circular" motion of eternity (133–145). The worm has finally become the angelic butterfly (*Pur*. X, 121–126), and Dante has, at long last, realized the destiny of the human race, born to fly upward even though many fail to realize this destiny and fall back (*Pur*. XII, 95–96). Neither buffetings nor the pursuit of worldly glories stayed Dante from the attainment of his goal. The vain rationalizations by which men defend human goals, whether honorable, like law and medicine, or dishonorable, like tyranny and idleness, had no permanent effect on him (XI, 1–12), and with Beatrice's help he finally achieved his aim.

Dante was brought to Paradise called by the beauty of the heavens (*Pur.* XIV, 145 ff.), but, above all, enticed by the sight of the luminous beauty embodied in those "beautiful eyes of which love made a noose to capture me" (XXVII, 11–12). The lure of beauty for the eyes and the eyes themselves as the most beautiful of bodily parts run as a unifying thread through Dante's works from the first visions of the *Vita nuova* to the final visions of the *Paradiso.*

In the *Vita nuova* (XIV, 33–47), the vision of Beatrice at the wedding party had robbed Dante of all his senses, except sight which remained alive because love had taken possession of the eyes. This sense had its vision of beauty which captured the eyes and took possession of the mind (XXVII, 88 ff.). Like all the visions of the *Vita nuova,* it obeys a principle which Dante presents early in this work when he assigns to the image of Beatrice's beauty abiding with him continually such virtue that at no time did it allow Love to rule over him without the faithful counsel of reason in those things in which such counsel would be useful. This love then is a true eros in that it is guided by judgment. It is a superrational or an arational, not an antirational, principle, complementing reason although the counsel of reason is not always applicable to its workings.

The beauty of the lady's eyes actualizes the potentiality of love in the lover; even where it does not exist potentially she can bring it into being (*Vita nouva,* XX and XXI). Commenting on the sonnet "Negli occhi porta la mia donna amore" (XXI), Dante contends that in the first stanza he portrays the lady as reducing the potentiality for love in the lover to actuality by means of her most noble part, the eyes.

In the previous sonnet, the famous "Amor e 'l cor gentil sono una cosa," the poet describes the beauty which appears in a wise lady as so pleasing *to* the eyes that it awakens in the heart a desire for the pleasing thing and thereby arouses the spirit of love (XX). These two sonnets show the dual aspect of Dante's conception of the relation of eyes or sight to beauty: the eyes themselves are lured by beauty and as the lady's most beautiful part are themselves a lure. This reciprocal relationship, analogous to that of act and potency, is also an image of the motive behind the erotic flight. The goal of this flight and its final cause Dante adumbrates in the closing sonnet of the *Vita nuova.* The lure of beauty evoking love finally leads the poet to an intuition of the world beyond space and time, an intuition not clearly understood except insofar as it involves Beatrice. After this sonnet Dante had a vision of such wondrous things that he determines to speak no more of Beatrice until he may treat of her more worthily. To this end he studies most diligently. The counsel of reason thus appears at the end of the *Vita nuova* as well as at the beginning. It is a love that both demands and seeks understanding, the full meaning of which the *Comedy* reveals to us: *Amor quaerens intellectum.*

When, in the *Purgatorio*, Dante's eyes again behold Beatrice's beauty on the summit of the mountain, they receive divine, ecstatic visions. Those same emeralds from which love once shot his darts at him (*Pur.* XXXI, 115–117) now reveal the double nature of Christ through the image of the Griffin (118–123). Again, at the very beginning of the *Paradiso*, Dante points out the importance of the eyes in the ascent. The relationship between Beatrice's eyes and those of Dante he describes as one of act and potency. A similar relationship prevails between Beatrice's eyes and the sunlight, so that the sun, Beatrice's eyes, and Dante's eyes constitute, through the light that connects them, a hierarchy of grades of actuality. The pilgrim ray of light, the actualizing principle, strengthens Dante's sight for a higher vision (I, 46–54). The eyes are the instruments through which he gradually attains higher and higher power of vision. Beatrice's power to actualize even higher degrees of vision grows with the ascent and coincides with her increase in beauty, especially the beauty of her eyes.

Dante makes it perfectly clear that Beatrice is always the most beautiful object in the journey through the spheres. In canto XIV he seems to be rating the divine song just heard above the beauty of her eyes, but, he explains, he merely brings this accusation against himself in order to deny it, without implying that the "holy delight" of her eyes is less important than the song. In fact, in this sphere of Mars, he has not yet looked into her eyes although he precisely defines their function. His desire finds rest in them; they are the "living seals" of all beauty, and their power and beauty become stronger and purer as they rise. Dante again conceives the relationship between Beatrice's eyes and himself in terms of act and potency, Beatrice acquiring greater beauty and actualizing power as they ascend and transmitting it to Dante so that he may follow her (130–139).

Throughout the *Paradiso* the great drama is played by the eyes as they seek light and find beauty, first in the eyes of another, then everywhere. This beauty is an external light which manifests an internal splendor. It is the principle of being and knowledge, shining in sensible particulars. A beautiful woman's organs are so arranged that she reveals the qualities of the rational soul, especially through those parts closest to the soul, the eyes and mouth, "balconies" looking out upon it (*Conv.* III, ii, vi, viii). But through these two noblest parts, "portals," not only does the soul look out, but the beloved's image enters the lover's soul (*Par.* XXVI, 13–15).

By looking at the eyes we know the soul's activity and

state. The smile is the "second beauty," a flash of the soul's joy, an outward light that manifests what is within. Thus in *Purgatorio* XXXI, 136–148, the theological virtues exhort Beatrice to add the second beauty of the smile to that of the eyes. The beauty of her eyes and mouth is there described as the splendor—a radiated form of light—of the eternal living light, a translation into an "outer light" of that inner light which the saints receive from their vision of the Uncreated Light Himself (142). Note that while in the mortal state the inner light is the soul and the outer light is bodily beauty, in the state of blessedness what was the inner light becomes an outer light, translating a radiation from the divine light which irradiates the heavenly host. Her beauty is light and ultimately a reflection of God's beauty and light.

The beauty of Beatrice's eyes and smile is thus affirmed throughout Dante's works with ever-greater insistence. Passing from the *Vita nuova* to the *Paradiso*, we learn more and more of what it means and how it works. This beauty possesses a revealing power and contains so much of the meaning of love that Dante often cannot fully describe it, though he knows it to be a function of that universal love which impels the soul to embellish the eyes and smile and which shines through those parts with His luminous beauty (XVIII, 7–21). This beauty, having a divine source, initiates and carries through a process of vision which ends in union with God; the primary function of both corporeal and disembodied beauty is to start and maintain this erotic flight to God. The earliest expression of this notion is found in the famous *canzone* "Donne, ch' avete intelletto d'amore" (*Vita nuova* XIX). Corporeal beauty centered in the eyes and lips functions as a superior grace established by God. The *Convivio* (esp. III, viii) more clearly expounds the idea that corporeal beauty starts the soul on its course toward God's immaterial beauty, and the clearest statement of all is found in the first lesson Beatrice gives to Dante on the summit of Purgatory.

Dante's confession, which Beatrice demands and obtains, is an admission of having turned away from her to false pleasures as soon as death had deprived him of her visible presence (*Pur.* XXXI, 34–36). But she was able to help him back to her and to salvation. Her death was thus a death of love, and her expectation had been that Dante would be attracted by a greater beauty which death bestowed. Yet he was seduced from the true course of erotic flight, and his wings were drawn downward by false "counter loves." But, we recall, Dante returned to the beautiful lures of Beatrice's eyes and lips and, by their guidance and power, climbed the ladder to God. When finally her beauty becomes so great that only God can see it (*Par.* XXX, 7 ff.), the lover and the artist have both reached their limits. As the life of moral choice leads to the eternal life of contemplation, so the finite modes of love and beauty are subsumed in their infinite source. Beatrice has finally accomplished her mission. She was the lady above who gained for him the initial grace which made the journey possible (*Pur.* XXVI, 59). But she also strengthened Dante for heaven (X, 91–93).

We have seen this strengthening in action. Her increasing light and beauty lure Dante up the ladder of love and actualize in him even higher degrees of vision and awareness, until she reaches her limit of power. In Dante's farewell to her he acknowledges her as the source of his salvation and addresses her for the first time as "tu," a sign of equality, of the complete actuality in him of all that she succeeded in actualizing (XXI, 79–84). Yet, finally, only the Virgin's light and brightness can prepare him to see Christ (XXXII, 85–87). Beatrice was able to lead him so far because she was, not simply a mortal miracle of beauty as in the *Vita nuova* (XXI, 22;

XXIX, 24–41), but through her death and salvation an immortal miracle (XVIII, 61–63). If in life she gave a foretaste of the joys of Paradise, as a saint she also reflects Paradise in her eyes, for her "lights" (*luci*, 52) look in upon the Eternal Joy or Beauty which shines directly upon her. In XVIII, 4 ff., Dante describes her as the lady who is leading him to God. Unlike her, he is not in God's presence; yet both are "present" to each other. Like the rest of the souls in Paradise her true place is in God's immediate presence, in the Empyrean. She shows as much mobility as Virgil; in fact, she descended into Hell to call him, appears in Eden, and resumes her place again in the amphitheater of the rose.

To the final imageless rapture his guide is St. Bernard, who appropriately distinguished two forms of mystical contemplation. Both are forms of ecstasy. In the lower form the soul withdraws from sensation and the images which flow into us from the outer world. In higher contemplation it withdraws even from the sensuous images; this is the contemplation of the Word of God, while the less proficient contemplatives consider the saints and angels in heaven. The lower form is still an external relation to God, equivalent to the whole of the *Paradiso* up to and including the heavenly rose. The higher form is the final rapture, a direct and internal relation to God.

As in Plato's ladder of love, the beloved must be transcended, but Dante does not leave his beloved on the first rung of the ladder. Beatrice guides her lover, intercedes for him, and leads him to the penultimate rung. For Dante, the beloved is continually active, in life and death, in the work of realization and of salvation.

IV

The Analogy of Creation in Dante

"ONE reasons by analogy under every aspect of intellectual activity [and such reasoning] relates to the very structure of our minds," writes M. Maurice Dorolle in his *Raisonnement par analogie*.[1] This observation has often been made, but only in recent times have we become more conscious of the pervasive character of analogical reasoning and of its possibilities and limitations. The development of science and philosophy during the last hundred years has served to make us aware of the importance of such reasoning in all the endeavors of creative thought. R. G. Collingwood, for example, in his *Idea of Nature* examines the history of cosmology *sub specie analogiae* and distinguishes the various analogies that, in his view, have governed philosophical views of the world: the analogy of *organism* (hylozoism), accepted from Thales to Kepler, which affirmed a living universe, pervaded by vitality and rationality; the *mechanical* universe of Cartesian science and philosophy which, in Collingwood's view, is now yielding to a cosmology based on the analogy of *process* or *development* or, as he says, to the *idea of history*.[2]

Science as well as philosophy and literature has always had its metaphors and analogies; ideas such as the concept of an electric fluid or a psychological "state" have proved useful analogies for guiding research. According to Morris R. Cohen, metaphor and analogy, particular and cosmic, have influenced the scientist perhaps more than the man of letters. Indeed, as he points out, the mythology of popular science is the result of a literal understanding of the scientific metaphor.[3]

Whether, in the past, scientific analogies were regarded as literal or metaphorical, in modern scientific and philosophical thought they are only a tentative means for establishing conclusions, although the history of science affords abundant illustration of prolonged adherence to analogies of limited utility. Alchemy, for example, deduced concepts like "salt" from crudely empirical and purely analogical resemblances between substances, whereas chemistry deduces its concepts of salts and sulphates from a body of experimental results. The chemist, unlike the alchemist, guides the analogy by a large body of evidence affording material for inductive techniques which in turn can help achieve more fruitful analogies. Thus an analogy is scientifically valid to the degree that it is susceptible of being linked to a clearer resemblance in the structure and mechanism of facts. There must first be a relationship between facts to give a base of affirmation and then the further possibility of systematizing the analogy in the framework of general systems of thought. As an example, Dorolle points out Newton's application of Galileo's law to lunar phenomena and his subsequent conclusion *ab uno* to the rest of the universe. One fact established in a uniformly mechanical system allows universal application of a formula derivable from that fact.[4] Newton's extension of Galileo's law to the universe is thus a fruitful example of analogical reasoning.

From the subjective point of view, one of the primary functions and effects of analogy lies in giving the perceiver the impression that he has understood some experience. He satisfies his desire to understand by transposing an acquired experience or an already formed idea into the terms of a new experience. Analogy is thus a kind of lever for research. However, it remains indecisive from the point of view of rigorous logic, and although it never affords a rigorous demonstration, it may provide an appreciable coefficient of affirmation. All generalization implies an analogy which directs thought in certain ways, but one does not arrive at a law except by a choice among possible analogies, the general direction of the choice being suggested by various experimental observations.

The value of an analogy in modern science is thus a function rather of the manner in which it is organized than of its terms. In this connection, Dorolle cites Aristotle's awareness of a relationship between gills and lungs. He did not deduce oxidation from this, but introduced a further analogy concerning the cooling powers of water concluding thereby that respiration cooled the body. The primary terms were correct, but their relation to the further analogy was not.[5]

Although modern thought is fully aware of the tentative

nature of analogical reasoning, earlier thought tended to consider an analogy as an end in itself and to rest content in an aesthetic and essentially poetic awareness of the feeling of understanding the analogy brought. The Renaissance works of Paracelsus or Bruno afford numerous examples of this tendency. Even when such thinkers gave indications of being aware of the metaphorical nature of their thought, they often adhere to inadequate analogies; for the probabilities of various analogies change with the state of science, and the degree to which a particular analogy is convincing is a function of the intellectual state or scientific culture of the concluding mind.

It is important to note here that the tendency of Renaissance quasi-science and philosophy to be satisfied in inquiry with aesthetic contemplation of a metaphor or analogy is parallel to the use of metaphor in poetry where it serves no further end and is offered as a final statement. We can begin to see that philosophers and poets of the Renaissance not only often shared a common vocabulary but the same *forma mentis*.

The distinguished German historian Karl Lamprecht, in the course of working out his psychological interpretation of history, characterized the Middle Ages as dominated by analogical reasoning.[6] Other scholars have agreed with this notion, but some of them have realized its inadequacy. Heinrich Schaller, for one, points out that, although Lamprecht's view seems to be correct so far as it goes, it is too broad. Since analogy is a universal characteristic of thought in any age, "we must further define and specify the nature of analogical processes of thought in the Middle Ages."

They are somewhat vague in many ways; fanciful, sentimental, metaphorical in meaning, intuitive, image-building, poetic, blending faith and knowledge, actuality and metaphysics, symbol and concept, the Inner and Outer world, in many ways naive and primitive, medieval analogies depend too little on experience and induction.[7]

Not only did the Middle Ages accept analogies which are no longer intellectually valid for us and apply analogy with little or no awareness of its limitations as an instrument of scientific investigation, but it applied analogy universally. Etienne Gilson finds in the principle of universal analogy a dominant trait of medieval thought, especially in St. Bonaventura and his followers. He maintains, however, that it was expanded and developed during the Renaissance with such persistence that it appears to be more characteristic of the thought of the Renaissance than of the earlier period.[8] This conclusion is, oddly enough, directly opposed to that of Lamprecht, who dates the decline of universal analogical reasoning from the fourteenth century. However, we do not have here a contradiction but a difference in points of view. It is clear that Lamprecht is talking about the tradition which culminates in the thought of Bacon, Galileo, and Descartes, whereas Gilson is probably thinking of Bruno, Paracelsus, Boehme, and other similar thinkers who in his view are more typical of the Renaissance. Most modern students of the Renaissance would tend to agree with Gilson, especially those who had tried to present a comprehensive view of the culture of the Renaissance in its own terms and not simply as it foreshadows the modern age.[9]

Windelband traced the growth of universal analogy in the Renaissance to the confluence and interaction of two cultural phenomena. On the one hand, the nominalism of the late Middle Ages had rejected "faith metaphysics" and made the world of experience the proper subject of philosophy. But while a method was being sought for the study of this new philosophical object, the Neoplatonic view of the cosmos was revived, so that the first solution of the new problem was in terms of universal analogies and cosmic affinities. The doctrines of the microcosm-macrocosm analogy, universal analogy, cosmic affinities, and varying versions of the *coincidentia oppositorum* (some of them, like Bruno's, based on a misinterpretation of the classical significance of this doctrine) were fully revived and became the basis for a new theory of knowledge. Thus knowledge became, in part at least, a form of self-knowledge, and man as microcosm was the mediator between himself and the universe; knowledge of one element in the microcosm-macrocosm analogy was analogical knowledge of the other.[10]

For both the Middle Ages and the Renaissance, analogy was nothing arbitrary or verbal. As Gilson points out, Bonaventura believed that universal analogy reveals that creatures are not merely things (*res*) but signs (*vestigia*) as well, signs which reveal the marks of the Creator in His creation. The analogical and symbolic potentiality of a thing is therefore not exterior or accidental to the thing but is derived from the very nature of creatures themselves and, indeed, is the law by which creatures were created. Thus exemplarism, or analogy between God and the universe, was not only necessary but inevitable. Aquinas, to a lesser extent, made use of analogical techniques and for the same reason as Bonaventura: analogy between God and His creatures solved the problem of pantheism by eliminating the univocal predication of "Being" to both God and His creatures. Bonaventura, however, was more interested in the unifying aspects of analogy, whereas Aquinas was concerned with the separative. Thomistic analogy led to the nicely ordered hierarchy of the *Summae*, and Bonaventura's led to the mass of symbols which is the *Itinerarium*. Thomas wished to establish every being in its own order so that no finite being might share in divine being;

Bonaventura was interested in the relationship that attaches creatures to their Maker.

In the Renaissance, however, we find the more extensive use of analogy among those thinkers, such as Bruno or Paracelsus, who are most pantheistic in tendency. Analogical techniques which had formerly been applied to understanding a transcendent God and had served to keep Him transcendent were now applied to an immanent Deity whose nature was revealed in the universal cosmic affinities that united the cosmos and in the basic identity of the contradictory aspects of experience. Renaissance analogism was thus not exemplaristic and was not directed toward solving the problem of pantheism. Those Renaissance thinkers who saw the world under the aspect of universal analogy seemed more interested in its unifying than its separative aspects. The unity sought, however, was not the purely analogical resemblance between God and His creatures but, as we might expect from pantheists, that unity which underlies the multiplicity of the universe and which is God Himself. The analogism of Bruno, for example, is "horizontal"; it does not seek exemplars of a transcendent divinity but rather tries to discover the "golden chain" which links all parts of the universe, however opposed they may seem to be.[11]

The Renaissance emphasis on universal analogy and cosmic affinities helped to make the *forma mentis* of Renaissance men richly metaphorical and symbolic. Cassirer justly remarked that one of the characteristics of Renaissance philosophy is the reluctance shown by philosophers of that period to be satisfied with an abstract statement. They sought instead the concrete expression of an idea, often by means of myths. They displayed a strong tendency to create an analogy, to understand it as an end to inquiry, and to feel an almost animistic identity of man with the great living world of nature. Indeed, the kind of analogical play often found in their works is really indicative of their tendency to intuit nature directly rather than think about it. Thus Paracelsus, Bruno, Campanella, and other Renaissance investigators of nature expressed themselves largely in linguistic statement and symbols rich in imaginative elements. Their criterion of the truth or falsity of a statement seems to have been its degree of richness in essentially "poetic" elements. It was this sense of "truth" which helps account, in part, for the great importance the Renaissance humanists placed on rhetoric, an emphasis which Ramus and others carried to the point of attempting to reduce the traditional scholastic logic entirely to rhetoric.[12] This same characteristic also helps us to understand the way in which the analogical sciences of the Renaissance, for example, alchemy and astrology, provided such abundant material for poets and were themselves expressed in a "poetic" manner.

It was not only the philosopher and investigator of nature but the poet as well who, by universal analogy, were to discover and express the unity of experience. Bruno begins his argument to *De gli eroici furori* with an attack on the Petrarchan theory of poetic inspiration. For the older notion of "amore" directed toward personal beauty, Bruno attempted to substitute the idea of "heroic love" directed toward the universe. This was also done by Ficino, but for Bruno this love is precisely the gift that the poet has for joining and unifying opposites or for making heterogeneous analogies. Thus, the principle of universal correspondences provides the basis for a unified theory of the imagination which joins the philosopher or investigator of nature and the poet.

It is interesting to compare this parallel between the poet

and the philosopher with the one Cassirer advances between the Renaissance mathematical physicist and the artist, whose respective endeavors were theoretically unified by means of the idea of measurement and proportion. Cassirer traced the origin of this unified theory of the mathematical and artistic imagination to Nicholas of Cusa, who maintained that all knowledge is a kind of proportion or measuring, a principle which was later applied aesthetically as well as mathematicologically and became one of the most profound motifs of Renaissance culture.

Thus, while the Renaissance theories of mathematics and art both sought "form" in experience, contemporary philosophers and poets demanded the revelation of the whole network of universal analogy. It would seem, therefore, that the concept of "form" and proportion on the one hand and the principle of universal analogy on the other are two categories of interpretation which help us to understand some of the motifs in the culture of the Renaissance.

These unified theories of the imagination persisted well into the seventeenth century and were weakened only by the victory of Cartesianism and Baconianism. Universal analogy, however, has an interesting subsequent history. Although analogism in Renaissance philosophy or investigation of nature gave way before the advance of science, it was kept alive in the form of the "occult." Under the influence of universal analogy, alchemical terminology became a system of universally applicable symbols and, with Boehme, a language suited to the expression of mystical experience. In this form, alchemy influenced several modern poets, such as Blake, Goethe, and Yeats. Universal analogy, especially as popularized by Swedenborg, revived the germ of Bruno's conception of the poet, and it was largely through the influence of Swedenborg that this notion of the poet was restated during the Romantic period and fully revived by Yeats and Baudelaire in the modern era. Even science has not entirely dispensed with universal analogy, as the thinking of contemporary schools of psychonanalysis, the school of Jung in particular, seems to demonstrate.

We can perhaps better clarify Dante's systematic and controlled use of analogical principles if we examine first the role of analogy in "metaphysical" poetry and thus compare more fully the workings of this principle in both the Middle Ages and the Renaissance.

I must beg the reader's indulgence for taking him on what may seem a roundabout approach to the problem of analogy in Dante; the seventeenth century is, however, like a great prism in our culture through which medieval intellectual traditions received their final diffraction. We can achieve, I think, a better grasp of the workings of analogy in the medieval tradition and in Dante if we first survey the end term in the series of transformations of analogical procedures for the organization and interpretation of experience.

Numerous theories of "metaphysical" poetry have been advanced ever since the appearance of Sir Herbert Grierson's great edition of Donne's poems in 1912 initiated the modern revaluation of the "metaphysical" poets. However, few of these theories seem to have approached the problem from the perspectives offered by sixteenth- and seventeenth-century literary critics themselves. One of the reasons for this oversight is the curious fact that there is no body of critical literature in English on the metaphysical movement written when that movement, under various names, such as "concettismo," "Marinismo," and "Gongorismo," was flourishing throughout Europe. Another reason is that we seem to have forgotten that the word "conceit," "concetto," or "concepto" also meant metaphor as well as "conceit" in the sense in which

Dr. Johnson used the word. This is especially surprising when we consider that many modern critics find the most striking characteristic of the metaphysical poet to be his desire to extend the range and variety of metaphorical expression.

The conception of the poet as one who discovers and expresses the universal analogies binding the universe together was later developed by the theorists of the conceit in the seventeenth century, the most familiar of whom are Baltasar Gracián in Spain and Emmanuele Tesauro in Italy, and was made the basis for a poetic of "concettismo" or, as I have called it elsewhere, "a poetic of correspondences." [13]

One of the cardinal tenets of the critics of the conceit is that the conceit itself is the expression of a correspondence which actually obtains between objects and that, since the universe is a network of universal correspondences or analogies which unite all the apparently heterogeneous elements of experience, the most heterogeneous metaphors are justifiable. Thus the theorists of the conceit justify the predilection of the "school of wit" for recondite and apparently strained analogies by maintaining that even the more violent couplings of dissimilars were simply expressions of the underlying unity of all things.

It is, of course, true that analogical thought is a fundamental property of the human mind in any age and that the notion of universal analogy has a long history which reaches back to Plato. The important point is that Bruno and the theorists of the conceit employed the principle as the basis of a poetic for the first time. The fact that they did so does not "explain" metaphysical poetry any more than Aristotle's *Poetics* "explains" Sophocles. This is not the function of a poetic or a theory of poetry. Rather, it formulates conceptually a concrete body of literature already in existence. As Hegel put it in his preface to *The Philosophy of Right*,

"When philosophy paints its gray in gray, a shape of life has grown old . . . it cannot be rejuvenated but only understood. The owl of Minerva spreads its wings at twilight."

What a poetic can do, however, is make explicit the cultural presuppositions which may govern a particular body of literature, a style, a genre. That Bruno and the theorists of the conceit should have based their poetic on the principle of universal analogy meant that they wished to justify and formulate philosophically the actual practice of metaphysical poets in making recondite and heterogeneous analogies and in using mundane and "learned" images.

The principle of universal analogy as a poetic, or the poetic of correspondences, offers, in my opinion, a theory of metaphysical poetry which is simpler, in great harmony with the evidence, and freer from internal contradictions than the major modern theories that have yet been formulated. It is in the light of this theory, contemporary to the metaphysical movement, that I propose to review the various modern theories.

One popular modern theory derives "metaphysical" poetry from the Petrarchan and troubadour traditions and describes it as a decadent and exaggerated version of these earlier traditions.[14] If this is so, we can hardly understand the deliberately "irregular" poets, such as Donne; the colloquial tone and the homely and technical imagery characteristic of "concettismo"; and the fact that Bruno, a "concettista" himself and the probable founder of Neapolitan "concettismo," began his *De gli eroici furori* with an attack on the Petrarchan and troubadour conventions and offered a clear and determined substitute theory. He, at least, was certain that he was doing something else, and the poetic creations of the "metaphysicals" are sufficient evidence that he succeeded. We can avoid this conclusion only if we insist on regarding the conceit as merely an odd or unusual image, in which case we can find it everywhere (and therefore nowhere) and even take its origin back to Martial. But it is clear that literary history cannot be made from superficial similarities and that the historian of taste must seek and determine the different cultural presuppositions that underlie the creations of minds as diverse as Bruno and Arnaut Daniel, without, at the same time, swallowing up the individual uniqueness and greatness of every distinguished artist and work of art in the general historical categories we construct for them.

Another theory would attribute the "metaphysical" style to the influence of Ramistic logic, but it seems to me that this view raises more questions than it answers. Norman E. Nelson has made an acute criticism of the confusion between poetry, rhetoric, and logic that the defenders of the Ramistic theory are apparently involved in.[15] It is at least questionable whether any system of inference or any empirical construction like rhetoric can have the kind of effect on a culture that the originators of this theory describe. If their almost deterministic view of the influence of logic and rhetoric were true, they would still have to explain away the fact that Milton, who wrote a Ramist logic and defended Ramist theories, was surely no "metaphysical" poet. The connection between "concettismo" and Ramism, if one can be established, is not a causal relationship. Rather, they are both expressive, in different ways, of what we might call the "rhetoricizing" tendency of Renaissance humanism, the belief shared with Ramus by Valla and others that literature or rhetoric, rather than the old scholastic logic, revealed the true path which the mind must take in its quest for truth.[16] It would seem that the confusion of logic and poetry characteristic of our modern "Ramists" is a result of the current use of the term "logical image" to refer to the kind of expanded metaphor characteristic of much "metaphysical" poetry. It is, of course, clear that the "logic" of development of an expanded metaphor has often very little to do with the logic of a syllogism or system of inference and is, indeed, directed toward a different end.

Another group of scholars relates the "metaphysical" style to the baroque, but variously, sometimes completely identifying it with the baroque and sometimes distinguishing the two. Croce, for example, calls "concettismo" a baroque phenomenon but considers anything baroque a negative aspect of Renaissance history whose only excuse for existence was to purge Western civilization from medievalism. It is otherwise with Hatzfeld, who, distinguishing "concettismo" and baroque, gives the honors to the latter, of which the conceit and its uses are, at most, degenerate parody.[17] It is difficult to discuss the views of this group, since the term "baroque" itself is, like "Renaissance" and "Romantic," so variable in reference. The notion has, however, been applied with greatest success to the study of the visual arts, where it is at least referable to specific techniques. I do not propose to complicate further this already complex problem, but it would seem desirable to keep the characteristics of baroque painting, sculpture, and architecture firmly in mind when we extend this term to other cultural spheres and not allow ourselves to be misled by chronological simultaneity alone. The original fruitful use of the concept of the baroque with reference to the plastic arts suggests that Cassirer's category of "form" and the principle of universal analogy might well be kept separated and that true "concettismo" belongs to the latter, whereas the baroque, as Croce suggested, is best understood as the transformation of the Renaissance interest in "form" into a preoccupation with "ornament." Baroque, according to Croce, also involves a weakening of the distinctions between the arts.

Perhaps the most widespread theory of the "metaphysical"

style is the emblem theory. This view, establishing a causal connection between the emblem movement or "emblem habit" and the conceit which is purportedly its result, is usually expressed in terms of a baroque theory of the "metaphysical" style. Mario Praz, the foremost representative of this group, bases his analysis on Croce's, without assuming the latter's negative attitude toward either the baroque or the "metaphysical" styles. However, his study of the actual creations of this literary movement leads him to a view of the conceit and the emblem which might be called the "game" theory, a position he assumes when he says of the conceit and emblem that they are of the nature of the charade or riddle—the by-products of an amusing, lighthearted verbal and pictorial game.[18] This is surely an astonishing description of a style in which some of the greatest religious poetry of all time was written, and it is, in effect, denied by the sensitivity of Praz's concrete criticism of John Donne and Richard Crashaw.

I believe that this conclusion is a consequence of Praz's insistence on the intimate relationship between emblem and conceit and between the mass of different styles, some of them quite absurd, which went under the name of "Marinismo," "Gongorismo," "seicentismo," "euphuism," and so on. However, not only are the resemblances between Donne and Lyly superficial at best, but the easy application of some notion of strangeness or eccentricity in style will find resemblances where none exist and will lead to false or useless descriptions of cultural phenomena. Praz seems closer to a working definition of the conceit when he says that it is to poetry what the illusory perspective is to art, although, in the light of both the theory and the practice of the "metaphysical" style, this insight is of somewhat limited utility and best describes a style like that of Crashaw.

Praz makes much of the fact that the emblem was usually

accompanied by an epigram, and, since he seems to hold that emblem and "metaphysical" poem are related to each other as cause and effect, he concludes that the epigram is the genre most characteristic of "concettismo." This conclusion, in turn, leads to his placing great emphasis on the diffusion of the *Greek Anthology* during the Renaissance as one of the important influences on the growth of the "metaphysical movement." [19] However, although the *Greek Anthology* stimulated many imitators, it seems to have had little effect on the best of the poets of wit. The long and "conceited" works of Marino, Gongora, Donne, and others preclude accepting this view, at least in the form in which it is stated. Praz's stress on the epigram also leads him to emphasize brevity as the most desirable quality of a good conceit, a quality which presumably helped make it "sharp" or "pointed." Brevity in the conceit was commended by the theorists of the conceit themselves, but they also recognized what we would call today the "expanded metaphor," and they often seem to mean by "brevity" a quality opposed to the Ciceronian notion of *copia*. There is, of course, no reason why an epigram should not have conceits, but there is also no apparent reason to establish a determined relationship between "concettismo" and epigram and, via the epigram, between "concettismo" and the emblem. I shall take up the more fundamental inadequacies of the emblem theory in detail when I discuss the view of Austin Warren below, since he presents this theory in purer form than does Praz. In the latter's version the emblem plays an important role, but mediately, through the epigram, which had to be brief, playful, and puzzling and was analogous to illusory perspective in the arts. Although this analysis is true of certain individual works, especially of some productions of the school of Marino, it is inadequate to the movement as a whole and gives no real clue to the *forma mentis* of a "concettista."

Indeed, this theory of the conceit was implicitly rejected by the seventeenth-century theorists of the conceit in whose works the emblem and *impresa*, as well as the epigram or "arte lapidaria," are treated as incidental topics involved in the analysis of conceit or metaphor. They were fully aware that any theory of the conceit had to be theory of metaphor or analogy, not a theory of genres. Emmanuele Tesauro, for example, analyzed all genres, literary and artistic, as forms of "acutezze" or types of metaphorical expression by extending the categories of rhetoric to include all literary and figurative creations.[20] Thus Tesauro himself realized that the sources of "concettismo" lay deeper than any classification of genres and were rooted in the nature of expression itself. Not only the epigram but all genres, including the lyric itself, had become "metaphysical."

Austin Warren, as already observed, shares some of Praz's conceptions about the emblem to an even greater degree. He says:

> The connection of the emblem with poetry was, from the start, close: indeed the term often transferred itself from the picture to the epigram which ordinarily accompanied it. . . . Thus the arts reinforced one another. The influence on poetry was not only to encourage the metaphorical habit but to impart to the metaphors a hardness, a palpability which, merely conceived, they were unlikely to possess. And yet the metaphors ordinarily analogized impalpabilities—states of the soul, concepts, abstractions. . . . Many emblems owe their undeniable grotesqueness to the visualization of metaphors, often scriptural, which were not intended to be visualized.[21]

In this particular passage, I take it that Warren means by "hardness" a kind of precision and by "palpability" a strong visual or sensuous element in the image. In any case the "metaphysical" image purportedly acquired these properties from the "emblem habit," which helped to develop metaphorical habits of mind and, presumably, habits for making recondite metaphors instead of commonplace ones.

However, as I have already explained, the theorists of the conceit either do not deal with the emblem at all or treat it merely as one aspect of the general theory of wit, making no direct connection between emblem and conceit. Taking our cue from them once more, we might observe that the qualities of precision and the strong sensuous element found in much "metaphysical" poetry can be accounted for, to the degree that any poetic "accounts for" a living and creative poetic tradition, by their theory of wit (*ingegno*, *ingenio*, *esprit*) as the faculty which, like Bruno's *genio*, finds and expresses the universal analogies latent in the data of experience. The desire to draw correspondences between heterogeneous things and thereby reveal the unity of what appears fragmentary and the desire to develop these correspondences are bound to give to the resultant imagery some of those qualities Warren discerns in the poets of wit.

From a more general critical point of view, the "palpability" or "hardness" of an image is, after all, a function of what the poet wishes to say and can say. In its own way Dante's imagery is as "hard" and "palpable" as one could wish. What the poet can say and the way he can say it are in part given by his culture, insofar as the culture makes him a man of a particular place, time, and environment, and in large part by his imaginative power, which enables him to "inform" and universalize his cultural and personal experience. No poetic has yet explained the secret of his power, although a poetic which is true to the concrete works of art that it attempts to describe can theoretically give us insight into the nature of the imagination by telling us what it did with what it worked with. Universal analogy and its later formulation as a poetic can thus tell us something about the

Renaissance imagination and throw light on Donne, Marino, Crashaw, and others, in spite of their differences. In this light, it would seem to be an error to attribute a movement such as "concettismo" to some secondary cultural phenomenon such as the "emblem habit" or Ramist logic and try, by so doing, to obliterate the differences between poets by swallowing them up in an influence.

Warren's version of the emblem theory of "metaphysical" poetry is based on a general theory of imagery involving the nature of the analogues in a metaphor:

> All imagery is double in its reference, a composite of perception and conception. Of the ingredients, the proportions may vary. The metaphorist can collate image with image, or image with concept, or concept with image, or concept with concept.[22]

After discussing the series of combinations according to which the "ingredients" of an image may be arranged, he continues:

> Then too, the metaphorists differ widely in the degree of visualization for which they project their images. The epic simile of Homer and of Spenser is fully pictorial; the intent, relative to the poet's architecture, is decorative. On the other hand, the "sunken" and "radical" types of imagery—the conceits of Donne and the "symbols" of Hart Crane—expect scant visualization by the senses.[23]

This passage is especially important because the author is here distinguishing between those poets called "metaphysical" (he also seems to include the modern "neometaphysicals") and all others. In this passage, however, Warren is not analyzing the school of wit and its imagery in terms of "palpability" or "hardness" purportedly derived from the emblem; indeed, he seems to be saying that the Donnean conceit is capable of "scant visualization." It would therefore lack the properties which the emblem supposedly gave to the conceit. In the passage previously cited, Warren closely connected the emblem to the conceit, whereas in this passage the conceit is completely severed from those properties which it was supposd to have derived from the emblem.

It is clear that we are involved in a contradiction. Unintentionally, Warren is pointing out one important thing about "metaphysical" poetry and about poetic imagery in general. The qualities of the "metaphysical" image seem to have nothing to do with whether or not it can be visualized or with the sensory content of the image itself, although it may be prominent. The qualities of the "metaphysical" image are a function of the *manner* in which the analogues are related, and it is this very point that the theorists of the conceit make when they insist that the wit is in the "form" of the conceit and not in the "matter."

A further reason for the inevitable inadequacy of the emblem theory is the historical fact that the emblem movement, initiated by the introduction of the *Hieroglyphica* of Horapollo to Renaissance Europe, is a cultural phenomenon distinct from the poetry of wit and has other cultural presuppositions. Although emblems and conceits were later found joined, they are found together at a relatively later date and usually in minor authors like Quarles, who gave emblems already in existence a verse commentary.[24] Granted that a poet might find an emblem suggestive of some image or another, the vast bulk of the creations of the school of wit do not seem to be related to the emblem literature in any intrinsic way. The very grotesqueness of many of the emblems is testimony to the fact that the conceit preceded—and was therefore independent of—its graphic expression. If anything, it was the conceit which made the emblem grotesque rather than the emblem's making the conceit "harder" and more "palpable."

Emblems drawn to many of the conceits of Donne or Crashaw or to much of the so-called "decorative imagery" of Homer would all be equally grotesque.

Perhaps the basic unexamined assumption in this whole theory is that there is a radical distinction in kinds of imagery. The sharp cleavage between what are called "decorative" imagery and "functional" imagery needs to be closely examined. We might begin by asking in what sense the imagery of Homer can be said to be decorative. It is clear even from a cursory reading of the *Iliad* that many of Homer's analogues for the events of battle are drawn from the world of peaceful endeavor. One of the obvious functions of these analogues is to heighten the pitch of the battle scenes and to bring the "great" world of peace into relationship with the "little" world of war. In this sense the *Iliad* is as much about peace as about war; metaphor is the link between these two worlds, revealing the nature of war through analogy with the events and experiences of peace. It follows that the poet's "choice" of analogues depends upon what he wants to say, upon what elements in the world of men he wishes to bring into the world of his poem. This is at least one sense in which the microcosm-macrocosm analogy is still profoundly vital.

When Homer compares an attacking army to a huge wave breaking on a beach, he would, in the opinion of some, be making a fully pictorial metaphor. All the reader has to do, however, is to try to think of the various ways in which an emblem might be constructed to represent this metaphor to see how grotesque the results could be. Two *separate* pictures could be drawn, and they could be photographic. But this would not result in the creation of an emblem, for the emblem would have to embody the whole metaphor at once in one representation. We must bear in mind that the metaphor is part identity and part difference. What Homer wants us to see is the way in which a wave under certain conditions is like an army under certain other conditions. By joining these two particular analogues, he selects those qualities of waves which can be transferred to armies. The pictorial quality is not in the whole metaphor or in the identity but in each analogue separately as a kind of sensuous residue remaining after the identity has been established, and as such it is part of the total effect of the image. Thus the pictorial quality remains precisely that aspect of the image which cannot be transferred from one analogue to the other.

It follows from this analysis that, when we speak of "pictorial imagery," we cannot mean that the metaphor can necessarily be absorbed into a pictorial representation or that, conversely, it was necessarily created by a graphic representation. Both historical evidence and theoretical necessity, therefore, require abandoning the emblem theory of "metaphysical" poetry. The emblem movement is more closely related to the tendency in the baroque plastic arts toward breaking down the barriers between the arts in the effort to create a universal art which would somehow combine all of them. Its great vogue was largely the work of the Jesuits, who found the emblem a useful pedagogic device for propagating the faith.

The failure to see the way in which the emblem is related, and the extent to which it is not related, to the conceit can lead to some further misinterpretations. Praz, for example, derives the limbeck image as used in the writings of the spiritual alchemists from the emblem tradition and believes that this image is a mere "conceit" or witticism.[25] But it was part of the religious and symbolic vocabulary derived from the symbols of empirical alchemy by application of the principle of universal analogy whereby they were extended to apply to all levels of existence. The limbeck was thus no mere suggestive and fanciful image but the symbol of a process that was recapitulated in every order of a universe seen *sub specie alchemiae*. The failure to realize the nature of this image leads Praz to misunderstand the significance of the work of Michael Maier, the alchemist who published an alchemical work containing both emblems and music to be sung to the various stages of the alchemical process, as a very strange example of baroque sensibility or "concettismo."[26] What Maier did, however, was to use the emblems for their pedagogic value, much as a chemistry textbook might have illustrations and equations. Music as a necessary part of the alchemical process was a characteristic result of the conviction that all things are universally related and affect each other through correspondences.

Although, as Warren maintains, "both the emblem and the conceit proceed from wit," they do not proceed from the same kind of wit, or in the same way.[27] The relationship is not, above all, filial but, at most, cousinly. Our own time is less "witty" than the time of Donne, and universal analogy has passed out of existence as a common habit of thought; the difficulty we have in penetrating this view of the world from within and somehow understanding it as "natural" and not "artificial" is, perhaps, the most important reason of all for the confusion about the nature of the poetry of wit. Many students of the movement have been aware that what may impress us as shocking, or recondite, need not have had the same effect on contemporaries. This has sometimes been attributed to habitual usage and "taste." However, the "metaphysical" poets and their contemporaries possessed a view of the world founded on universal analogy and derived habits of thought which prepared them for finding and easily accepting the most heterogeneous analogies.[28]

Now let us turn to the medieval tradition of analogy and

specifically to Dante where we will find that his analogical relations are drawn not only between sets of parallel entities but, even more significant, between levels of reality. In this case each level explains and unfolds a reality on the next lower level to which it is related analogically.

The idea of creation was one of the central problems of patristic and medieval thought, and some of the most original contributions of scholastic philosophy are by-products of the attempt to define creation *ex nihilo* and to work out the implications of that concept.[29] The divine act of creation, the conferral of existence, came to be considered the act of creation in the proper sense of the word while all other forms of what we would call creation were analogically or mimetically related to it.[30] There was thus a sharp distinction between creation by the First Cause and the activity of the secondary causes of nature. The latter did not really create at all; they actualized what God had already created in potency, perhaps as *rationes seminales*, or transmitted His power and thus were capable only of "generation." Man could *make* but neither create like God nor "generate" except as he is himself an instrument of nature and possesses thereby the power to reproduce himself.[31]

The main point of departure for the centuries of speculation on the idea of creation was of course Genesis. However, there soon was joined to this text the *Timaeus* of Plato, in spite of the fact that the Demiurge does not create *ex nihilo*.[32] In the later Middle Ages, it was the cosmographers and poets of the school of Chartres, William of Conches, Alan of Lille, Bernard Silvestris, and others, who were most concerned with creation theory. They took as their ideal task the interpretation of both Genesis and the *Timaeus* in the light of each other and attempted to harmonize and synthesize these two works.[33]

The Chartrians began by affirming that the world or nature is the most beautiful of created things. Nature is not only perceived as possessing aesthetic value but it is understood as being beautiful because it is the work of the Divine Artificer. Like any artifact, it possesses two aspects which pronounce it as a creation: sensory matter and an intelligible order. On the other hand, nature also has a quasi-creative power of its own, and this proclaims it a divine creation.[34]

The metaphysic on which this aesthetic was based can be formulated as a set of analogical "trinities," some divine and some natural, all of which reflect each other. The divine Trinity is the first: *Pater*, *Filius*, *S. Sanctus*. Its synonyms are *unitas*, *aequalitas*, *amor et connexio*; *potentia*, *unitas*, *bonitas*; and *causa efficiens*, *causa formalis*, *causa finalis*. These names also apply to nature in an analogical way and are related to another purely natural "trinity," *natura primordialis*, *forma rerum*, *anima mundi*. It is thus that created being reflects all those divine attributes which proclaim it to be the work of the Absolute.[35]

Nature is the artifact produced by the first of three kinds of productive work, the work of the Creator who endowed it with an actualizing power of its own. This it manifests through the familiar processes of generation and corruption which embody and perpetuate the species—manifestations of the divine archetypal ideas—through the production of successive individuals. The third kind of work is that of man, who makes by imitating nature in a manner analogous to the way that nature imitates God.[36]

Where we would use the term creativity loosely, patristic and medieval thinkers used it with great care to refer only to the work of the Creator. The term which could be applied to the agents of creation, generation, and making equivocally was *auctor*. An *auctor* is one who brings about the existence of anything or fosters its increase and well-being. An *auctor* is not necessarily the originator. He may simply be the preserver and perpetuator. Thus in classical usage the word held many meanings: creator, maker, author, inventor, father, teacher, leader, cause, and so on. God, nature, and man are all *auctores* on a descending scale, with creation appropriate only to the first.[37]

The first creation is that without any pre-existing matter, such as the creation of the elements or spirits or of those things that occur against the course of nature, such as a virgin giving birth. Nature needs the seeds or germs of things and is the perpetuator of similar individuals out of similar ones. It possesses an innate productive power, whereas man makes things simply because of his insufficiency.[38] He needs clothes, shelter, and other necessities; but nature and, above all, God need nothing. They create or generate, as the case may be, simply out of "goodness," out of a kind of excess of being or power, to reveal and manifest their intrinsic value and wisdom.[39] In addition, that which God directly creates is eternal, the work of nature is eternal in the species only, the individual coming to be and passing away, and anything made by man is perishable.[40]

Thus any human making is utterly different in kind and quality from that of either nature or God. Its products cannot perpetuate themselves, much less endure. Moreover, as we have noted, the productions of the higher *auctores* possess revealing power—they are creations whose intention is simply the manifestation of goodness and wisdom. Theoretically, therefore, human artifacts are primarily utilitarian, although the possibility of their possessing beauty or revealing power is not explicitly excluded.[41] As will be brought out, the beauty of human artifacts (painting and poetry, for example) was usually formulated theoretically as the faithful representation or description of a pre-existing beauty anterior and external to the work itself.

The analogy of creation was further elaborated through a second analogy between the artist who creates according to an inner model and the Creator God who did the same kind of thing on a much higher and qualitatively different level. This analogy is traceable at least to St. Augustine, who in the tradition of Middle Platonism placed the ideas of all things in the mind of the Creator God Himself.[42]

Now it is God, in this scheme, who possesses the true Idea and, therefore, the true creative power. What the artist has both as idea and as creative power is something remotely like it. The image of the *Deus Pictor* or *Deus Artifex* in medieval or patristic thought is not intended as a glorification of the artist. It is rather an attempt to understand divine creation by using the artist as an analogue. Medieval theory, basically Plotinian, never gave to human creativity a positive or active role in relation to nature.[43] Such a conception was the conquest of the Renaissance. Still less was there any notion of the artistic activity as something "divine." The artist or maker never creates in a metaphysical sense, although he has an inner "quasi-idea" and resembles the Deity in his use of a pre-existing model. A painting or statue was not ever primarily considered as the imitation of a natural object, but simply as the representation of the inner idea. Theoretically there was no essential difference between painting and architecture, for the artist had no relation to nature. There is simply a parallelism between divine creation, whose product is nature, and human quasi-creation, whose product is some artifact or other. The work of art does not involve an adaptation or accord between man and nature, but emerges from the imposition of an interior form on an external matter. Medieval art theory remained an extension of medieval cosmology.

The notion of the universe as somehow like a work of art antedates the Christian conception of it as a creation. It is a central assumption of Greek Platonism and Aristotelianism that the universe is to be understood on the analogy of an art work, in terms of form and matter. Thus, *morphe* is the shape conferred on *hyle*, literally wood, although the elaboration of this basic conception took different forms with different thinkers.[44] It is important to bear in mind that the main alteration of this guiding analogy which took place in Christian thought was the notion of the world as a creation, an actual *oeuvre*, not simply something *like* a made work, for the universe in Greek thought was coeternal with God and not His handiwork.[45]

Let us now turn to the work of Dante to see what use he made of this widespread analogy of creation, and consider first the creativity of God. Primarily, His artifact is the universe, and secondarily it is the immortal human soul individually created for each of us.

The divine goodness creates because it is utterly free of envy, it creates out of an excess of love. This love with which the Divinity is aflame translates itself into a creative activity which is at the same time a manifestation of its eternal beauties. Whatever issues forth immediately from this divine creative activity—angels, souls, the heavens—is eternal, for the immediate imprint of the divine is imperishable. The stars, new things compared to God and themselves immediate creations made to be the ministers of nature, cannot control other immediate creations such as the human soul. All such direct creations bear the greatest similitude to their Creator, for the divine love which irradiates all things as luminous beauty is brightest in that which is most like itself.[46]

The first act of creation, the properly divine act, created the angels, the heavenly bodies which are their instruments, and the primal undifferentiated matter on which they operate. Even the four elements—in this Dante differs from the Chartrians—the cosmological building blocks of the universe, were subsequently brought into being by the actualizing power of the intelligences operating through the light of the heavenly bodies. The elements in being were further actualized into vegetative and animal life. Thus the primal matter contained potentially all the things that now fill the universe—with the exception of man—and it was the work of the light and motion of the stars which made that true divine creation actual. Man, both body and soul, was originally a divine creation and so created was entirely imperishable. The human soul is, of course, still immortal, but the body temporarily lost its immortality through original sin, although it is destined to regain its bodily immortality upon the completion of the drama of salvation.[47]

Dante turns again to an exposition of the creation theme in discussing the creation of the angels, brought into being out of pure benevolence simply to reflect God's splendor back to Him by using their capacity for consciousness and love. They, pure form and actuality, came into being along with time, pure formless potential matter, and the heavenly bodies which are compounds of both form and matter. This was the creation of order, and it came into being instantaneously, just as light diffuses itself through a transparent medium.[48]

Dante's creation doctrine is *Timaeus* doctrine adapted to Christian theism. God directly created or, in the case of the intellectual soul, still does create, incorruptible things: the angels, the heavens which are the instruments of their angelic movers, and primary matter. The intelligences through their spheres created or, better, generated mutable things out of the potential complex according to the divine eternal archetypes. The species is eternal because it primarily exists in God, whereas the individual is perishable because it is created by nature (in the medieval sense of the word by which nature includes angels, beings we would consider supernatural). Given God and what He directly creates, the rest of the process is *Timaeus* doctrine with its three elements: a divine archetype, middle causes corresponding somewhat inaccurately to the Demiurge, and an unformed matter which they inform. Note, too, that Dante follows the tradition of the Chartrian *Timaeus* commentators in distinguishing between the creativity of nature and that of God according to the permanence of the artifact.

There has been some scholarly controversy on Dante's theory of creation. The problem is stated as whether Dante teaches a doctrine of direct creation or a doctrine of indirect as well as direct creation, the latter perhaps heterodox in nature. It seems clear that Dante adheres to a doctrine of both direct and indirect creation and carefully distinguishes the role of the angels from God's role in the creation of the universe. It is true that the idea that angels created things by the use of their intellects was condemned, but this is not the same thing as allowing them some secondary or ancillary task. Gundissalinus and Dietrich von Freiburg, for example, attempted to reconcile some notion of angelic creativity with Christian theism.[49]

No one denied, of course that the angels had some kind of control over creation either as governors or ministers. The only question was whether and to what extent the angels participated in the hexameral work. It was by no means necessarily unorthodox to have allowed the angels such a role. Heterodoxy could be involved only if the angels were said to have created the human soul or if their generation of anything else was thought to be *ex nihilo*.[50]

The highest level of creation, that of the divine creation of the four *coaequeva*, the four coevals of matter, time, the heavens, and the angelic nature, was appropriately enough discussed in the *Paradiso*.[51] This is the greatest and primary act of creation and demands for its apprehension all that Dante the pilgrim had learned in the preceding *cantiche*. The *Purgatorio* treats of human creativity, as will be shown, and of one other act of divine creation, that of the immortal soul. This act is discussed earlier in the poem because it is the divine creative act superimposed on the postlapsarian natural generation of the body. The human being is now the work of both nature and God, and His essence is more comprehensible at the purgatorial level of consciousness.

When, in *Purgatorio* XXV (37 ff.), Dante approaches the seventh terrace, the ledge on which lust is purged, Statius explains to him the process of reproduction. The semen, a more "perfect blood," is generated in the man's heart and possesses an informing, active power which, when mixed with the passive blood of the female, forms the embryo. In its growth the embryo develops the vegetative faculties, and, when these are complete, it acquires all the sensitive or animal faculties. At this point Statius tells us that Averroës, a wiser man than Dante, erred by denying that the possible intellect, the faculty of intellection, was an individual possession of the human soul because he could find no organ for it. He was thus led erroneously to deny a special divine act of creation for each soul. Dante learns, however, that this immortal intellectual soul is an individual possession created by God and infused into the fetus at the right moment. It then absorbs all the lower souls or faculties, making them its own and carrying them with it beyond the grave.[52]

This analysis of creation has a multiple purpose in the context. It serves to explain how, in the fiction of the poem, the souls make new organs from the surrounding air, and, more important, it gives the pilgrim knowledge of the true purpose and function of reproduction, a human act the result of which God completes. The pilgrim is now ready to enter upon the purgation of lust. This human aspect of divine creativity with its profound moral implications properly precedes the cosmological, since it is necessary knowledge in the retraining of the will.

Dante had earlier considered this same problem during the period of the *Convivio* (III, vi, and IV, xxi), and there is a question whether the earlier doctrine may not be heterodox. Let us consider the most important passage in question before we take up the pros and cons:

> And therefore I say that when the human seed falls into its receptacle, that is, into the matrix, it bears with it the virtue of the generative soul, and the virtue of heaven, and the virtue of the elements it combines, that is to say, its complexion; and it matures and disposes the material for the formative virtue which the soul of the generator gave. And the formative virtue prepares the organs for the celestial virtue which draws the soul from the potentiality of the seed into life. And the moment it is produced it receives from the virtue of the mover of heaven the possible intellect, which potentially brings in itself all the universal forms, according as they exist in its Producer, but in a lesser degree in proportion as it is more removed from the prime Intelligence.[53]

On this question Busnelli and Vandelli argue that Dante's theory of the creation of the soul and generation of the body is Thomistic.[54] Bruno Nardi has shown, however, that Dante owes more to Albertus Magnus; and Nardi accepts, as do Busnelli and Vandelli, a harmony between the versions of the *Convivio* and *Purgatorio.*[55] Nancy Lenkeith does not accept such a harmony and argues without adducing much textual evidence or source material that the theory in the *Convivio* eliminates the part of the Creator in the production of the intellectual soul, a position corrected in *Purgatorio* XXV.[56]

The problem really hinges on what Dante meant in the *Convivio* by the phrases *la vertù celestiale* (IV, xxi, 4) and *la vertù del motore del cielo* (5). Busnelli and Vandelli maintain that both phrases refer to God so that the vegetative and sensitive souls as well as the rational soul are all created by God in one act, as one soul which replaces the perishable souls that pre-existed it in the purely biological phase of the embryo's development. Such at least is the opinion of St. Thomas with which they equate Dante's.[57]

Nardi argues that *la vertù celestiale* is the active result of the formal principles constituting each heavenly body whereas *la vertù del motore del cielo* is the power of God Himself. Thus, the heavenly bodies produce the lower souls, and the intellectual soul, "the possible intellect," is divinely created. This last soul then absorbs the lower souls, constituting them in one unit. Although this is certainly the doctrine of *Purgatorio* XXV, where there is an explicit reference to the First Mover who can be nothing else but God, it is not completely clear that *la vertù del motore del cielo,* or even *la prima intelligenza,* unequivocally refers to God. At least, that is what I think that Lenkeith's interpretation implies, although she is not explicit. In this case *la vertù del motore del cielo* would refer to the power of a celestial intelligence, perhaps that of the lunar sphere, who moves it and who, in the thought of Averroës, is the source of the possible as well as the active intellect.[58] Dante, as Nardi has shown, never refers to the active intellect but seems to have adopted some doctrine of illumination to account for the actualizing power of thought.[59]

To be consistent, we must also take *produttore* and *prima intelligenza* as referring not to God but to the first intelligence in the sense that the mover of the first sphere might be so called. If, as Lenkeith seems to maintain, Dante's view in the *Convivio* is Averroistic in assigning to angelic intelligences and the spheres the origin of both body and soul, then *Purgatorio* XXV must be read as another of Dante's many self-corrections in the *Comedy*.[60]

In *Paradiso* XIII, St. Thomas Aquinas explains to Dante that the creative processes of nature in the generation of the human being worked perfectly on only two occasions, in the creation of Adam and of Christ. The pre-eminence of Solomon among all men, attested in Scripture, refers only to his kingly wisdom. This distinction is made in the framework of another discourse on creation. Immortal things, such as the angels and the heavens, and mortal things, the creatures of the sublinary sphere, are all nothing but the luminous manifestation of the Idea, the Son eternally generated from the Father through Love, the Holy Spirit which is one with the other two persons of the Trinity. This shining source of light, simultaneously one and three, manifests itself first in the angelic hierarchy, nevertheless remaining one. From the angelic hierarchy this light descends from rank to rank in the great chain of being to progressively lower and lower actualities until its creative power makes only minerals and organic beings, "things generated with or without seed."

The molding Idea working as light and the imprinted matter, a kind of wax, are not always most propitiously related to one another so that the form of a thing does not always dominate the matter, with the result that the individuals of a species are not perfect specimens. Indeed, in the course of the ordinary operations of nature, the "wax" is never molded perfectly, and the heavens are never at the height of their power. With the exception of the two instances of Adam and Christ, when there was divine intervention, nature works like an artist who possesses the skill of his art but whose hand trembles when he tries to externalize his inner idea.[61]

Dante here implies a number of related creation analogies. As the artist's or artificer's activity has a triple aspect, so has nature. The artist possesses an internal idea, an externalizing faculty and its instrument, and he uses a matter which he stamps with his internal idea. So nature has the Idea which exists in the mind of God, a faculty which externalizes it and its instrument—the angels and the heavenly bodies—and a matter which is formed.[62] Nature, however, is not capable of fully realizing the divine idea unless the Divinity, as the Holy Spirit, the burning love, intervenes. When it is autonomous, as it usually is, nature works defectively.[63]

In the *Convivio* (II, iv, 1–6) Dante has entertained a different conception of the status of the Idea although it is not clear whether he was committed to this view. He attributes to Plato, "a man of supreme excellence," the view that there are as many intelligences or angels as there are kinds of things as well as movements in the heavens. Each angel or class concept generates the particulars of which it is the universal, working as the exemplar to its many images. There is an angel-universal for man, one for gold, and so on, and each is a generator of its own kind. These the gentiles called gods and goddesses.

Here the Idea would be the angel-universals considered collectively, not the forms in the divine mind as in the *Comedy*. That Dante might have temporarily accepted this view would be in harmony with the interpretation of his theory of the generation of the soul in the *Convivio* which maintains that he excluded the Creator's role.[64]

Two of the three levels of creation in the works of Dante have now been considered. Before proceeding to the third, let us summarize the first two. The first and primary act created the four coevals. Such a divine act is continued only in the creation of each human soul, an act which completes the purely natural and therefore always defective generation of the body. Two instances, Adam and Christ, are examples of the Divinity interfering to raise nature to its perfection so that nature momentarily operated as a perfect instrument of the divine intention.

Nature herself, however, is usually autonomous. As *natura naturans* she works through her proper instruments, the heavenly bodies which, moved by angelic intelligences, impress the image of the divine archetypes on primary matter. The heavens, the angels, and the human soul, since they are direct creations of the Deity, are all immortal. The human body temporarily lost its immortality through sin, but it too will repossess it as by the original divine intention.

The third analogy of creation is human, and Dante explains this in a well-known passage of the *Inferno* in which the moral scheme of Hell is expounded. The analysis of human productivity is prefixed to an explanation of the unnaturalness of usury, for one theory of human making accounted for all artifacts, whether strictly utilitarian or what we should call aesthetic.[65]

Nature, Virgil explains to Dante, copies the divine mind and its art, its creative activity, and tries to embody the divine ideas in its own secondary creation. Man in turn, as Aristotle tells us in the *Physics* (II, 2, 194a, 21–25), creates by trying to imitate nature, so that his activity is, as it were,

God's grandchild. Man must make things, as Genesis (1: 28–29) tells us, because of his neediness. So Scripture and Aristotle complement each other in teaching that human industry must create if we are to survive and that man must create by imitating nature. Man comes into the world unequipped by nature to meet his needs for survival instinctually. Art, the activity of making or creating, by following nature makes the human environment more hospitable than the environment of fallen nature herself.[66]

This is creation *propter indigentiam* and is all that the pilgrim can truly understand of the analogy of creation at the "infernal" level of consciousness. Human productivity is next discussed in the *Purgatorio* after the vision of irremedial moral evil is over, when the pilgrim has received more grace and understanding, a clearer and higher vision. There the poet learns about the arts, the activities which meet the human need for beauty and which, although they arise out of the desire to fill a void, do not meet the indispensable needs alluded to in the *Inferno*. It is there that the talk is filled with considerations of poetry, the visual arts, and music and that the arts are judged, implicitly and explicitly, in relation to revelation and the moral life. Casella's beautiful song must not stay the task of re-education of the sinful will (*Pur.* II, 112 ff.). That poetry which gives the truth dictated by love is distinguished from mere rhyming (*Pur.* XXIV, 99 ff.), and the relationship between Statius and Virgil dramatizes the paradoxical differences which may obtain between the poet's artistic and eternal destinies. Virgil, an instrument of both divine and artistic grace for Statius, has incomparably the higher artistic status but is removed forever from the beatific vision which he unconsciously helped to obtain for his follower.

The most powerful consideration of the higher forms of

human creativity in the *Purgatorio* occurs on the first terrace where pride is purged. Here Dante's criticism, direct and oblique, of the radical sin is strongly focused on artistic creativity, and even other occasions of pride and the opposite virtue of humility are presented through the divinely wrought sculptures on the wall of the terrace.

He first sees divine sculptures on the wall representing examples of humility. They are such that they would put both nature and Polyclitus, the greatest of sculptors, to shame (*Pur.* X, 31–33). This is a kind of sculpture where the speech of the figures is somehow visible (95), heard while it is unheard, and where the incense depicted in the wall is smelled without being smelled (58–63). They are work of the Divine Craftsman (*fabbro*, 99). Such would sculpture be if God decided to do it, an art which would be life and still remain art.

Similarly, the sculptures seen at the end of the purgation of pride, those that show the proud brought low, exceed the power of the greatest masters "of brush or chisel" (*Pur.* XII, 64). The dead seem dead and the living seem living in perfect verisimilitude. Between these two confrontations of the sculpture of the Divine Craftsman, Dante meets Oderisi, the famous illuminator who tells him of the vanity of human artistry from the standpoint of eternity.

> In painting Cimabue thought to hold the field and now Giotto has the cry, so that the other's fame is dim; so has one Guido taken from the other the glory of our tongue, and he, perhaps, is born that shall chase the one and the other from the nest.[67]

Dante here couples the visual arts with poetry, but it is important to realize that he does not attempt a theory of poetry in terms of the analogy of creation. Rather he uses a theory of inspiration, an adaptation of theories of prophecy and of mystical vision, to account for the "newness," the non-imitative character of the products of the poetic imagination. If Dante's theory of beauty in nature and the visual arts is one of imitation or participation in a divine or natural beauty, respectively, his conception of poetry is that a true poem is participation in divine wisdom and that its function is the salvation of himself and others (*Par.* XXXIII, 37 ff. and 67 ff.). The poet is the scribe of the Holy Spirit, the only true creative Agent in existence, and from Him come truly new images. Hence the novelty of the poem to which Dante so often calls our attention, especially by invoking supernatural aid and lamenting his inability to render his vision fully.[68]

In this conception of poetry Dante departs from the main current of medieval theory, usually an elaboration of the Horatian notion of *ut pictura poesis*. Both painting and poetry were generally thought to present us with "descriptions" of the ideal beauty of the world of sense.[69] This conception of poetry was part of a scheme according to which there were three modes of contemplating the beauty of the world. The first way, exemplified by Hugh of St. Victor and the poets, was to see it with the eyes of the flesh, to delight in its very visibility. A second and higher mode was to see it as does the thinker, permeated with order, regularity, and harmony. The Chartrians were pre-eminent among those who saw it in this manner. The third and highest mode was to see the universe's beauty with the eyes of the spirit, whereby one saw everywhere in the created universe spiritual significations and analogies. Such were St. Bernard, the Victorine mystics, and St. Bonaventura.[70]

It is obvious that the *Divine Comedy* includes all these modes of vision and does not stop at the purely descriptive or visual mode which was all that the creation analogies of Dante's time could offer poetic theory.

Although man creates primarily to survive, he also captures beauty. But creation for the sake of beauty is primarily the intention of the Divine Artist. Indeed, the creation of the universe was an act of divine self-manifestation as beauty. This divine beauty is most evident in the internal order of the mind and in the order of the luminous heavenly bodies, as the rational and "moral law within, and the starry heavens above."

Looking on His Son with the Love which the One and the Other eternally breathe forth, the primal and ineffable power made with such order all that revolves in mind or space that he who contemplates it cannot but taste of Him. Lift up thine eyes with me then, reader, to the lofty wheels, directing them on the part where the one motion strikes the other [the Ecliptic], and from that point take thy pleasure in the art of the Master, who so loves in His heart that His eye never leaves it.[71]

Not only does nature possess this revealing beauty, but so does Beatrice. Indeed, her beauty is such that it surpasses both that of nature and that of art. All beauty is a divine lure, and Beatrice is pre-eminent among all of the myraid manifestations of that single divine beauty. Beatrice's beautified soul, made directly by God and therefore one of the creations which most manifests Him, is always the most beautiful object in that part of the *Paradiso* which unfolds itself in nature's categories of space and time (cantos I–XXIX). According to the creation concepts we have considered, Beatrice, as a specimen of God's art brought to perfection by being in God's presence, could not but surpass all the beauty that reveals itself in space and time—the celestial landscape—and all the beauty that man might capture—the poet's power to render or suggest her beauty.

The enamoured mind that wooes my Lady continually burned more than ever to bring back my eyes to her; and if nature or art have made baits to take the eyes so as to possess the mind, in human flesh or in its portraiture, all these together would seem nothing beside the divine delight that shone on me when I turned to her smiling face.[72]

The beauty that Dante goes seeking through the levels and kinds of creation is not, of course, the beauty of the poem. What the pilgrim experiences as beauty is not the same thing that we experience as beauty. Yet it is beauty, divine and natural, created and uncreated, which lures the pilgrim through the universe of the poem, and it is in the power the poet has to make us believe that he has tracked beauty to its source that the beauty of the poem, in part, resides.

V

Dante and Epicurus: The Making of a Type

THE figure of Epicurus in the *Divine Comedy* has been a problem for Dante scholars in their attempt to determine how the poet approaches the problem of heresy and, by extension, whether the poet himself may not have been entangled with heretical doctrines. Why is Epicurus, a pagan, in the circle of heretics? Why symbolize heresy by what Dante believed to be Epicurean doctrine? The answers to these problems will involve a consideration of typological allegory and symbolism, a study of Dante's knowledge of Epicureanism, and, in between, an analysis of what I believe to be another of the numerous self-corrections we find as we read through the works of Dante. Dante not only changed his mind about Epicurus and Epicureanism but found in the evidence at his disposal the motive for making a "type" of heresy in the same way as other figures of sacred and secular history appear as "types" in the *Divine Comedy*.

The allegorical interpretation of Scripture antedates Philo Judaeus, although he was the major influence on Origen and the Eastern fathers who preferred his rather abstract, moral, and philosophical reading of Scripture.[1] In the West, the work first of Tertullian and then of St. Augustine signalized the triumph of a more concrete and historical way of interpreting Scripture which has since come to be known as typological allegory or, as the late Professor Auerbach called it, "figuralism." [2] This is the method of interpreting Scripture whereby the persons and events of the Old Testament are seen as figures or realities which are also simultaneously prophetic signs of the drama of salvation unfolded in the New Testament. The New Testament in turn is prophetic of the events and realities of the Last Judgment, not only when it is obviously prophetic but in the very events of New Testament history themselves. Unlike the Eastern tradition in allegorical interpretation of Scripture which tended to weaken the literal and historical verity of the Old Testament, the "figural" method based itself fully on the literal and historical value of the events recorded in Scripture. This method is unlike ordinary allegory or symbolism in that both terms in the analogy are literally and historically real and not merely signs. Thus Moses, Adam, and Joshua are types of Christ, but they are also Moses, Adam, and Joshua. The Deluge is a type of baptism, but there was a real deluge. The sacrifice of Isaac was a type of the sacrifice of Christ, but there were a real Isaac and Abraham. In short, the relationship between the terms of a figural analogy is not that of sign to reality signified but that of shadow (*umbra*) or *imago* to its fulfilled truth, although both are concrete, real, and historical realities.[3] Only the link between them is abstract.

This method of interpretation in the Christian tradition begins as early as St. Paul. Thus the Jews in the wilderness are types of ourselves (I Cor. 10: 6 and 11). The Jewish law is a shadow of what is to come (Col. 2: 16 ff.). Adam is both a type and an antitype of Christ (Rom. 5: 12 ff., and I Cor. 15: 21). The relations between the law and grace, bondage and freedom is prefigured in the relationship between Hagar and Ishmael or Sarah and Isaac (Gal. 4: 21–31).

This Pauline method of interpretation was rooted in rabbinical allegorical exegesis, the Midrash, but St. Paul modified it and turned it into an instrument in his attack of the Judaizing Christians. His main intention was to deprive Judaism of its normative character because of his deeply felt convictions on the paradoxical and antithetical relations between law and grace, justification by faith or works. In effect he tried to reduce the Old Testament to a prediction. In so doing, he made the particular history and mythology of a particular people accessible—in an enormously altered way, to be sure—to gentiles; but it contained the seed of a philosophy of history.[4]

St. Augustine, in this as in other matters for the Western Christian tradition, gave definite shape to figural interpretation as well as to exegetical techniques and practices.[5] Along with rather abstract moral and philosophical allegories of a familiar sort we discover many typological analogies. Noah's ark is a prefiguration of the Church, Moses is a figure of Christ, the priesthood of Aaron is a shadow and figure of the eternal priesthood, Hagar is a figure of the earthly Jerusalem or the Old Testament, and Sarah is a figure of the New Testament, the heavenly Jerusalem, or the City of God. Jacob and Esau are figures of Jews and Christians, and so on.[6]

Even in the case of immoral acts in the Bible, St. Augustine insists that they are to be taken literally. However, they are also to be taken figuratively, and the interpreter is to use the figurative interpretation alone.[7] The literal polygamy found in the Old Testament is to be understood as a special divine dispensation appropriate to a certain time in the history of the drama of salvation. Nevertheless, even though these acts are no longer permissible, they have an eternal reference, a figurative moral meaning which is always applicable and a prophetic meaning which will last until the end of history. Thus, although the events of Scripture are to be read historically and literally, they are also to be read figuratively and prophetically.[8]

We can easily grasp here one of the ideas which, especially after it was secularized, could lead to the possibility of countenancing apparently immoral contemporary actions on the grounds that they were providentially ordered, an important conception which underlies much of the apologia for later Christian tyrants.

The nature of figural interpretation and its historiographical implications might be clarified if we compare it to modern historical interpretation. The latter places events in a sequence moving, so to speak, horizontally toward an ever-receding horizon. The meaning of any single event is given in a development to a further event which defines what went before. Hence each generation must write its history anew, for each event alters the significance of the past. On the other hand, in figuralism, the meaning comes from above; it is given by a vertical dimension, by the operation of divine grace and judgment. The pattern of events is not a uniform series. There are breaks, mistakes, miracles, and conversions.[9]

There are thus intrusions of eternity into time, and, for Christianity, the central event was the Incarnation, "unto the Jews a stumbling block and unto the Greeks foolishness." Each such intrusion is both a historical reality and a promise. While for secular historiography the immediate fact is regarded as secure and the interpretation naturally incomplete, in figuralism the general interpretation is given through revelation, and the dates are subject to it not only for interpretation but even for selection. Each event possesses an archetypal meaning whose fulfillment lies in the mind of God. Thus *figurae* and the Incarnation are signs of a future temporal fulfillment but also signs of something existing in the hereafter. The complete meaning, now hidden, will be revealed to both sense and thought when the Redeemer returns.

They are not only preparatory and prospective of temporal events but are preparatory of the eternal and otherworldly, pointing not only forward to the future but "upward" to eternity, where they already exist as complete in the mind of God. Time is thus the moving image of eternity. Paradoxically, the effect of this prophetic history was not to negate the historical sense but finally to strengthen it. It is no accident that autobiography, the sense of the self as a product of the past, arose first within Christianity. The radical historicity of the individual man is a corollary of the radical historicity of the Christian view of the world. History is a drama of salvation with a beginning, revelation, and a coming end to history. God's grace works in mysterious ways and inscrutably. It selects a chosen people whose apparently unimportant history must be read as a record, partly in cypher, of God's revelation. A humble unlettered carpenter becomes the vehicle of the infinite, and in the realm of daily life the greatest drama of all unfolds itself. Christianity not only made history more historical, but also widened its range to include areas of life and experience not included before. The trivial, the humble, both on the historical scene and in daily life, might all be vehicles of grace.[10]

As time went on, figural interpretation became a kind of second nature to Christian intellectuals, and pagan material came to be figurally interpreted. The Sibyl, Virgil, the Grail story, the legend of the Seven Sleepers, Charlemagne, and others were all conceived at least in partially figural terms. The most striking and familiar application of this technique to secular materials is Dante's *De monarchia* where not only is there posited a correspondence between secular and sacred history but the great characters of Roman history are given some of that exemplary and figural character they will have in such a striking degree in the *Divine Comedy*. As Auerbach points out, some of our surprise at finding Cato in Purgatory and not in Limbo or the Wood of the Suicides disappears if we look at him as a figure of liberty.[11]

From the point of view of figural interpretation, the *Divine Comedy* is a historical vision in which the prospective meaning of men and events is seen in its fulfillment. The figures in it are not mere allegories or abstractions. Their historical and earthly identity is preserved in eternity in that final essential meaning which they created for themselves and which was what they signified in the plan of providentially ordained history. It is important, too, to understand that not everything a man does or believes is carried beyond the grave or enters into his fulfillment. St. Bernard despised Rome and the Romans, but he is a dweller in that Rome of which Christ is a Roman. Cato was the enemy of Caesar and a suicide, but his final essence did not lie in these but in the height of his sacrifice for civic virtues and freedom. Siger of Brabant may have been a heretic, but he discovered some important truths. Eternity baffles judgment and indeed may even surprise the historical individual's idea of himself. Would Virgil ever have dreamed that he would be a light unto others although himself doomed to dwell in darkness forever? Virgil in the afterlife is essentially what he was on earth, a poet and guide, although not as he was on earth, for he now knows more of his own influence as a poet and of his capacity to lead even where he was unconscious of that capacity. A conscious poet of universal empire, he comes to know that the empire he celebrated is a figure of an eternal Christian empire—he was the conscious prophet of Rome and the unconscious prophet of Christ. In a sense, the *Comedy* is a fulfillment of the *Aeneid* considered as figura.[12] Dante applies similar categories of interpretation to his other characters and to secular as well as sacred history. Even the texture of his metaphors and the character of his symbols and episodes are influenced by this all-pervasive perspective of figuralism.[13]

I have dwelt at some length on typological interpretation in order to be certain that its fundamental principles are clear before turning to the figure of Epicurus in Dante's works.

In the course of his life Dante changed his mind on a number of important intellectual and aesthetic problems. Perhaps the most obvious of these self-corrections occurs in Canto II of the *Paradiso* on the question of the causes of the spots on the moon. In the *Convivio* (II, xiv), Dante had erroneously maintained that the dark areas on the moon were caused by the rarity of its substance in those parts. Beatrice, however, tells Dante that the cause of his error lay in not having understood that the luminosity of the heavenly bodies is a function of God's power and that of His angels. This power manifests itself as light and shines in different degrees in different parts of the universe, just as the soul manifests its power variously in different parts of the body. Dante thus finally exchanged his earlier quantitative explanation of the presence of spots on the moon for a qualitative one.[14]

Another obvious correction that Dante makes is on the ordering of the angelic hierarchy. In the *Convivio* (II, vi), Dante adopted the order given by Brunetto Latini who in turn took it from Isidore of Seville. In *Paradiso* XXVIII, however, Dante decided on the Dionysian order, rejecting both his own earlier view and that of Gregory the Great.

Indeed, Dante changed his mind on matters which are even more important than these. There is a steady development of Dante's views, both implicit and explicit, from the *Vita nuova* to the *Divine Comedy* on such questions as the origin of language, the worth and proper use of the vernacular, and literary genres and their application to appropriate subjects.[15] His conception of the role of the poet and the nature of allegory and metaphor and of poetic expression in general also underwent significant change.[16] Although certain central elements of his political thought remained constant, there seem to have been shifts of emphasis even if there has been a good bit of disagreement about the degree and direction of change.[17] And every student of Dante is familiar with the greatest change of all, the "return" to Beatrice from the *donna gentile* and the puzzling interrelationship between the "Lady Philosophy" of the *Convivio* and the Beatrice of the *Vita nuova* and *Comedy*. This is perhaps the crux of Dante scholarship, and Witte, Moore, Wicksteed, Nardi, and practically every great name in the scholarship of the last few generations tackled the problem of what the poet's shift in interpretation of these figures signifies.[18]

In view of Dante's continual reconsideration of so many questions, it is odd that G. Busnelli and G. Vandelli, the latest major editors and most exhaustive commentators on the *Convivio*, should interpret Dante's references in that work to Epicurus and Epicureanism in the light of the ninth and tenth cantos of the *Inferno*. In both the commentary on the apposite passages and in an appendix on Dante's presumed doctrinal tolerance, they assume that the poet held the same view of Epicureanism throughout his life and that the Epicureans of the *Convivio* are the archheretics of the *Inferno* "who make the soul die with the body." [19] I hope to demonstrate that they read back into the *Convivio* what is clearly another of Dante's later corrections of an earlier error. To make this matter clear, we must consider Dante's various references to Epicurus and Epicureanism in the light of the sources and definitions available to him and relate as precisely as possible his changing views to his use of different sources at different times. We shall then discover that Dante knew two entirely different versions of Epicurus, one of which we find in the *Convivio* and the other in the *Inferno*. The former is Ciceronian and classical whereas the latter is based on the medieval Christian tradition, best exemplified by Isidore of Seville.

Before we examine these sources, it would be useful to review the more important interpretations of the philosophical character of the *Convivio* and thus suggest some of the possible larger implications of our examination of Dante's shift in attitude toward Epicureanism. Much has been written on this difficult work, but it seems to me that the best literature on the subject, regardless of whatever final interpretation is made, recognizes the eclectic character of Dante's thought. He is surely not a Thomist in any really meaningful sense of the word as the footnotes of the Busnelli-Vandelli edition would seem to imply. Bruno Nardi's many studies have convinced virtually all scholars of the poet's debt to the medieval tradition of Aristotelianized Neoplatonism [20] and of the non-

Thomistic character of Dante's solutions to various important philosophical questions.

Etienne Gilson, the leading student of St. Thomas in our time, also recognized the non-Thomistic character of Dante's thought and advanced an Averroistic interpretation of the *Convivio*, and Nancy Lenkeith attempted to show that Dante's view of philosophy is neither Thomistic nor Averroistic, but Neopelagian.[21] According to the latter interpretation Dante drew on medieval Aristotelians and Platonists, but gave to philosophy and philosophical activity a virtually charismatic power to create in the philosopher both the moral and the theological virtues. Philosophy even had this power for pagan thinkers, so that they were able to achieve salvation through its efficacy. Thus, in the *Convivio* Dante saved pagans in a pagan way, through the power of thought and human effort rather than through the special and miraculous grace which saved Trajan and Ripheus in the *Paradiso*. The *Comedy* thus shows a radical re-evaluation of the great pagan thinkers, since it placed them all in Limbo and, in the case of Epicurus, even farther down.

This interpretation of the *Convivio* has the real merit of recognizing a change in Dante's evaluation of the nature of philosophy and especially of Epicureanism, although whether one ought to deduce from this that Dante was a Neopelagian heretic in the full sense of the word heretic is open to question. There is no question that Dante reveals himself in the *Convivio* as very optimistic about the range and scope of philosophy, to the extent that he virtually identifies it with theology, and equally optimistic about what human nature can accomplish through its own intellectual and moral effort. Although the case for the Neopelagian character of the *Convivio* may be essentially sound, it is more important to interpret the poet's changing views in the light of his relation to different currents of opinion on the nature of classical thought and the character of classical thinkers than to decide whether or not he was a heretic.

Dante's presumed heresy and his treatment of heresy in the *Inferno* have been the subject of much discussion and sometimes of bitter debate. But there are more than one way of being a heretic and more than one kind of heretic. The researches of two generations of scholars would seem to show that Dante had little precise knowledge of heresy, along with great independence of mind and equally great reverence for the Catholic faith, and that he was not possessed by that consistency which is the hobgoblin of little minds. Whatever the heretical implications of his thought in the *Convivio* may be—and I think it does have such implications—few doubt that Dante's sense of his own position was that it was orthodox, and still fewer doubt that the *Comedy*, both in its thought and in the implications of its thought, is sufficiently orthodox.[22]

Those passages in the *Convivio* in which Dante discusses Epicureanism should next be considered. In chapter fourteen of the third book of that work, Dante tells us how and why love may be said to be the very soul and form of philosophy. Divine, immaterial light, as that form of intellectual light by which we know whatever we know, descends immediately and directly upon the intelligences or angels and, through their mediation, to the rest of creation. Men also receive this light directly from its divine source, and it functions in them as a divine power which conforms human love to its own likeness, gives it eternal wisdom, the Word Himself, for its object, thus eliciting that love of supreme wisdom which is philosophy (*Conv.* III, xiv, 1–7). As this love grows, all other lesser loves or desires are quenched (7–8). It was this love of wisdom which led the great pagan philosophers such as Democritus, Plato, and Aristotle to condemn temporal goods and personal advantage and led others such as Zeno, Socrates, and Seneca to despise their very lives (8–9). This divine power descends upon men as it does upon the angels, Dante tells us again; and it is significant that he should repeat this idea immediately after the parade of examples drawn from the great thinkers of classical antiquity (9). For they received that "celestial thought" which is philosophy from heaven itself and participated in an activity which is more than human (11–12), displaying that particular kind of love which philosophy kindles wherever it exists (13).

We possess the power to look upon philosophy in high degree not only that we may behold what she reveals, but also that we may desire those things which she keeps hidden:

> Whence even as by her name much is perceived in its reason and in its sequence which without her appears a marvel, so by her means it becomes credible that every miracle may have its reason for a loftier intellect, and consequently may take place. Whence our excellent faith hath its origin, from which cometh the hope of that for which we long and which we foresee, and from this is born the activity of charity; by which three virtues we rise to philosophize in that celestial Athens where Stoics and Peripatetics, and Epicureans by the art of the eternal truth, harmoniously unite in one will.[23]

According to Busnelli and Vandelli in their commentary on this passage, all that Dante means is that the three sects unite in seeking the *summum bonum*, not in finding it. Yet Dante says quite unmistakably that it is the "art" or power of the eternal truth which unifies the wills of all three philosophical schools. "To philosophize in that celestial Athens" can mean nothing else than the loving contemplation of Wisdom, the beatific vision, in whose sight all the mundane differences of intellectual opinion and ethical ideals which separate lovers of truth disappear. The three great schools which Dante mentions were for him, following Cicero, the three great ethical schools of antiquity primarily concerned with the active life, with the volitional aspect of consciousness. They not only differed on the nature of the *summum bonum,* but failed to realize that the highest mode of life was contemplative, not active. Once they rise, however, to that "celestial Athens" and philosophize as the blessed do in the beatific vision, by loving and knowing the eternal truth, not only are their intellectual differences reconciled, but their conflicting wills are harmonized. They not only know clearly what the *summum bonum* is, but unite in having it as the one object of their love.

It seems to me, as it does to Lenkeith, that Dante does actually say that Stoics, Peripatetics, and Epicureans find the *summum bonum,* for it is nothing other than eternal truth as the object of love or desire, and it is by the art of this eternal truth that the various sects unite in one will. Before they could so unite it was necessary that they know the eternal truth, and they would seem to have achieved such knowledge after death. What is even more striking is that Dante identifies with Christ that wisdom which has always been the goal of philosophy by citing the opening of St. John's Gospel (*Conv.* III, xiv, 7), thus clearly indicating that the object of the philosophical love of the pagan philosophers was really Christ as the Logos, even though they were not aware that this was the goal of their striving. Furthermore, they unconsciously sought Wisdom or Christ, and moved toward Him, because of the divine power and light which descended to them from that source (4–5 and 7–8).

So interpreted, this passage would mean that the pagan philosophers not only sought the Word, but were able to rise to some kind of knowledge of supernatural truth in this life and to complete knowledge in the afterlife. Their seeking was thus fulfilled in heaven, where what they sought in this life but could not completely find was finally given to them, that ultimate truth which transcends and reconciles all their differences.[24] Indeed, the three theological virtues are conceived as growing out of the intense prosecution of philosophical activity. Such activity, love of wisdom, quenches all the lesser loves and so develops the moral virtues, as it obviously did in the pagan philosophers. Continued further, however, philosophy leads, by way of belief in the ultimate comprehensibility of miracles, to faith, from which issue hope and charity. The distinctions between theology and philosophy seem blurred, and the realm of nature appears to lead directly into the realm of grace. Even pagans seem to have been capable of acquiring a sufficient degree of theological insight and virtues in this life so that their knowledge could be completed in the celestial city of philosophy.[25]

Dante again refers to Epicureanism in Book IV of the *Convivio* where he discusses the final good posited by the Stoics and Epicureans. His argument here is drawn entirely from the *De finibus* of Cicero, and he seems to evaluate these pagans as generously and tolerantly as his source.

There were then certain very ancient philosophers, of whom the first and chief was Zeno, whose view and belief was that the goal of this human life is solely rigid integrity; that is to say rigidly to pursue truth and justice, without respect to aught; to show no grief, to show gladness at nothing, to have no sense of any emotion. And this is how they defined this integrity, "That which, apart from utility and apart from result, is, for its own sake to be praised by reason." And they and their sect were called Stoics, and of them was that glorious Cato of whom I dared not to speak above.

There were other philosophers whose view and belief was different from theirs; and of these the first and chief was a philosopher who was called Epicurus; who, seeing that every animal as soon as it is born, and as though directed by nature to the due goal, shuns pain and seeks pleasure, said that this our goal was voluptuary (I do not say "voluntary" but write it with a *p*), that is to say, delight without pain. And moreover, between delight and pain he placed no middle term, saying that "voluptuous" was no other than "without pain"; as Tully seems to recount in the first of the *Goal of Good*. And of these who are called Epicureans after Epicurus, was Torquatus, the noble Roman, descended from the blood of the glorious Torquatus of whom I made mention above.[26]

The final reference to Epicurus in the *Convivio* occurs in chapter twenty-two of Book IV. Dante begins to discuss the goal of human life and the progress the souls make in reaching it. He chooses the opinion of Aristotle and the Peripatetics, leaving aside those of Zeno and Epicurus:

Letting be, then, the opinion on this matter which the philosopher Epicurus had, and that which Zeno had, I purpose to come at once to the true opinion of Aristotle and of the other Peripatetics. As said above, from the divine excellence sown and infused into us from the beginning of our generation there springs a shoot which the Greeks call *hormen*, that is, natural appetite of the mind.[27]

This is the principle of self-love which grows and differentiates itself by distinguishing between higher and lower objects of its appetite and finally comes to rest in the love of the exercise of the highest part of the self, the mind, including both the will and the intellect. Dante departs from his source, *De finibus*, here and, in harmony with contemporary Peripateticism and, indeed, with Boethius, places the contemplative over the active life.[28] However, even though the latter is superior, the operation of both the practical and speculative intellects is equally the fruit of the seed of divine excellence naturally implanted in us in the process of generation. But at this point we should consider exactly what Dante means by the seed of divine excellence.

God gives most men a kernel or seed of grace which is the principle of the natural growth of virtue. This seed of blessedness is nobility, a strictly personal quality which cannot be obtained through inheritance. It is the indispensable prerequisite of virtue, and virtue necessarily grows out of it. God gives it to a soul which has a body perfectly disposed in every part so that it may in turn dispose the soul to receive the seed of grace which is nobleness (*Conv.* IV, xx, esp. 7–9). Now the way in which nobility descends on man may be explained in two ways, first, by natural science and, second, by theology. If we consider the process of conception from the aspect of purely natural science, we learn that the physical conditions which determine the process are not always the same. The impregnating seed may vary because of its elemental composition or because of the degree of generative power it received from its Creator. In addition, the celestial influences which govern the moment of impregnation are not always at their most propitious. All these differences in turn determine the way in which the receptive, passive "matter" of the female is physically prepared to submit to the action of the male generative power, the way in which the generative power acts in forming the fetus, and the way in which the potential life-giving principle of the seed is actualized by the celestial power transmitted through the light of the stars (IV, xxi, 1–4). When the fetus is sufficiently grown to receive it, the intellectual principle is divinely superinduced in it, and the human being is complete (4–5).

To the extent that all these aforementioned conditions are

closer to perfection, to that degree are divine excellences multiplied in the soul (7–9). Dante then adds that it is theological science which permits us to say that these excellences are the gifts of the Holy Spirit and to enumerate them (11–12). However, if all the natural conditions are actually perfect, then "so much of the Deity would descend thereon that it [the person] would be almost an incarnate God: and this is almost all that can be said by way of natural science" (10).[29]

Dante then adds "by way of theological science" that when God sees a creature so prepared by natural process to receive His benefactions He commits to it as much as it can take of them (11). These are the gifts of the Holy Spirit automatically bestowed on the perfectly disposed recipient—they are wit, wisdom, understanding, counsel, strength, knowledge, piety, and the fear of God (12). All these (in strict orthodoxy they are gifts of grace which God confers in secret counsel) are treated as virtually natural endowments.

Dante concludes his analysis of what the need of nobleness is by saying that its most fitting offshoot is that mental appetite which the Greeks call *hormen*. This along with other offshoots of the seed must be cultivated and nurtured; otherwise it would have been better not to have had any seed at all. Evil is thus implicitly presented as a kind of deviation from natural growth. Hence Dante emphasizes the need for training and education of the person in well-doing and restraint in order to correct any propensity toward evil, citing both Aristotle and St. Augustine (of all people!) for authority in this matter (14). This analysis leaves, for Dante, a question. What of that person in whose begetting the various natural factors failed to operate as they should so that he has some defect or lacks the seed of nobleness altogether? This is answered after the discussion of the unfolding of *hormen* when Dante says that "by much correction and cultivation some portion of the outgrowth of this seed may be so led to a place where it did not originally fall as to come to fruit. And this is, as it were, a kind of engrafting of another nature on a diverse root. And so there is none who can be excused; for if man has not this seed from his natural root, he may at least have it by way of engrafting." [30] Thus, where the divine seed of grace does not exist, it may be engrafted by education through a virtuous agent, the outgrowth of this seed.

After *hormen* has finally unfolded itself and become the love of the mind, the operation of the practical and the speculative intellect, the choice then becomes which of these two activities to follow. The highest is, as we have seen, contemplation, and this is what the three ancient sects of the active life did not achieve. In a striking interpretation of the story of the three Marys at the tomb, Dante equates the three ladies with the Stoics, Peripatetics, and Epicureans:

But in truth the one of these exercises is more full of blessedness than the other, to wit, the speculative, which, without any admixture, is the exercise of our most noble part, which, by reason of that fundamental love which has been spoken of, is chiefly to be loved, to wit the intellect. And this part cannot in this life have its perfect exercise, which is to see God (who is the supreme object of the intellect), save in so far as the intellect considers him and contemplates him through his effects. And that we should supremely demand his blessedness and not the other (to wit that of the active life), the Gospel of Mark instructs us, if we would rightly consider it. Mark says that Mary Magdalene and James' Mary and Mary Salome went to find the Saviour at the tomb, and found him not, but found a man dressed in white, who said to them: "Ye seek the Saviour, and I say unto you that he is not here. Nevertheless, fear ye not, but go and say to his disciples, and to Peter, that he will go before them in Galilee, and there ye shall see him as he said unto you:" By these three ladies may be understood the three schools of the active life, to wit, the Epicureans, the Stoics, and the Peripatetics, who go to the tomb, that is, to the present world, which is the receptacle of corruptible things, and demand the Saviour, that is, blessedness, and find it not; but they find a man in white garments, who, according to the testimony of Matthew, and also of the others, was an angel of God. And therefore Matthew said: "The angel of God descended from heaven and came and rolled away the stone and sat upon it; and his aspect was as lightning and his garments were as snow." [31]

This angel is nothing less than our nobleness which descends from God and which tells our reason that beatitude cannot be found in the active life but in speculation. He informs both those who are seeking beatitude and those who have gone astray where it lies. Thus all the pagan sects erred in not knowing where to find beatitude, having evidently not listened sufficiently to the voice of our naturally implanted indwelling nobleness. Even though Dante uses a scriptural story to get his argument across, he is not discussing Christianity or theology, for this allegory simply concludes the argument of "Aristotle and the other Peripatetics." Notice the apparent inconsistency in Dante's references to Peripatetics, for he first implies that they are "contemplatives" and later cites them as "actives." The second definition is Ciceronian. Either Dante has not noticed his own inconsistency, or he assumes that the reader will make the necessary distinction between "the true opinion of Aristotle and the other Peripatetics" and what Cicero says that they taught. In any case the Schoolmen and Dante's contemporaries knew that Aristotle gave the palm to the contemplative life, and Dante seems to use both conceptions of Aristotle even though they are contradictory.

Whatever Dante's inconsistency, it is manifestly clear that

he is passionately enthusiastic about philosophy, and the *Convivio* is filled with her praises. Indeed, his love of wisdom is so great that it makes him claim that virtually perfect happiness can be achieved on earth through philosophy alone (III, viii, 5 ff.). It is, after all, a divine virtue which descends on man in an angelic fashion. Dante's own love of philosophy extinguished every other thought from his mind, even Beatrice (II, xii, 7–8), as, let us recall, the love of wisdom which fired the pagan philosophers quenched all their lesser loves. It has this effect precisely because the happiness it gives transcends all other kinds. Indeed, philosophy functions like grace in that its beauty can make a new nature in those who gaze on it, a miraculous thing which aids our faith (II, viii, 20).

The idea of precedent merit, the ability of man to ennoble himself, the obscuring of the sharp distinctions between philosophy and theology, the intense rationalism which simultaneously culminates in mysticism—all of these are certainly not Thomistic ideas even if they are not as heterodox as some interpreters would make them (cf. *Conv.* II, xiv; III, xi, esp. 12 ff.; III, xii, esp. 11 ff.). One thing, however, is clear. In every reference Dante makes to Epicurus or the Epicureans, his tone and attitude give no indication whatsoever that he then thought that they denied the immortality of the soul. In fact, in Book II of the *Convivio* he denounces such people in no uncertain terms: "I say that of all the stupidities that is the most foolish, the basest, and the most pernicious, which believes that after this life there is no other." [32]

Dante then claims as authority for this statement not only the Scriptures, but all the philosophers and sages, specifically referring to the Stoics, Aristotle's *De anima*, Cicero's *De senectute*, and the pagan poets, and all nations, even Jews,

Saracens, and Tartars. Although Dante does not mention the Epicureans here, their omission signifies nothing. If the immortality of the soul was such a crucial question for him and if Dante at this time knew that Epicurus held this doctrine, he surely would have given some indication and would not have spoken of his followers as if they were as good as the Stoics and the Peripatetics. However, his knowledge of Epicureanism at this point was based entirely on Cicero's *De finibus*. He was as yet unaware of what Epicureanism had come to mean in the Christian tradition and was not acquainted with the *Tusculan Disputations* from which he might have learned what he could not from *De finibus*, that the Stoics held a doctrine of limited immortality whereas the Epicureans did not believe in it at all.[33]

We ought now to consider Dante's source, Cicero's *De finibus*, and try to specify Dante's relation to it. It will be seen that he not only adopted a number of its philosophical ideas and arguments, but also assumed Cicero's evaluation of Epicurus and Epicureanism. Indeed, he follows Cicero so closely that he includes the Peripatetics among the teachers of the supremacy of the active life, at the same time that he argues from "the true opinion of Aristotle" that the contemplative life is supreme.[34]

For his discussion of the principle of universal self-love which culminates in the highest good, Dante also drew on *De finibus*,[35] and his agreement with the Peripatetics means adopting as the ultimate Good living "in accordance with nature and in that condition which is the best and most suited to nature that is possible." [36] There are other important borrowings from *De finibus*. The argument that Epicurus finds the chief good in pleasure and the natural evidence for this view are simple recapitulations of Book I, ix, 29–30. Similarly, that there is no such thing as a neutral state of feeling between pleasure and pain is drawn from Book I, xi, 38. Dante stresses his use of the word *voluptate* to prevent the reader from confusing it with *voluntate* or will. So Cicero discusses at length the rendering of Greek *hedone* by Latin *voluptas*.

Over and above the borrowings of doctrine, there is the assimilation of an attitude. Of course Cicero's work is a set of dialogues in which various people attack and defend various positions. Yet not one says a harsh word about Epicurus. In Book II (xxix–xxx, 95–96) there is a long discussion of the nobility of Epicurus' death, for he died with a display of fortitude in enduring pain which would seem to be in contradiction to his principle that pain must be disregarded. He was a good, kind, humane man, with many friends. It is his intellect and not his character that is called into question. Only frivolous Greeks attack a man's ideas through his character.[37]

In reference to Epicurus' fondness for making classifications of desires, he is called a great and famous philosopher who has a right to maintain his dogmas boldly.[38] He corrected the error of reprobating pleasure and extolling pain and is a great explorer of human truth and the master builder of human happiness.[39] At no point in *De finibus* is Epicurus impugned. Only Zeno, of the three great teachers of the active life, gets any personal criticism, and that happens only once when he is called a crafty Phoenician (Book IV, xx, 56). Otherwise, even he gets plenty of respect. More important than Cicero's attitude toward Epicurus is the fact that at no point in *De finibus* is there any clear indication that Epicurus taught that the soul dies with the body. The closest Cicero comes to this is in a passage in which he says that Epicurus taught that sensation ceases after death so that there is no need to fear it. "For he repeatedly argued at length, and also stated briefly and plainly in the book I have just mentioned, that 'death does not affect us at all; for a thing that has experienced dissolution must be devoid of sensation; and that which is devoid of sensation cannot affect us in any degree whatsoever.' "[40]

With our knowledge of Epicurean doctrine we would read this passage as denying the immortality of the soul. Yet what Cicero says is that *sensation* ceases after death, a statement which, taken as such, need not disturb a Christian conscience. Cicero correctly assumes that Epicurus taught that absence of sensation would mean the absence of consciousness, but Dante need not have drawn this conclusion. Sensation is a corporeal function, and with the dissolution of the body and the organs of sense, the faculty of sensation would naturally cease. In the system of Epicurean materialism, as Cicero well knew, the loss of the body would mean the loss of consciousness. However, in Dante's thought and that of the Schoolmen, the loss of sensation in death was assumed and did not interfere with the survival of consciousness and memory. In fact, it was this loss which was so often used to argue for the necessity of the resurrection of the body. The human being would not be complete without the sensory functions, and for those he needs a body. I would suggest that Dante read this passage to mean that dying would not be painful because it is simply the loss of the vegetative and sensitive souls. It therefore could not be experienced as pain or pleasure.

It is clear that, at the time of writing the *Convivio*, Dante did not know what Epicureanism really meant and that he was able to accord it the respect he apparently felt for it precisely because he did not know what it meant. This conclusion follows with particular force when we consider that his source for his knowledge of Epicureanism was *De finibus* and that he everywhere shows his dependence on it, both on what it omits as well as on what it includes. Dante also shared the respectful attitude of his source toward Epicurus as well as toward the other great thinkers of antiquity. He saw no inconsistency in his own reverent attitude toward Epicurus and his condemnation of those who deny the immortality of the soul.

If we accept a Neopelagian interpretation of the *Convivio*, which implies that Dante there gave to pagan thinkers a knowledge of saving truth, then his change in attitude toward ancient thought was very marked indeed, for all pagan thinkers spend eternity deprived of the beatific vision in the *Comedy*. But even if we do not accept this view, we are still faced with an interesting question. Why is Epicurus the only great thinker of antiquity deprived of the companionship of his peers in Limbo when he stands together with them in the *Convivio?* Before we can answer this problem, we must consider briefly the fortunes of Epicurus' reputation. The early history of Epicureanism in the Christian period is interesting because Epicurean arguments against the pagan religion were widely used by Christian polemicists. Later, however, he was also employed against Christianity, so that St. Jerome and St. Ambrose both consider Epicureanism a menace, although St. Augustine treats it as pretty well dead. By the time of Isidore and Rabanus Maurus he is *Epicurus de grege porcus*, morally corrupt, even though St. Jerome praised his life at the same time that he condemned his doctrine.[41]

By the tenth century the term Epicurean had lost any really specific reference to the actual teachings of the classical followers of Epicurus and had become a general term for "materialist." Thus, Alvarus of Cordova designated them as the most dangerous fomenters of heresies, and by heresies he meant determinism, the idea that the soul is corporeal (although immortal), denied of the immortality of the soul, and opposition to both marriage and to continence. So vague had the meaning of "Epicurean" become that the Cathari and other medieval heretical sects were called by that name, and even the great Italian Ghibelline opponents of the papacy were accused of "Epicureanism," although precisely what this may have meant in their case is not clear. It is in the tenth century also that atomism and determinism are seen to have an intrinsic connection with one another and that the former also comes to be condemned as heretical after having been an innocent doctrine in the Carolingian period.[42]

It is this attitude toward Epicureanism which we find in the *Inferno*, a view which Dante may have obtained from a number of places but for which the most important medieval source was the *Etymologies* of Isidore of Seville or the *De universo* of Rabanus Maurus, the latter a rather faithful copy of the former. That Dante had read these two authors is very probable since he glorifies them in the *Paradiso*, Isidore in canto X (131) and Rabanus in canto XII (139). Let us now turn to Isidore and see what he has to tell us about the pagan philosophers and especially the Epicureans. We will then, I think, be able to specify the exact nature of the shift in Dante's evaluation of the latter.

Isidore gives one section of his encyclopedia the title "On the Pagan Philosophers" ("De philosophis gentium") and begins by classifying them according to their "sects" (*haeresis*). Some, such as the Platonists and Epicureans, take their names from their founders, others such as the Peripatetics and Stoics from their meeting places. The Platonists, named after Plato, believe that although God creates souls the angels create bodies, and they also believe in reincarnation.[43]

Zeno was the founder of the Stoics, who believed that no one can be blessed without virtue. There are no degrees of sin according to them, so that the man who steals chaff is as guilty as the man who steals gold, and the man who kills a gull is as guilty as the man who kills a horse. The crime is thus measured by the state of the soul and not by the animal killed. They believe that the soul perishes with the body and that continence is not a virtue, and they strive after eternal glory although they say that they are not eternal.[44]

Isidore reports that the Stoics and the Epicureans deny the immortality of the soul. There is a great difference, however, in his ethical and moral evaluation of these two "sects." Epicurus was not a true lover of wisdom, he said, but a lover of vanity. He wallowed in carnel filth and placed the highest good in bodily pleasure, so that the philosophers themselves called him a pig. He denied divine providence and maintained that the origin of things lay in the fortuitous concourse of atoms. His followers denied that God does anything and claimed that everything was corporeal including the soul. Epicurus said, "I will not be once I am dead."[45]

Although both the Stoics and the Epicureans denied the immortality of the soul, the former were virtuous and had a strenuous morality, whereas the latter were hopelessly corrupt. They were equally in error about the nature of God, the Stoics confusing Him with the world and the Epicureans placing Him beyond all concern for the world. All of the pagan thinkers, saying they were wise, were made fools.[46]

The ancient philosophers held varying erroneous opinions concerning the nature of the world. The Platonists thought it was incorporeal, the Stoics corporeal; Epicurus thought it made of atoms, Pythagoras out of numbers, and Heraclitus and Varro of fire. The last two named held the foolish opinion that death was the result of the loss of fire and that the world died when it lost such fire through lightning. These errors of the philosophers brought many heresies into the

Church, including Arianism, the heresies of Valentinus and Marcion (the latter heresies deriving from the Stoics), the denial of the immortality of the soul which is the work of Epicurus, and the denial of the resurrection of the body, a teaching of "the vain school of all the philosophers." Where God is identified with matter, we detect Zeno, and where with fire, Heraclitus. It was such ideas which circulated among the heretics and the philosophers and which are to be rejected.[47]

Whatever little merit Isidore's garbled account of classical philosophy, Gnosticism, and Arianism may have as history, it is clear that philosophy and heresy are for him virtually synonymous and that Christian heresies derive from the errors of pagan philosophers. Indeed, Isidore classifies Christian heretics and pagan philosophers under the genus of those who chose to believe whatever seemed better to them, ignoring the truth promulgated to the world by the Apostles, who received it from Christ. It is the Apostles of God who are the *auctores*.[48]

I think it is now abundantly clear that Dante had two entirely different conceptions of Epicurus and Epicureanism at the time of writing the *Convivio* and the *Inferno*. His later view gives us the Epicurus of medieval tradition, the pagan philosopher who above all was the breeder of heretical errors. I would suggest that it was the medieval conception of Epicurus as morally corrupt which, among other reasons, may have helped prompt Dante to single him out as the symbol and type of heresy. The Stoics too, as he could have learned from Isidore, denied the immortality of the soul, but this denial was pre-eminently an Epicurean position. In addition, the Epicureans were immoral and materialistic in the broad sense of the term. The Stoic hero appealed so to Dante that he finds room for Cato in the *Purgatorio*, for whatever their intellectual errors, their moral virtues were undeniable.

Oddly enough, Dante in this matter reversed what was to be the trend of the future. He went from a better understanding of Epicureanism available in Cicero's *De finibus* to the characteristic medieval view, which was less accurate to say the least. The diffusion of *De finibus* gradually led to a rehabilitation of Epicureanism until in Valla's *De voluptate* we find an attempt at reconciling important Epicurean tenets with Christianity. Dante later, however, placed the authority of Isidore and Rabanus over that of Cicero, modifying his earlier "humanism" in the light of Christian medieval tradition.

Dante in the *Comedy* saves only those pagans who received a special grace and knew of the redemption which was to come or which had come—Ripheus and Trajan. Cato, as he is found in the *Purgatorio*, is not saved in the sense that he shares in the beatific vision, although he will apparently share in it at the general resurrection. He is certainly saved from the boredom of Limbo, evidently because his singular virtues make him a suitable agent for helping to operate the machinery of the other world. The virtuous pagans, all the rest —Aristotle, Plato, and Democritus "who ascribed the world to chance"—are in Limbo, Averroës too is there, a Moslem who might have been placed with Mohammed and Ali among the fomenters of discord. What places all of these in Limbo and not elsewhere is the exemplary character, according to Dante, of their lives. They were *virtuous* pagans. They are not placed in Limbo because they held particular intellectual positions, even those which might have approximated orthodoxy, or because they knew a great deal, but because they were able to use what truth they had to lead moral lives. Epicurus, treated as the peer of other great pagan thinkers in the *Convivio*, was later discovered to be, as medieval tradition held, *de grege porcus*. He was not a virtuous pagan, and Dante then could use him as the symbol of heresy that he was for so many medieval theologians.

That Dante omits mentioning the Cathari, Patarini, and other contemporary heretics with which some scholars have identified his Epicureans has been a problem.[49] It is clear, however, when we consider Isidore's definition of heresy and its presumed source in pagan thought, especially that of Epicurus, that Dante is using a traditional typological figure of the heretic to symbolize them all and that he singles out one heresy—denial of the immortality of the soul—as a type of all the rest. That Dante should have thought this the most serious heresy of them all should not surprise us when we reflect on his passionate belief in justice and the extraordinarily subtle differentiations and gradations of rewards and punishments in the *Divine Comedy*. If the soul does not survive death, then the good may receive no reward and the evil may escape all punishment. This is a heresy which destroys the very foundations of the moral life, its sanctions and its fulfillment, and which denies the existence of universal order and justice in its most important area.

Whatever revaluation Dante may have made of pagan thought, he never shared remotely in the ignorant contempt and fear of it of such as Isidore. He knew too much and admired the greats of antiquity too much for that. Yet he may well have learned from Isidore what the eternal destiny of virtuous pagans *could not* be, rather than what it had to be. He finally had to deprive his ancient sages of the beatific vision, but he could save them from active torment because of their nobility of character, something Isidore would not have been ready to do. The exception, of course, is Epicurus, and after Dante learned what he thought was the truth about the man, he neither could nor would do anything else with him than what he did.[50]

Dante corrects another aspect of his earlier thought on the source and origin of virtue, moral and intellectual. It will be recalled that in the *Convivio* (IV, xxi) Dante argued that, if all the natural conditions in the generation of the fetus are in their highest state, so much of the Deity would automatically descend on the person that it would be almost another incarnate God. Theologically considered, these gifts of the Deity are the gifts of the Holy Spirit committed by Him to a creature perfectly disposed by natural processes to receive them. Let us compare this notion with another in the thirteenth canto of the *Paradiso*. There Dante is puzzled by the assertion that none ever rose to equal Solomon in his wisdom, for was not all human knowledge possessed to perfection by Adam and Christ? St. Thomas answers him by explaining that all things are simply a reflection of the divine idea which remains one in itself while manifesting itself in countless creatures. However, the power of the heavens, "the seal," and sublunary matter, "the wax," are not always ideally situated in respect to one another so that the heavens can exert their full influence. In fact, nature is *always* faulty, like an artist who has the skill of his art but whose hand trembles (76–78). Perfect natural conditions occurred and will occur only twice in history, once at the creation of Adam and for the second and last time when the Virgin conceived, and these natural conditions reached such perfection by the *active* intervention of the Holy Spirit (79–81). In the *Convivio*, the Holy Spirit waited upon nature to do its work and whenever natural conditions were perfect—and there is no specific limitation of the number of times such conditions would occur—conferred its gifts on the recipient. In the *Paradiso*, nature is made the instrument of the Holy Spirit on two specific and great occasions in the history of the world, the creation of man and the Incarnation.

Solomon's gift was purely that of kingly rule, and his wisdom is thus qualified (88–111). St. Thomas then warns Dante to take extreme caution in making deductions, for even those that seem obvious may have to be carefully qualified (112–142), a warning which surely signals a self-correction.[51]

Nature still has a large role to play, and it is precisely because it "trembles" that there is the diversity of human gifts and attributes. But perfection is here clearly beyond it, and only on those two occasions when God actively intervened was it achieved. Of itself it never can create the conditions which would induce the Holy Spirit to give it such an abundance of gifts as to make another incarnate God.

Appendix

The "Sirens" of Purgatorio *XXXI, 45*

AFTER Dante encounters Beatrice in their reunion beyond the grave and completes his confession of error, Beatrice rebukes him a second time in order to be sure that he will be stronger should he again hear the "sirens" (*Pur.* XXXI, 44–45). She reminds him of his grief at her death and of the failure of his love to journey with her beyond the grave. Her beauty while she was alive had surpassed any of the beauties brought into nature or men. When she died, it had not disappeared, as Dante evidently thought for a time, but had been translated to an ever-greater beauty by becoming purely spiritual. Dante had evidently forgotten the great principle that a quality detected in corporeal embodiment is simply a defective manifestation of that which more truly exists in an immaterial mode. Therefore, his love for her should have increased in proportion to her new and greater beauty. Temporarily it did not, and for a time Dante failed to perceive that no mortal good should have lured him away from Beatrice and so deflected his love from his "transhumanized" beloved who now stood in the presence of God.

Nevertheless, in order that thou mayest now bear the shame of thy wandering and another time, hearing the Sirens, be stronger, lay aside the sowing of tears and hearken; so shalt thou hear how my buried flesh should have directed thee the other way. Never did nature or art set before thee beauty so great as the fair members in which I was enclosed, and they are crumbled in the dust; and if the highest beauty thus failed thee by my death, what mortal thing should then have drawn thee into desire for it? Truly thou oughtst, at the first shaft of deceptive things, to have risen up after me who was such no longer. No young girl or other vanity of such brief worth should have bent thy wings downward to await more shots.[1]

Tuttavia, perchè mo vergogna porte
  del tuo errore, e perchè altra volta,
  udendo le sirene, sie più forte,
pon giù il seme del piangere ed ascolta:
  sì udirai come in contraria parte
  mover dovìeti mia carne sepolta.
Mai non t'appresentò natura o arte
  piacer, quanto le belle membra in ch'io
  rinchiusa fui, e sono in terra sparte;
e se 'l sommo piacer sì ti fallio
  per la mia morte, qual cosa mortale
  dovea poi trarre te nel suo disio?
Ben ti dovevi, per lo primo strale

> delle cose fallaci, levar suso
> di retro a me che non era più tale.
> non ti dovea gravar le penne in giuso,
> ad aspettar piu colpi, o pargoletta
> o altra vanità con si breve uso.

In a general way the nature of Dante's error is clear. He simply failed to continue to love Beatrice after she died with the even greater love she merited. The real problem, however, is the exact nature of the counterlures which Beatrice refers to as "sirens" and "young girl" (*pargoletta*, line 59).

Let us first turn our attention to the *pargoletta*. Is she figurative or literal or both? If she has a figurative meaning, is that meaning poetry or philosophy? The best approach is furnished by recognizing that Dante's *forma mentis* was such that he always sought in any real event its transcendental meaning, the allegorical and symbolic value inherent in any thing or person. A thing was always a sign as well as itself.[2]

Grandgent, starting with this premise, identified the *pargoletta* with the *donna gentile* of the *Vita nuova* and *Convivio* and argued that she stands for both an amorous and an intellectual deviation from the true path without, however, overlooking the difficulties of the solution:

> As far as we can see, Dante's devotion to Philosophy never ceased. . . . That she ever was a dangerous companion for him or that he ever thought of his pursuit of her as excessive, there is no clear indication. He could scarcely have referred to her, at any time, as a "short-lived vanity." If then, we are to see in the *pargoletta* of the *Commedia* anything more than a woman, it is likely that she represented, to Dante's repentent mind, a whole mode of life and thought, a practical, imaginative, and artistic materialism.[3]

A minority tradition beginning with Dante's son Pietro identifies the *pargoletta* with poetry. Yet there is no evidence that the art of poetry as such ever constituted a moral threat to Dante. Any danger would have been in the *doctrina* that the poet sang, the philosophy and theology he adopted. On the other hand, the evidence that Dante passed through a period of what he considered intellectual error is abundant. As every student of Dante knows, the exact nature of the successive changes of the poet's thought is one of the major problems of Dante scholarship. Since Karl Witte there is hardly an important Dante scholar who has not traced the poet's changing views on one question or another, linguistic, political, scientific, and theological. One of the questions still disputed concerns the nature of Dante's views on the interrelationship between philosophy and theology. The opinions vary considerably, and the most radical is that Dante moved from a Neopelagian view of philosophy in the *Convivio* to a position of Christian rigor in the *Comedy*.[4] This view is perhaps extreme, but it points to a real change in the thought of the poet on the relations between philosophy and revelation, reason and grace. If we consider that the fate of one's immortal soul might be decided by the correct solution of this problem, it does not seem too strange to believe that Beatrice could have referred to a certain kind of philosophy as a "vanity of brief worth." On the whole, one is inclined to agree with the general direction of Grandgent's interpretation, that the *pargoletta* is the *donna gentile* in both her aspects as the *donna pietosa* and *filosofia* and that the one figure is both a person and a meaning.

Now what of the sirens? Grandgent suggested that they may symbolize the sirens of poetry which Boethius banished for the consolations of philosophy, the muses pleasant to the point of destruction but unable to heal the prisoner of his spiritual distress.[5] Such an interpretation would mean that Dante was in error for *not* turning to philosophy and would conflict with Grandgent's own reasonable assumption that the *pargoletta* is to be identified with "Lady Philosophy." It is also clear that when the image of a siren appears earlier in the *Comedy*, during Dante's dream in his second night on Purgatory (*Pur.* XIX, 19 ff.), she clearly represents the sins of the flesh. This was a traditional interpretation and the one recorded by Isidore of Seville, who identifies them with prostitutes.[6]

If, however, we could find an interpretation of the sirens which makes them stand for knowledge, for the temptations of the mind as well as the temptations of the flesh, we would then have an exact parallel to Grandgent's interpretation of the *pargoletta* as simultaneously the *donna pietosa* of the *Vita nuova* and the "Lady Philosophy" of the *Convivio*, "she" who temporarily eclipsed Dante's first love and whose positive qualities were later absorbed into the Beatrice of the *Comedy*.

Such an interpretation is available in an important section of Cicero's *De finibus*. It is clear that at the time of the composition of the *Convivio* much of Dante's knowledge of the character and history of the classical schools of philosophy was drawn from Cicero's treatise, and he even echoes the preferences and attitudes of his author.[7] More important still, Bruno Nardi has shown in an admirable essay that the core of Dante's magnificent conception of Ulysses in *Inferno* XXVI is a passage from Cicero's *De finibus* (V, xviii–xix, 48–50).[8] The passage in question is not only interesting as a source, along with Horace's first Epistle (2, 20 ff.), for Dante's Ulysses, but it is precisely in this passage that we find the sirens allegorically interpreted as standing for knowledge. It is worth, therefore, citing it at some length:

Again, take persons who delight in the liberal arts and studies; do we not see them careless of health or business, patiently enduring any inconvenience when under the spell of learning and of science, and repaid for endless toil and trouble by the pleasure they derive from acquiring knowledge? For my part I believe Homer had something of this sort in view in his imaginary account of the songs of the Sirens. Apparently it was not the sweetness of their voices or the novelty and diversity of their songs, but their professions of knowledge that used to attract the passing voyagers; it was the passion for learning that kept men rooted to the Sirens' rocky shores. This is their invitation to Ulysses (for I have translated this among other passages of Homer):

> Ulysses, pride of Argos, turn thy bark
> And listen to our music. Never yet
> Did voyager sail these waters blue, but stayed
> His course, enchanted by our voices sweet,
> And having filled his soul with harmony,
> Went on his homeward way a wiser man.
> We know the direful strife and clash of war
> That Greece by Heaven's mandate bore to Troy,
> And whatso'er on the wide earth befalls.
>
> [*Odyssey*, 12, 184 ff.]

Homer was aware that his story would not sound plausible if the magic that held his hero immeshed was merely an idle song! It is knowledge that the Sirens offer, and it was no marvel if a lover of wisdom held this dearer than his home. A passion for miscellaneous omniscience no doubt stamps a man as a mere dilettante; but it must be deemed the mark of a superior mind to be led on by the contemplation of high matters to a passionate love of knowledge. What an ardour for study, think you, possessed Archimedes, who was so absorbed in a diagram he was drawing in the dust that he was unaware even of the capture of his native city! What genius do we see expended by Aristoxenus on the theory of music! Imagine the zeal of a lifetime that Aristophanes devoted to literature! Why should I speak of Pythagoras, or of Plato, of Democritus? For they, we are told, in their passion for learning travelled through the remotest parts of the earth! Those who are blind to these facts have never been enamoured of some high and worthy study.[9]

Dante seems to have echoed this passionate praise of a heroic dedication to wisdom and knowledge in the *Convivio* (III, xiv) when he expounds on the manner in which love is the very soul of philosophy and how divine love descends directly upon the angels and the human mind eliciting that love of knowledge and wisdom which overcomes all other loves of any kind whatsoever, presumably even Beatrice. Thus the ancient philosophers showed by their mode of life that they paid attention to nothing else besides wisdom. Democritus did not cut his beard, hair, or nails. Plato, the son of a king, ignored his royal dignity. Aristotle put truth before his own best friend, Plato. Zeno, Socrates, Seneca, and many others sacrificed their very lives for that love of wisdom which is philosophy.[10]

In the *Comedy* we find all these heroes of thought in the Limbo of the virtuous pagans presented to us with a judgment quite different from that in the *Convivio*, for we finally learn beyond any doubt that even the most dedicated pursuit of knowledge without revelation is not enough. The great thinkers of antiquity are no longer seen as intellectual heroes who gave up all for knowledge. Rather it is Ulysses who is so delineated. It is interesting to compare Dante's earlier enthusiasm for a passionate dedication to knowledge with the judgment implicit in the Ulysses episode. There, the Greek hero becomes the symbol of a particular kind of intellectual *hybris*, a virtually Faustian desire to storm the citadel of experience and truth, oblivious of all the divinely imposed limits, the social and moral bounds which ought to restrain a man. Ulysses betrayed his duties as a son, husband, and father to pack as much awareness as possible into this "brief vigil of the senses" and, as an evil counselor, persuaded others to follow him on the forbidden journey. He is punished in eternity for this bad advice, but one feels that it was his monomaniacal devotion to knowledge of the "vices and the worth of men" which as much as anything kept him out of Limbo. From another point of view Ulysses represents what we might call the horizontal dimension of the love of knowledge, the boundless desire to explore the world and discover all of its secrets without reference to the demands of the moral life or what it is necessary to know to be saved. For the Dante of the *Comedy*, love of wisdom by itself can save no one. At best, when it is used to implement the moral virtues, it can lead to Limbo. At its worst, it becomes demonic even in its very heroism and merits actual punishment. True philosophy will point to the revelation which transcends it.

Could the sirens of knowledge, the temptation for this kind of overweening desire for philosophical truth, have lured Dante to a betrayal of the bond with Beatrice? This interpretation seems to me to be plausible and, if we take the *pargoletta* as both the "Lady Philosophy" and the *donna gentile*, then the interpretation of the sirens as simultaneously the sins of the flesh and a misuse of knowledge would permit us a more consistent interpretation of the passage along the lines suggested by Grandgent.

Notes

I: *The Medieval Concept of Hierarchy*

1. See my *Structure and Thought in the Paradiso* (Ithaca, N.Y., 1958), ch. ii, for a review of the literature on Dante's allegory and further comments.

2. John Wisdom, "Philosophy, Metaphysics, and Psycho-analysis," in *Philosophy and Psycho-analysis* (Oxford, 1953), 248–282.

3. On the reader's point of view for the *Divine Comedy*, see C. S. Singleton, "The Irreducible Dove," *Comparative Literature*, IX (1957), 129–135.

4. Hubert Merki, *Homoiosis theoi: Von der platonischen Angleichung an Gott zur Gottähnlichkeit bei Gregor von Nyssa* (Freiburg in der Schweiz, 1952), 65. Cf. Plotinus, *Enneads* V, 8, 12; I, 6, 8.

5. Merki, *op. cit.*, 66.

6. *Ibid.*, 69–71.

7. Rudolf Bultmann, *Primitive Christianity in Its Contemporary Setting*, trans. R. H. Fuller (New York, 1956), 19 ff.; Merki, *op. cit.*, 75 ff. and 83 ff.

8. Ernst Cassirer, *The Myth of the State* (Anchor ed.; New York, 1955), 163; original ed., New Haven, Conn., 1946.

9. St. Thomas Aquinas, *Summa theologiae* 1, q. 13 a. 2–3, 5–6. My discussion of the doctrine of analogy in Dionysius draws heavily on M. V. Lossky, "La notion des 'analogies' chez Denys le pseudo-Areopagite," *Archives d'histoire doctrinale et littéraire du moyen-âge*, V (1930), 279–309.

10. Lossky, *op. cit.*, 280 ff.

11. Dionysius Areopagita, *De divinis nominibus* V, 8, in Migne's *Patrologia Graeca*, 3, col. 824 A-C. Migne's two series, *Patrologia Latina* and *Patrologia Graeca*, will hereafter be cited as *P.L.* and *P.G.* respectively.

12. *Ibid.*, and cf. Lossky, *op. cit.*, 284–286.

13. Lossky, *op. cit.*, 289.

14. *Ibid.*, 294–296.

15. *Ibid.*, 297–301.

16. *Ibid.*, 306–307.

17. My discussion of Dionysius' conception of hierarchy draws heavily on the work of René Roques, "La notion de hiérarchie dans le Pseudo-Denys," *Archives d'histoire doctrinale et littéraire du moyen-âge*, XXIV (1949), 183–222, and XXV–XXVI (1950–1951), 5–44. These have been incorporated into his later book, *L'univers dionysien: Structure hiérarchique du monde selon le Pseudo-Denys* (Paris, 1954).

18. *De coelesti hierarchia* III, 1; *P.G.* 3, col. 164D. This work is hereafter abbreviated as *C.H.* Dionysius expresses the concept of order primarily through the use of three terms: *taxis* or "military" order; *kosmos*, the notion of the universe as good order, a term with aesthetic overtones; and *metron*, the concept of measure also applied to God as the measuring principle. These terms along with "harmony" refer both to the idea of order and to a particular order.

19. *C.H.* III, 2; *P.G.*, 3, col. 165A.

20. *C.H.* III, 2; *P.G.*, 3, col. 165B.

21. *C.H.* I, 1; *P.G.*, 3, cols. 120B–121A.

22. *C.H.* I, 1; *P.G.*, 3, col. 120A.

23. *C.H.* VIII, 2; *P.G.*, 3, col. 240D.

24. *C.H.* V; *P.G.*, 3, col. 196A.

25. *C.H.* VII, 3–4; *P.G.*, 3, cols. 209C–212A.

26. *C.H.* VII–X; *P.G.*, 3, cols. 205B–273C.

27. *Dictionnaire de théologie catholique*, XVI, pt. II, "Hierarchie," by B. Dolhagaray, 2362–2382.

28. *De ecclesiastica hierarchia* I, 4; *P.G.*, 3, col. 376C. Hereafter this work is abbreviated as *E.H.*

29. *E.H.* V, I, 4, 7; *P.G.*, 3, cols. 504C–505A, 508C–509A.

30. Cf. *C.H.* X, 3; *P.G.*, 3, col. 273C.

31. *E.H.* V, I, 2; V, III, 10; II, 1; *P.G.*, 3, cols. 501B–D, 440A, 392C.

32. *E.H.* I, 2; *P.G.*, 3, cols. 373D–376A.

33. *E.H.* I, 1; *P.G.*, 3, cols. 372A–B.

34. *E.H.* VII, III, 11 and 4–5; *P.G.*, 3, cols. 568D–569A, 560B.

35. Cf. Erich Auerbach, "Dante's Addresses to the Reader," *Romance Philology*, VII (1954), 268–278, and Leo Spitzer's reply, "Dante's Addresses to the Reader in the 'Commedia,'" *Italica*, XXXII (1955), 143–165.

36. For a monumental edition of all the Latin translations of the Dionysian corpus see *Dionysiaca* (2 v.; Bruges, 1937), by the monks of the Abbey of Solesmes. The edition also includes the Greek text of the oldest manuscript and the text of Morel.

37. *Die pseudoaristotelische Schrift ueber das reine Gute bekannt unter dem namen Liber de causis*, ed. Otto Bardenhewer (Freiburg im Breisgau, 1882), 5, p. 168.

38. *Ibid.*, 19, p. 181; 30, p. 190; 16, p. 179.

39. The most useful study of St. Bernard's thought is G. B. Burch, *The Steps of Humility*, trans., with introd. and notes, as a study of his epistemology (Cambridge, Mass., 1950). See also the editions of *De diligendo Deo* by W. W. Williams and *De gradibus humilitatis et superbiae* by B. V. R. Mills in *Select Treatises of St. Bernard of Clairvaux* (Cambridge, 1926).

40. See Burch, *op. cit.*, 106. This scale is parallel to one of twelve degrees of pride: curiosity, frivolity, foolish mirth, boastfulness, singularity, conceit, audacity, excusing sins, hypocritical confession, defiance, freedom to sin, habitual sinning.

41. St. Bernard's vocabulary of love needs some clarification. By the thirteenth century, *amor*, *dilectio*, and *caritas* often but not always

refer to different aspects of love. *Dilectio* usually means *amor spiritualis* or "emotional charity" (*caritas affectualis*). This is to be distinguished from both *amor carnalis*, equivalent to *concupiscentia*, and *caritas actualis*, which is active charity. Thus *amor* may refer sometimes to spiritual love (Burch, *op. cit.*, 58) and *concupiscentia* always to carnal love.

Later, with St. Thomas, *amor* refers to the natural disposition of an appetite for its good and to the spiritual motion of the soul toward what it apprehends as good and beautiful. *Dilectio* is more restricted and implies the exercise of choice as to the object loved. See St. Thomas, *In lib. beati Dionysii de Div. Nom. comm.* cap. iv, lect. 9, and *Summa theologiae* 2, 1, q. 26 a. 3.

42. *De grad. hum.* ch. ix, 24: Ad quod tamen jam, ipso juvante, quo et vocante, mihi scalam erexi.

43. Cf. St. Bonaventura, *The Mind's Road to God*, trans. with an introd. by George Boas (New York, 1953), 7, n. 1. The Latin text of the *Itinerarium mentis ad Deum* together with the *Breviloquium* and the *Reductio artium ad theologiam* is conveniently available in the edition of the Franciscan fathers in *Tria opuscula* (5th ed.; Quaracchi, 1938). An English version of the *Breviloquium* is that of E. E. Nemmers (St. Louis and London, 1946), of the *Reductio* that of Sister E. T. Healy (with text introd. and commentary; St. Bonaventura, N.Y., 1939).

44. *Itinerarium* I, 2: Cum enim secundum statum conditionis nostrae ipsa rerum universitas sit scala ad ascendendum in Deum.

45. St. Bonaventura, *Breviloquium*, prologus, 3, 3: Est enim pulchritudo magna in machina mundana, sed longe maior in Ecclesia pulchritudine sanctorum charismatorum adornata, maxima autem in Ierusalem superna, supermaxima autem in illa Trinitate summa et beatissima. All translations from the *Breviloquium* are mine.

46. *Breviloquium*, prologus, 4, 4: Quoniam autem Deus non tantum loquitur per verba, verum etiam per facta, quia ipsius dicere facere est, et ipsius facere dicere, et omnis creata tanquam Dei effectus innuunt suam causam.

47. *Itinerarium* II, 13: Dum per haec lumina exteries data ad speculum mentis nostrae, in quo relucent divina, disponitur ad reintrandum.

48. *Breviloquium* I, c. 6, 3 and 4; see also I, c. 8, 2.

49. *Itinerarium* I, 9: Quoniam igitur prius est ascendere quam descendere in scala Iacob, primum gradum ascensionis collocemus in

imo, ponendo totum istum mundum sensibilem nobis tanquam speculum, per quod transeamus ad Deum, opificem summum, ut simus veri Hebraei transeuntes de Aegypto, ad terram patribus repromissam.

50. *Ibid.*, II, 11: Omnes creaturae istius sensibilis mundi animum contemplantis et sapientis ducunt in Deum aeternum, pro eo quod illius primi principii potentissimi, sapientissimi, et optimi, illius aeternae originis, lucis et plenitudinis, illius, inquam, artis efficientis, exemplantis et ordinatis sunt umbrae, resonantiae et picturae, sunt vestigia, simulacra et spectacula nobis ad contuendum Deum proposita ed signa divinitus date. Cf. *Breviloquium* II, 11. The *Deus artifex* created the world expressly to make himself known as in a vestige or mirror.

51. *Breviloquium* II, c. 5, 2.

52. *Itinerarium* II, 12.

53. *Ibid.*

54. *Ibid.*

55. *Ibid.*, IV, 4. Cf. a typical and especially apposite statement of St. Bernard's in *De consideratione* V, c. 5, n. 12, cited by St. Bonaventura: Deus in Seraphim amat ut caritas, in Cherubim novit ut veritas, in Thronis sedet ut aequitas, in Dominationibus dominatur ut maiestas, in Principatibus regit ut principium, in Potestatibus tuetur ut salus, in Virtutibus operatur ut virtus, in Archangelis revelat ut lux, in Angelis assistit ut pietas.

56. *Breviloquium* VI, c. 3, 1.

57. *Ibid.*, VI, c. 12.

58. *Itinerarium* II, 10: Numerus est praecipuum in animo conditoris exemplas et in rebus praecipuum vestigium decens in Sapientiam. St. Bonaventura is here elaborating on Boethius' *De arithmetica.* See Quaracchi edition of St. Bonaventura's *Opera omnia,* V, 11, n. 6.

59. *Itinerarium* VII, 1.

60. *Breviloquium* II, c. 1, 2. These various aspects of God's causality lead to the various names by which he can be called. Thus the wisdom of God is the cause of knowing all things known and as such is called light. Insofar as it is the reason for knowing things seen and approved, God may be called a mirror, a term usually reserved for creatures. Insofar as God is the reason for knowing things beforehand and their disposition, God is the exemplar in which realities pre-exist. Finally, insofar as knowing things predestined and reprobated, God's wisdom is called the book of life (*ibid.*, I, c. 8, 2).

61. *Itinerarium* III, 6.

62. *Ibid.*, I, 7.

63. The idea of the Trinity as a hierarchy of persons might seem somewhat unorthodox, but it is clear that St. Bonaventura is not arguing for any real subordination in persons, merely pressing his analogies as far as they will go.

64. *Breviloquium*, prologus, 3, 1.

65. *Itinerarium* IV, 4; Boas translation, *op. cit.*, 30. The Latin for the nine stages is *nuntiatio, dictatio, ductio, ordinatio, roboratio, imperatio, susceptio, revelatio, unctio.* Professor Boas reads *unitio* for *unctio*, and I am inclined to accept his emendation.

66. *Breviloquium* VI, c. 6.

67. *Itinerarium* I, 4.

68. Cf. *Itinerarium* IV, 1.

69. *Itinerarium* III, 1; V, 1.

70. *Ibid.*, I, 5, and II, 1: Sed quoniam circa speculum sensibilium non solum contingit contemplari Deum per ipsa tanquam per vestigia, verum etiam in ipsis, in quantum est in eis per essentiam, potentiam et praesentiam; et hoc considerare est altius quam praecedens.

71. *Ibid.*, I, 6.

72. *Breviloquium* V, c. 6, 6. For an analysis of the modes of prophecy in medieval thought and the distinctions between contemplation and speculation see my *Structure and Thought in the Paradiso*, ch. iv.

73. Cf. *Itinerarium* VI, 6–7, VII, 5–6, and Ernesto Jallonghi, *Il misticismo bonaventuriano nella Divina Commedia*, ed. D. Scaramuzzi (Padova, 1938), 141 ff. See also the remarks of Rudolf Palgen on the theme of assimilation to God in St. Bonaventura and the *Divine Comedy* and his remarks on the influence of the tradition of Scotus Erigena, the substitution of the Timaeus creation doctrine for the six days' work of Genesis, deification and the return to God, and the notion of a twofold Paradise, one of natural felicity and one of mystical ecstasy, in "Scoto Eriugena, Bonaventura e Dante," *Convivium*, n.s., XXV, no. 1 (1957), 1–8.

Bonaventura makes a distinction between luminous, transparent, and opaque nature which suggests the visual atmosphere of Dantes' *Inferno*, *Purgatorio*, and *Paradiso* (*Breviloquium* II, c. 2, 3).

74. See Robert Grinnell, "The Theoretical Attitude towards Space in the Middle Ages," *Speculum*, XXI (1946), 141–157; the quotation is on p. 156. Concerning the influence of the Dionysian ideas, as trans-

mitted through Scotus Erigena, on Abbot Suger in the building of the Saint-Denis Church, see Erwin Panofsky, *Abbot Suger on the Abbey Church of St.-Denis and Its Art Treasures* (Princeton, 1946), "Introduction," 1–37. See also the same author on the analogy between the hierarchical principles in scholastic philosophy and Gothic architecture, *Gothic Architecture and Scholasticism* (Meridan Books; New York, 1957), 45 ff. And see Otto von Simson, *The Gothic Cathedral: The Origins of Gothic Architecture and the Medieval Concept of Order* (New York, 1956), and Robert Grinnell, "Franciscan Philosophy and Gothic Art," in *Ideological Differences and World Order*, ed. F. S. C. Northrup (New Haven, Conn., 1949), 117–136.

75. On the question of medieval doctrines of love with special reference to Dante see my *Structure and Thought*, esp. ch. iii.

76. For a very penetrating essay on the concepts of the Middle Ages and Renaissance and the real value of those concepts in spite of so much criticism, see Federico Chabod, "The Concept of the Renaissance," in *Machiavelli and the Renaissance*, trans. David Moore (London, 1958), 149–200. On feudalistic values see Carl Stephenson, *Medieval Feudalism* (Ithaca, N.Y., 1942), 17–18.

77. See the penetrating study of Maurice de Wulf, *Philosophy and Civilization in the Middle Ages* (Princeton, N.J., 1922), ch. iii, esp. 54 ff. The functional and hierarchical character of medieval political theory drew its scriptural authority from St. Paul's metaphor of the Church as members of a body (Romans 13: 1 ff).

78. On this question see the brilliant pages of Chabod, *op. cit.*, 175 ff.

79. For a lucid exposition of the kinds of chivalry, feudal, courtly, and religious, and their interactions see Sidney Painter, *French Chivalry* (Baltimore, 1940).

80. Cf. Jurgen Ruesch and Gregory Bateson, *Communication: The Social Matrix of Psychiatry* (New York, 1951), 158.

81. Cf. Johan Huizinga, *Homo ludens: A Study of the Play-Element in Culture* (New York, 1950), 104. Huizinga also points out that a direct line runs from the knight to the *honnête homme* of the seventeenth century. The Latin countries of the West added the ideal of the gallant lover to the feudal ethic of loyalty so that both feudal and courtly chivalry soon became completely interwoven. By the end of the seventeenth century the ideal of the gentleman split into two distinct kinds, that of the *honnête homme* proper, a worldly and

aristocratic type, and the *homme de bien*, a moral and middle-class, even religious conception. This betrays the incompatible and inconsistent origins of the concept in religious, courtly, and feudal chivalry proper. See André Léveque, " 'L'honnête homme' et 'l'homme de bien,' " *PMLA*, LXXII (Sept. 1957), 620–632.

82. On this concept see R. G. Collingwood, *An Essay on Philosophical Method* (Oxford, 1933), 54 ff.

83. Cf. Bernard Stambler, *Dante's Other World* (New York, 1957), 13 and 168.

84. Mazzeo, *Structure and Thought*, ch. iii. See also C. S. Singleton's brilliant *Essay on the Vita Nuova* (Cambridge, Mass., 1949) for an extensive analysis of the displacements and transformations of love.

II: The Light-Metaphysics Tradition

1. Clemens Baeumker, *Witelo: Ein Philosoph und Naturforscher des XIII Jahrhunderts*, Band III, Heft 2, of his *Beiträge zur Geschichte der Philosophie des Mittelalters* (Münster, 1908), 358 ff.

2. Edgar de Bruyne, *Etudes d'esthétique médiévale* (3 v.; Bruges, 1946), III, 17 ff.

3. Baeumker, *Witelo*, 362 ff.

4. St. Augustine, *De Genesi ad litteram* IV, c. 28, n. 45; *P.L.*, 34, col. 315.

5. Baeumker, *Witelo*, 362–372.

6. St. Augustine, *Soliloquia* I, 8, 15; *P.L.*, 32, col. 877: Ergo quo modo in hoc sole tria quaedam licet animadvertere, quod est, quod fulget, quod illuminat: ita in illo secretissimo Deo, quem vis intelligere, tria quaedam sunt, quod est, quod intelligitur et quod cetera facit intelligi.

7. *Soliloquia* I, 1, 3; *P.L.*, 32, col. 870: Deus intelligibilis lux, in quo et per quem intelligibiliter lucent quae intelligibiliter lucent omnia.

8. Cf. Baeumker, *Witelo*, 377.

9. St. Augustine, *Contra Faustum Manichaeum* XX, 7; *P.L.*, 42, col. 372: Quando enim discrevistis lucem qua cernimus ab ea luce qua intelligimus? . . . Et tamen etiam hoc lumen [i.e., intelligible] non est lumen illud quod Deus est. Hoc enim creatura est, creator ille; hoc factum ille qui fecit.

See also St. Augustine, *De Gen. ad litt. liber imperfectus* 5, 20; *P.L.*, 34, col. 288, where St. Augustine distinguishes between uncreated light and created light whether corporeal or incorporeal: Alia est lux de Deo nata, et alia lux quam fecit Deus: nata de Deo lux, est ipsa Dei Sapientia; facta vero lux est qualibet mutabilis sive corporea sive incorporea.

10. *De Gen. ad litt. liber imperfectus* 5, 21: Et fortasse quod quaerunt homines, quando angeli facti sunt, ipsi significantur hac luce, brevissime quidem tamen convenientissime et decentissime. (Cf. Baeumker, *Witelo*, 374–375.)

11. St. Augustine, *De libero arbitrio* III, 5, 16; *P.L.*, 32, col. 1279.

12. For an excellent study of Augustinian light speculation with special reference to his theory of knowledge see Regis Jolivet, *Dieu soleil des esprits: La doctrine augustinienne de l'illumination* (Paris, 1933). For *sui generis* light cf. *De Trinitate* XII, 15, 24; *P.L.*, 42, col. 1011.

13. De Bruyne, *op. cit.*, III, 17–18. See also A. C. Crombie, *Robert Grosseteste and the Origins of Experimental Science, 1100–1700* (Oxford, 1953), 91–134, for a thorough treatment of the scientific importance of light speculation, as well as his *Augustine to Galileo: The History of Science, A.D. 400–1650* (London, 1952), 19–43. The bibliographical material in the Grosseteste volume is most complete.

Concerning the reason for Grosseteste's interest in light metaphysics Crombie says, "The analogy between the corporeal *lux*, whose mathematical laws he held to underlie the operations of physical things, and this spiritual *lux* gave an additional force and interest to Grosseteste's belief that the study of geometrical optics was the key to knowledge of the natural world, and it must be reckoned among the reasons for the popularity of optics and mathematical science in the Oxford School" (p. 131).

Grosseteste claimed that it was by divine illumination that man has certain knowledge of reality, in this following St. Augustine. Crombie refers to the following series of analogies which Grosseteste makes between corporeal and spiritual light: the operation of light illustrates the relationship between the persons of the Trinity, the operation of grace on free will which is like light shining through colored glass, the nature of the relationship betwen the various orders in the ecclesiastical hierarchy, the bishop, for example, "reflecting" power to the clergy like a mirror. Crombie adds, "With some of his followers in Oxford the physical science of optics became a method of arriving at a sort of analogical knowledge of spiritual reality and truth."

From a more philosophical and theological point of view the general treatment of light metaphysics in the second volume of Ueberweg-Heinze's *Grundriss der Geschichte der Philosophie* is perhaps the best (see Bernhard Geyer, *Patristische und scholastische Philosophie* [Basel, 1951; reprinted without change from the 1927 edition], 287–325 and 257–280).

14. De Bruyne, *op. cit.*, III, 18. The *De intelligentiis* was first attributed to Witelo by Baeumker and dated about the third quarter of the thirteenth century. This attribution was later withdrawn, and dating of the work was moved back to about Grosseteste's period, or the first few decades of the century. Some manuscripts indicate that the work may be by an Adam Pulchra Mulier or Adam Mulier Pulcherrima and that it originated in Paris. The book, in any case, enjoyed considerable circulation. See Baeumker's article, "Zur Frage nach Abfassungszeit und Verfasser des irrtümlich Witelo zugeschriebenen Liber de intelligentiis," 87–102, in *Miscellanea Francesco Ehrle: Scritti di storia e paleografia*, vol. I, *Per la storia della teologia e della filosofia* (*Studi e testi* 37; Roma, 1924).

15. St. Thomas Aquinas, *II Sent.* d. 13 q. 1 a. 2 (Fretté and Maré, vol. VIII). The references to St. Thomas' Commentary on the four books of sentences of Peter Lombard are to the so-called Vivès edition of the *Opera omnia*, ed. S. E. Fretté and P. Maré (34 v.; Paris, 1871–1880).

16. St. Thomas Aquinas, *II Sent.* d. 13 q. 1 a. 3 (Fretté and Maré, vol. VIII).

17. St. Thomas Aquinas, *In Aristotelis librum de anima commentarium*, ed. A. M. Pirotta (3d ed.; Turin and Rome, 1948), Bk. II, lectio XIV. All the references to this work are from lectio XIV, Bk. II. The paragraph numbers are cited in the text.

18. St. Thomas Aquinas, *Quodl. VI* q. 11 a. 19 contr. 1 (Fretté and Maré, vol. XV), which contains all the *Quaestiones quodlibetales*): Liber de intelligentiis non sit auctoritatis alicujus; nec etiam verum sit quod omnis influxus sit ratione lucis, nisi lux metaphorice accipiatur pro omni actu, prout omne agens agit inquantum est ens actu.

19. St. Thomas Aquinas, *Summa theologiae* 1, q. 1 a. 9. The citations from the *Summa theologiae* are from the Leonine edition of the *Opera omnia* (Rome, 1882–).

20. St. Thomas Aquinas, *In I Sent.* prol. q. 1, 5 c. 3 and ad 3 (Fretté and Maré, vol. VII).

21. St. Thomas Aquinas, *Commentarium in II libros Arist. posteriorum analyticorum* I, lectio 1 (Fretté and Maré, XXII, 105). On the conflict between scholasticism and poetry in the thirteenth and fourteenth centuries see Ernst Robert Curtius, *European Literature and the Latin Middle Ages*, trans. from German by Willard R. Trask (London, 1953), 203–227, 480–484. Cf. St. Thomas *In Metaphysicam Aristotelis commentaria*, ed. M. R. Cathala (3d ed.; Turin, 1935), nn. 61–63, where he comments on Aristotle's remark that the poets maintain that the gods are jealous of men (Bk. I, ch. ii, 12–14, 982D–983A). Thomas says that the poets were liars in this as they were about many other things, as the "common proverb goes": Sed poetae non solum in hoc, sed in multis aliis mentiuntur, sicut dicitur in proverbio vulgari (n. 63).

22. *Liber de intelligentiis*, ed. Baeumker in *Witelo*, c. VI, p. 8: Prima substantiarum est lux. Hoc manifestari potest per auctoritatem beati Augustini in II super Genes. [the author means to cite *De Genesi ad litt.* IV, c. 28, n. 45; *P.L.*, 34, col. 315] ad litteram dicentis, quod Deus non dicitur lux, sicut dicitur agnus. Dicitur enim agnus translative et non proprie, lux autem dicitur proprie et non translative.

23. *Ibid.*, c. VI, p. 8: Manifestari etiam protest per hoc quod ipsius est natura una, per prius et posterius secundum magis et minus participat; et hoc est in eis maxime divinum et nobile. Quod autem in istis sensibilibus apparentibus maxime est nobile, hoc est lux.

24. *Ibid.*, c. VII, p. 8: Omnis substantia influens in aliam est lux in essentia vel naturam lucis habens. . . . Si enim a substantia prima est influentia in omnibus aliis, omnis autem substantia influens in aliam est lux in essentia vel naturam lucis habens.

25. *Tractatus de luce Fr. Bartholomaei de Bononia* in *Antonianum*, vol. VII, fascs. 2–4, ed. with annotations by P. Irenaeus Squadrani, O.F.M. (1932), pars IV, caput 7, p. 478.

26. *Ibid.*, IV, 7, p. 479.

27. *Ibid.*, IV, 1, pp. 370–371.

28. *Ibid.*, IV, 1, p. 371: Sicut autem lux haec conciliat et ad quandam amicitiam reducit illas maioris mundi principales partes, quae ad invicem contrarietatem habent scilicet quattuor elementa, ita etiam per lucem divinum, postquam fuerit in mentem per adventum gratiae recepta, ad amicitiam et conciliationem reducit minoris mundi, scilicet hominis, principales partes, carnem scilicet et spiritum, ad invicem rebellionem ac pugnam habentes.

29. *Ibid.*, IV, 4, p. 469.

30. *Ibid.*, IV, 4, p. 470.

31. *De intelligentiis* c. VIII, p. 9.

32. Albertus Magnus, *De causis et processu universitatis*, Lib. II, tract. 1, c. 25, p. 475a (Borgnet, vol. X). The citations from Albert are from the *Opera omnia*, ed. by Augustus Borgnet from the Lyon edition of 1651 of P. Jammy (38 v.; Paris, 1890–1899). See Baeumker, *Witelo*, 407–414, for the inconsistencies in Albert's thought brought about by the conflict between his Christian theism on the one hand and his Neoplatonism on the other. The *De intellectu et intelligibile* in vol. X and the commentaries on the works of Pseudo-Dionysius in vol. XIV are the works in which Albert presents his speculations on the metaphysics of light.

33. *De causis et proc. univers.* I, 4, 5, p. 419a.

34. De Bruyne, *op. cit.*, III, 21, n. 4.

35. *De intelligentiis* c. VIII, p. 9: Unaquaeque substantia habens magis de luce quam alia dicitur nobilior ipsa. . . . Nobilitas vero in omnibus attenditur secundum appropinquitatem maiorem et participationem esse divini.

36. *De intelligentiis* c. IX, p. 11: Lux in omni vivente est principium motus et vitae calore disponente. Natura lucis est in omnibus; non tamen in omnibus operatur motem et vitam; et defectus est ex parte materiae.

37. *De philosophischen Werke des Robert Grosseteste*, ed. Ludwig Baur, in Baeumker's *Beiträge zur Geschichte der Philosophie des Mittelalters*, vol. IX (Münster, 1912), *De luce*, p. 51: Lux per se in omnem partem se ipsam diffundit, ita ut a puncto lucis sphera lucis quamvis magna generetur nisi obsistat umbrosum. . . . Atqui lucem esse proposui cujus per se est haec operatio: scilicet per seipsam multiplicare et in omnem partem subito diffundere.

38. *De intelligentiis* c. IX, p. 11.

39. De Bruyne, *op. cit.*, III, 19.

40. Grosseteste, *De luce*, ed. Baur, p. 51.

41. *Ibid.*

42. St. Bonaventura, *II Sent.* d. 12 a. 2 q. 1, p. 318a (Quaracchi; vols. I–IV contain the four books of *Sentences* respectively).

43. *Ibid.*, d. 12 a. 2 q. 2 arg. 4, p. 304b.

44. *Ibid.*, d. 13 a. 2 q. 2, p. 320b.

45. *Ibid.*, d. 13 a. 2 q. 2, p. 321a.

46. *Ibid.*, d. 13 a. 2 q. 2, p. 321a.

47. *Ibid.*, d. 12 a. 2 ad. 5, p. 321b.

48. *De intelligentiis* c. VIII, p. 10.

49. *Ibid.*, c. IX, p. 12. Cf. Aristotle's conception of the generative powers of the sun in *De coelo* II, 12, 292B, 28–30. In *De intelligentiis* we also read that this light emanating from the empyrean is a divine power or causes a divine power because of which it can "vivify." Cf. c. IX, p. 12, referring to the light of the empyrean: Quae lux diffusa vel est virtus divina, vel deferens virtutem divinam, propter quam ipsa habet virtutem vivificativem.

50. St. Bonaventura, *II Sent.* d. 13 a. 2, q. 2 f. 4, p. 319a.

51. *IV Sent.* d. 19 dub. 3, p. 496a.

52. *II Sent.* d. 15 a. 1 q. 3 f. 2 ad oppos., p. 379 b.

53. *Ibid.*, d. 14 p. 1 a. 3 q. 3, p. 348b.

54. Bartholomew of Bologna, *Tractatus de luce* IV, 4, p. 467.

55. Cf. Baeumker, *Witelo*, 401 ff.

56. *De intelligentiis*, c. IX, p. 13: Sive sit lux corporea, sive incorporea; semper enim est multiplicativa sui et suae virtutis in aliud.

57. For example, the following passage from Bartholomew says that all created things depend on Christ just as *lumen*, *radius*, and *splendor* depend on *lux* (I, 2, p. 235, on *Christus Lux*): Est etiam stabilissimam, et sic non cadit circa ipsum flexibilitas; et absolutissimum, et sic non cadit in eo ulla dependentia, imo potius ab ipso dependet quaelibet alia natura creata, quemadmodum a luce dependet aliorum trium natura, scilicet radii, luminis et splendoris, ut ostensum est supra.

The imagery suggests emanation of all things from the Son, but it is clear that he is using a corporeal exemplar to explain a theological truth. Baeumker says that the *De intelligentiis* does not follow out the pantheistic tendencies implicit in its doctrine and that the emanationism it propounds is not "substantial" or "inherent." Its emanationism is *sicut in deferente*. There is, however, a community of being between the divine light and the light of the universe. See *Witelo*, p. 603, and note on p. 432.

58. St. Bonaventura, *II Sent.* d. 13 a. 1 q. 1 obj. 3, p. 311b: Lux de spiritualibus et corporalibus dicitur proprie, magis tamen proprie de spiritualibus quam de corporalibus, sicut dicit Augustinus super Ge-

nesim ad litteram. Propriissime enim Deus lux est, et quae ad ipsum magis accedunt, plus habent de natura lucis.

59. *Ibid.*, d. 13 a. 2 q. 1 ad 4, p. 318a. Spiritual light whether created or uncreated is fully actual.

60. *Ibid.*, d. 13 a. 2 q. 1 f. 2, p 319a: Lux inter omnia corporalia maxime assimilatur luci aeternae, sicut ostendit Dionysius de Divinis Nominibus, et maxime in virtute et efficacia.

61. Bartholomew, *Tract. de luce* II, 2, p. 349: Ad evidentiam autem aliorum trium modorum quibus descendunt mentales illuminationes ab hac prima luce, notandum est pro unoquoque illorum modorum materiale exemplum de emanatione materialium luminum.

62. *Ibid.*, II, 2, p. 349.

63. Bartholomew's elaborations of light analogies are the most fanciful of all; for example, in I, 3, p. 236, he says that Christ chose to be born in Jerusalem because it is the center of the world and therefore the doctrine of salvation might "radiate" out from a "central source."

64. The unpublished manuscript of Grosseteste's *Hexaemeron*, Lond. Bibl. Reg. 6 E.V., fol. 147 v, cited in De Bruyne, *op. cit.*, III, 23.

65. St. Bonaventura, *Comment in Sapientiam* VII, 10, p. 153 (Quaracchi, vol. VI). Cf. *Breviloquium* II, 5, 6.

66. Bartholomew of Bologna, *Tract. de luce* IV, 4, pp. 467–468.

67. *Ibid.*, IV, 5, p. 472: Quanto enim lucis subiectum magis exaltatur versus caelum, tanto, ceteris paribus, lucis natura decorat ipsum. Abundantius enim decoratur a luce ipsum empyreaum quam cristallinum, et cristallinum quam stellatum. Per maiorem in eo lucis aggregationem, ut patet in sole respectu aliarum stellarum, et in aliis stellis respectu aliarum partium orbis.

68. *De intelligentiis*, c. X, p. 14: Proprium et primum principium cognitionis est lux. Si autem exordium cognitionis inspexerimus, dicemus: lux est ipsa virtus cognoscitiva. Principium cognitionis est lux, sensitivae autem operationis calor.

69. *Ibid.*, c. XI, p. 15: Omnis substantia cognoscitiva quanto lux purior est et simplicior, tanto magis in ea apparent rerum species, et potentia eius se extendit ad plura. Si enim luci debetur virtus cognoscitiva: quanto simplicior est et purior, magis cognoscet et magis rerum species apparebunt in ea; sicut in speculo materiali quanto magis politum est et tersum, tanto magis in eo apparent imagines.

70. *Ibid.*, c. XII, p. 16: Lux inter omnia apprehensioni est maxime

delectabile, secundum vero naturam calor. Quod est quia maxima delectatio est in conjunctione convenienti. Ergo, si subiectum cognitionis vel virtus cognoscitiva est lux, ex unione lucis exterioris cum ipsa erit delectatio maxima.

71. *Ibid.*, c. XII, p. 16: Visus inter omnes sensus maxime habet de actione animali et maxime cognoscitivus est . . . operatio autem visus fit mediante luce, et ipsa lux maxime delectabilis est. Unde Plato beneficium oculorum ostendens dixit: "Quibus carentes debiles caecique maestam vitam lugubremque agunt" (*Timaeus*, p. 47b).

Delectatio is Aristotelian *hedone*, or Italian *piacenza* and *piacimento*. These terms have both an objective and subjective meaning. Subjectively they mean pleasure, but objectively they mean beauty or that which pleases. See Witelo's *Perspectiva* in Baeumker's *Witelo*, pp. 172–174, esp. p. 172: Fit enim placentia animae, quae pulchritudo dicitur.

72. St. Thomas Aquinas, *Summa theologiae* 1–2, q. 27 a. 1.

73. *Ibid.*, 1–2, q. 27 a. 2.

74. *Ibid.*, 1–2, q. 4 a. 4 ad. 4.

75. *De intelligentiis*, c. XVIII, p. 23: Amor in eodem naturaliter antecidit cognitionem; perficitur tamen per cognitionem et deliberationem. . . . Delectatio autem vel amor est complementum appetitus sed rationalis appetitus amor, cuiuscunque vero delectatio nec tamen omnino amor completus est, nisi participetur; et ideo per cognitionem et deliberationem perficiter, quia cognitio sit complementum amoris, sed quia ex cognitione multiplicatur et viget in se ipso, cognitio enim ordinat appetitum cum suo appetibili, in qua unione perficitur amor et delectatio; ex cognitione enim perficitur amor. Non tamen cognitio est perfectio eius, sed potius e contrario; ad delectationem enim et amorem ordinatur cognitio. Unde sicut actus prior est potentia in eodem, sed incomplete, potentia tamen ab actu perficitur: ita et amor in eodem antecedit cognitionem, sed incompletus; per cognitionem vero postea in se ipso multiplicatur et cognitionem perficit et in se ipso perficitur.

76. Baeumker, *Witelo*, 512–513.

77. *De intelligentiis*, c. XIX, p. 24: Delectatio enim est ex coniunctione convenientis cum convenienti. Quae coniunctio vel unio fit per appetitum naturalem in substantia non cognoscenti, per desiderium et amorem in substantia sensibili, per voluntatem in rationali. Unde appetitus, desiderium vel voluntas media sunt per quae ordinantur vel

unitur potentia activa cum exemplari, ex ea unione relinquitur delectatio.

78. Baeumker, *Witelo*, 24.

79. St. Bonaventura, *II Sent.* d. 13 a. 1 q. 1 ad. 3, p. 313a.

80. Rupertus Tuitens, *In Genesin* I, 11; *P.L.*, 167, col. 207: Nec vero pro similitudine, sed pro re vera lucem dicimus appellatam (sc. angelicam naturam), id est non ideo quod similitudinem visibilis lucis habet. Nam ista potius visibilis lux, haec astra visibilia secundum similitudinem lucis illius sunt facta, ut cognoscat spiritualis homo, sic sanctos angelos in eadem felicitate differentis esse honoris et gloriae sicut "stella differt a stella in claritate" (I Cor. 15, 41). Sic eos in comparatione solis aeterni, scilicet creaturis sui, veram lucem non esse, sicut stellae circa solem in toto hemisphaerio nequent sum lumen ostendere.

81. *Purgatorio* XIV, 145; I always cite the translation from *The Divine Comedy of Dante Alighieri* by John D. Sinclair (3 v.; New York, 1948) and text from the edition of the Società Dantesca Italiana (Firenze, 1921):

Quel fu il duro camo
che dovria l'uom tener dentro a sua meta

Ma voi prendete l'esca, sì che l'amo
dell'antico avversaro a sè vi tira;
e però poco val freno o richiamo.
Chiamavi 'l cielo e 'ntorno vi si gira,
mostrandovi le sue bellezze etterne,
e l'occhio vostro pur a terra mira;
onde vi batte chi tutto discerne.

82. St. Bonaventura, *Sermones de tempore, Dominica in Albis*, Sermo I, 2, p. 290 (Quaracchi, vol. IX).

83. *Die pseudoaristotelische Schrift ueber das reine Gute bekannt unter dem namen Liber de causis*, ed. Otto Bardenhewer (Freiburg im Breisgau, 1882), 1, p. 164.

84. *Ibid.*, 5, p. 168.

85. Johannes Scotus Eriugena, *Super ierarchiam caelestem S. Dionysii* 1, 1; *P.L.*, 122, col. 128D.

86. Cf. *De causis*, 19, pp. 181–182 in Bardenhewer.

87. Maurice de Wulf, *History of Medieval Philosophy*, trans. E. C. Messenger, I (London, 1952), 104.

88. Dionysius Areopagita, *De coelesti hierarchia* III, 1 and 2; *P.G.*, 3, cols. 164D–165A, 165B. Cf. also *Epist.* X; *P.G.*, 3, 1117A–1120A.

89. Dionysius, *De divinis nominibus* IC, 1; *P.G.*, 3, col. 693B.

90. *Ibid.*, IV, 4; 697B–700C, esp. 700B. Paragraph numbers are given in text.

91. *Ibid.*, IV, 5; 700C–701A.

92. *Ibid.*, IV, 7; 701C.

93. *Ibid.*, IV, 7; 704A–704B.

94. *Ibid.*, IV, 8; 704D.

95. De Bruyne, *op. cit.*, III, 37 and 58 ff. See also Ven. Thomae abbatis Vercellensis Sancti Andreae, Ord. S. Bened., *Commentarius Hierarchicus in Canticum Canticorum*, in pt. 1, cols. 504–690, vol. II (1721) of *Thesaurus ancedotorum novissimus seu veterum monumentorum praecipue ecclesiasticorum, ex germanicis potissimum bibliothecis adornata collectio recentissima*, Opera et studio Bernardo Pezio et P. Hueber, Augustae vindelicorum et graecii (6 v., 1721–1723).

96. De Bruyne, *op. cit.*, III, 65, 66, 60.

97. In an appendix to his edition of Bartholomew's *Tractatus de luce*, Squadrani has edited the *Sermo in nativitate Domini fratris Bartholomaei de Bononia:* Videtur lux increata per nudam et revelativam inspectionem, scilicet in patria, ubi pupilla oculi Sanctorum facta est aquilina (et) videt solem in sua rota. . . . Secundo modo Verbum exponit se nobis visibile . . . in assumpta humanitate. . . . Tertius modus videndi illud Verbum est per speculum, et isto modo lux increata exponit se nobis visibile in quolibet creato (pp. 488–489).

On the spiritual senses see Rahner Kurt, "Le début d'une doctrine des cinq sens spirituels chez Origène," *Revue d'ascétique et de mystique* (Toulouse), XIII (April 1932), 113–145, and "La doctrine des 'sens spirituels' au moyen âge en particulier chez Saint Bonaventure," *ibid.*, XIV (July 1933), 263–299.

III: Light Metaphysics in the Works of Dante

1. *Conv.* III, vii, 2–3. All citations from the *Convivio* are from the *Opere di Dante*, in an extensively commented edition begun under the direction of Michele Barbi and still in progress (vols. IV and V): *Il Convivio*, ridotto a miglior lezione e commentato da G. Busnelli e G. Vandelli con introduzione di Michele Barbi (Firenze, vol. I, 1934, vol. II, 1937). Vol. I has Books I–III, and vol. II has Book IV.

2. *De causis*, 19, pp. 181–182 in Bardenhewer.

3. Busnelli and Vandelli cite appropriate passages from Albertus in Appendix III to Book III, vol. I, pp. 460–463, in their edition of the *Convivio*, esp. *De intellectu et intelligibile* i, 1, tr. 3, 2 (Borgnet, vol. IX).

4. *Conv.* III, vii, 3–4.

5. *Conv.* III, vii, 5.

6. *Conv.* III, vii, 6.

7. *Conv.* III, vii, 6–7.

8. Aristotle, *Ethics*, VII, 1, 2, 1145a.

9. *Conv.* III, vii, 7.

10. *Conv.* III, vii, 8.

11. *Conv.* III, viii, 3.

12. *Conv.* III, viii, 11.

13. *Conv.* III, viii, 8.

14. *Conv.* III, viii, 9. Dante cites the passage from *De partibus animalium* III, 10, 673a, in *Ep.* X, 26, and *Vita nuova* II, 1.

15. *Conv.* III, xii, 6–8.

16. *Conv.* IV, xxii, 17.

17. *Conv.* III, xiv, 4–6.

18. *Conv.* II, vi, 9. Cf. III, xiv, 4.

19. *Conv.* II, iii, 8–10.

20. *Conv.* III, ii, 14.

21. *Conv.* IV, i, 11.

22. *Conv.* I, xi, 3–4.

23. *Ep.* X, 1, ll. 375 ff.: Quia ex eo quod causa secunda recipit a prima, influit super causatum ad modum recipientis et repercutientis radium, propter quod causa prima est magis causa. Et hoc dicitur in libro *De Causis*, quod "omnis causa primaria plus influit super suum causatum, quam causa universalis secunda." Sed hoc quantum ad esse.

All citations and translations from the letter to Can Grande are from *Dantis Alagherii Epistolae: The Letters of Dante*, emended text with introd., trans., notes, and indexes and appendix on the *Cursus* by Paget Toynbee (Oxford, 1920).

24. *Ep.* X, 21, ll. 400 ff.: Propter quod patet quod omnis essentia et virtus procedat a prima, et intelligentiae inferiores recipiant quasi a radiante, et reddant radios superioris ad suum inferius, ad modum speculorum. Quod satis aperte videtur Dionysius de coelesti hierarchia

loquens. Et propter hoc dicitur in libro *De Causis* quod "omnis intelligentia est plena formis." Patet ergo quomodo ratio manifestat divinum lumen, id est divinam bonitatem, sapientiam et virtutem, resplendere ubique.

The phrase *omnis intelligentia est plena formis* is to be understood in the light of the principle that the effect is contained eminently in the cause and that the possession of causality, of spontaneous efficacy and force, belongs pre-eminently to spiritual beings.

25. *Ep.* X, 23, ll. 428 ff.: Bene ergo dictum est, quum dicit quod divinus radius, seu divina gloria, "per universum penetrat et resplendet"; penetrat quantum ad essentiam; resplendet quantum ad esse. Quod autem subicit de magis et minus habet veritatem in manifesto, quoniam videmus in aliquo excellentiori gradu essentiam aliquam, aliquam vero in inferiori; ut patet de coelo et elementis, quorum quidem illud incorruptibile, illa vero corruptibilia sunt.

26. Cf. Geyer in Ueberweg-Heinze, *Grundriss,* 549–551.

27. *Ep.* X, 24, ll. 473 ff.: Et postquam praemisit hanc veritatem, prosequitur ab ea, circumloquens Paradisum; et dicit quod fuit in coelo illo quod de gloria Dei, sive de luce, recipit affluentius. Propter quod sciendum quod illud coelum est coelum supremum, continens corpora universa et a nullo contentum, intra quod omnia corpora moventur (ipso in sempiterna quiete permanente), a nulla corporali substantia virtutem recipiens. Et dicitur empyreum, quod est idem quod coelum igne sive ardore flagrans; non quod in eo sit ignis vel ardor materialis sed spiritualis, qui est amor sanctus sive caritas.

28. *Ep.* X, 5, ll. 454 ff.: Quod autem de divina luce plus recipiat, potest probari per duo. Primo per suum omnia continere et a nullo contineri; secundo per sempiternam suam quietem sive pacem. Quantum ad primum probatur sic: Continens se habet ad contentum in naturali situ sicut formativum ad formabile, ut habetur in quarto *Physicorum.* Sed in naturali situ totius universi primum coelum est omnia continens; ergo se habet ad omnia sicut formativum ad formabile; quod est se habere per modum causae. Et quum omnis vis causandi sit radius quidam profluens a prima causa, quae Deus est, manifestum est quod illud coelum quod magis habet rationem causae, magis de luce divina recipit.

29. Cf. Aristotle, *De caelo,* III, 2, and IV, 3 and 4.

30. *Ep.* X, 26, ll. 471 ff.: Quantum ad secundum probatur sic: omne

quod movetur, movetur propter aliquid quod non habet, quod est terminus sui motus; sicut coelum lunae movetur propter aliquam partem sui, quae non habet illud ubi ad quod movetur; et quia sui pars quaelibet non adepto quolibet ubi (quod est impossibile) movetur ad aliud, inde est quod semper movetur et nunquam quiescit, et est eius appetitus. Et quod dico de coelo lunae, intelligendum est de omnibus praeter primum. Omne ergo quod movetur, est in aliquo defectu, et non habet totum suum esse simul. Illud igitur coelum quod a nullo movetur, in se et in qualibet sui parte habet quidquid potest modo perfecto, ita quod motu non indiget ad suam perfectionem. Et quum omnis perfectio sit radius primi, quod est in summo gradu perfectionis, manifestum est quod coelum primum magis recipit de luce Primi, qui est Deus. . . . Sic ergo patet quod quum dicit "in illo coelo quod plus de luce Dei recipit," intelligit circumloqui Paradisum, sive coelum empyreum.

31. *Ep.* X, 27, ll. 510 ff.: Praemissis quoque rationibus consequenter dicit Philosophus in primo *De Coelo* quod coelum "tanto habet honorabiliorum materiam istis inferioribus, quanto magis elongatum est ab his quae hic." Adhuc etiam posset adduci quod dicit Apostolus ad Ephesios de Christo: "Qui ascendit super omnes coelos ut impleret omnis." Hoc est coelum deliciarum Domini; de quibus deliciis dicitur contra Luciferum per Ezechielem: "Tu signaculum similitudinis, sapientia plenus et perfectione decorus, in deliciis Paradisi Dei Fuisti."

32. On light metaphysics in Dante, in addition to the works of Baeumker and De Bruyne already cited, see also G. Poletto, *Amore e luce nella Divina Comedia, ragionamento critico* (Padova, 1876); G. B. Zoppi, *Il fenomeno e il concetto della luce studiati in Dante* (Rovereto, 1886); Giuseppe Tarozzi, *Luce intellectual, piena d'amore: Nota sul concetto della natura del "Paradiso" di Dante* (Torino, 1888); Stanislao Prato, "Essenza ed imagini simboliche della luce e delle tenebre confermate da vari passi della 'Divina Commedia' a specialmente del 'Paradiso,'" *Giornale dantesco*, XIII (1905), 199–236. There are two recent studies: Allan Tate, "The Symbolic Imagination: A Meditation on Dante's Three Mirrors," *Kenyon Review*, XIV, no. 2 (1952), 256–277, and G. di Pino, *La figurazione della luce nella Divina Commedia* (Firenze, 1952).

33. On light as the principle of causality in the works of Dante cf. *Conv.* II, vi, 9–10; III, vii, 1–5; III, xiv, 3–4; *Pur.* XXV, 89; *Par.* VII,

74; VIII, 2–3; XIX, 90; XXIX, 29. The *primum mobile* which divides the temporal and spatial universe from eternity is conceived as both corporeal and incorporeal, itself "surrounded" by intellectual light and love (*Par.* XXX, 38).

34. Cf. *Pur.* XV, 66, where Dante had Virgil explain how spiritual good increases by being shared. The relation of love between the eternal goodness and the blessed is likened to light reflected between mirrors. Without expressly saying so, he bases his analogy on light's reputed ability to "multiply itself" when transmitted through the diaphanum.

35. Cf. light as the principle of knowledge in *Par.* II (106–111). Beatrice says to Dante that she will fill his mind with a light so living or vivid that it will sparkle when he sees it. In line 110, I prefer the reading "verace" for "vivace," in which case she would fill his mind with a true or truth-giving light:

Or come ai colpi delli caldi rai
  della neve riman nudo il suggetto
  e dal colore e dal freddo primai,
così rimaso te nell' intelletto
  voglio informar di luce sì vivace [or "verace"]
  che ti tremolerà nel suo aspetto.

The verb "informar" is a technical term from light speculation describing light as the principle which gives form as the principle of being and, in this case, as the principle of knowledge.

36. Cf. XXVIII, 107–115, where Dante explains how the angelic hierarchy participates in various degrees in the beatific vision and love. The degree of vision (which engenders love) is proportional to merit, which in turn is proportional to grace and rectitude of will. We must deserve the "sight of Truth," and God must freely give it before we can love Him. The process here described takes place in eternity; it is not, stricly speaking, an answer to the question whether love of God precedes knowledge of Him or knowledge precedes love of Him as applied to the mortal state. The state of the blessed is one of amorous knowing or of knowing-amorous-ness, a state which presupposes the unity of will, intellect, and sense. Intellectual vision and love are therefore two moments of one function. Of course, God must in some sense be known before He can be sought; indeed, the quest for Him is a kind of knowing.

37. Dante carefully used the term *splendore* in the technical sense of some form of reflected light in XXIX, 1, 15, and again in XXX, 95, where it is through the splendor of God, His reflected light, that Dante saw the kingdom of truth. So God's motive in creating the angels was to let His reflected light shine back on him from them, because His overflowing goodness led Him to create self-conscious substances as mirrors for His light. Cf. IX, 61; XIII, 58–60; XXIX, 58–60. Dante makes God the Mind which is the origin of the categories, substances, and accidents, an idea quite different from the Neoplatonizing tradition. Yet the Primal Light "materializes" itself at and pours down from the *primum mobile.* The principle of emanationism is often affirmed in terms which could have been taken from Proclus.

38. God is also the true light or light of truth (*vera luce*) in XIII, 55, and the Trinal Light (*trina luce*) in XXXI, 28–29. As eternal light cf. also XI, 20.

39. Bruno Nardi, *Nel mondo di Dante,* 218–225.

IV: The Analogy of Creation in Dante

1. Maurice Dorolle, *Le raisonnement par analogie* (Paris, 1949), 115; my translation. I owe the largest debt for the first section of this chapter to Dorolle's work. The following works have, however, been very useful: Harold Höffding, *Der Begriff der Analogie* (Leipzig, 1924) and *Der menschliche Gedanke* (Leipzig, 1911); Paul Grenet, *Les origines de l'analogie philosophique dans les dialogues de Platon* (Paris, 1948); Dorothy M. Emmet, *The Nature of Metaphysical Thinking* (London, 1949); W. M. Urban, *Language and Reality* (New York, 1939); Luigi Stefanini, *Imaginismo come problema filosofico,* vol. I (Padua, 1946).

2. R. G. Collingwood, *The Idea of Nature* (Oxford, 1945), 8.

3. Morris R. Cohen, *A Preface to Logic* (New York, 1944), 84–85.

4. Dorolle, *op. cit.,* 128, 161–165.

5. *Ibid.,* 107–113, 170–177.

6. Karl Lamprecht, *Moderne Geschichtswissenschaft* (Freiburg, 1905); see the first two of the five lectures which constitute the book.

7. Heinrich Schaller, *Die Weltanschauung des Mittelalters* (München-Berlin, 1934), 11; also cf. 11–15 and 45. (Translation is mine.)

8. Etienne Gilson, *La philosophie de Saint Bonaventure* (2d ed.; Paris, 1943), ch. vii, esp. 156 ff.

9. For example, Ernst Cassirer, *Individuum und Kosmos in der Philosophie der Renaissance* (Stud. der Bibl. Warburg, vol. X; Leipzig, 1927). Among the scholars who have concerned themselves with the literature of the Renaissance, the most important of those using analogy as a category of interpretation are E. M. W. Trillyard, *The Elizabethan World Picture* (London, 1948) and *Shakespeare's History Plays* (New York, 1947); Theodore Spencer, *Shakespeare and the Nature of Man* (2d ed.; New York, 1949); Marjorie H. Nicholson, *The Breaking of the Circle* (Evanston, Ill., 1950). A philosophical work which clarifies the doctrine of cosmic affinities in the Renaissance is Paul O. Kristeller's *The Philosophy of Marsilio Ficino*, trans. into English by Virginia Conant (New York, 1943).

10. Wilhelm Windelband–Heinz Heimsoeth, *Lehrbuch der Geschichte der Philosophie* (14th ed.; Türbingen, 1950), 314 ff. The Renaissance played numerous variations on this theme, and it had important consequences for the development of modern science. Nicholas of Cusa's mathematico-mystical reading of the "book of nature" is a corollary of his interpretation of the microcosm-macrocosm analogy; eventually Galileo was led to a fruitful reading of that same "book." Cusanus' contribution was to advance the notion that the "book" could be literally deciphered mathematically instead of merely contemplated (Cassirer, *op. cit.*, ch. ii).

11. Gilson, *op. cit.*, 29 ff. In addition, whereas Thomas sought to preserve the category of equivocal application of names, it would seem that Bruno deliberately discarded the notion that analogy was ever equivocal and that similitude was ever extrinsic. Gerhard Fricke in his study *Die Bildlichkeit in der Dichtung des Andreas Gryphius* (Berlin, 1933) points out that it is in this latter sense that similitude was interpreted by the German theorists of the "Barocklyrik." He quotes one of them, Buchner, as follows: Nec enim ulla res est, quocumque censeatur nomine unde similitudinem non possis ducere (p. 19). Cf. St. Thomas, *Summa contra gentiles*, Lib. I, cap. 33.

12. Cassirer, *op. cit.*, ch. iv, *passim.* The animistic sense of identity between man and nature persists well into the seventeenth century. Henry Vaughan's view of nature, mistakenly called Wordsworthian, is based on the idea that internal and external nature are one.

13. See Mazzeo, "A Seventeenth-Century Theory of Metaphysical Poetry," *Romanic Review*, XLII (1951), 245–255, and "Metaphysical

Poetry and the Poetic of Correspondence," *Journal of the History of Ideas,* XIV (1953), 221–234.

14. Helmut Hatzfeld, "A Clarification of the Baroque Problem in the Romance Literatures," *Comparative Literature,* I (1949), 115–116.

15. This theory in its essentials is advanced primarily by Rosemond Tuve, *Elizabethan and Metaphysical Imagery* (Chicago, 1946). Nelson's study *Peter Ramus and the Confusion of Logic, Rhetoric, and Poetry* is in the series University of Michigan Contributions in Modern Philology, no. 2 (April 1947).

16. This view was characteristic of many humanists who were also nominalists and who therefore banished all previous metaphysical assumptions from logic. The new rhetoric-logic was to teach men how to follow in their voluntary thinking the same "natural" laws that were followed in involuntary thinking. Hence the numerous literary examples to be found in Ramist logics. However, although Ramus abandoned the old metaphysical assumptions, he reintroduced the old categories, arranging them by dichotomies in a purely arbitrary and empirical order.

17. See René Wellek, "The Concept of Baroque in Literary Scholarship," *Journal of Aesthetics,* V (1946), 77–109, for a discussion of the concept of baroque and for a bibliography of the subject. The following treat the "metaphysical" movement or "concettismo" as a manifestation of the baroque: Benedetto Croce, *Storia della età barocca in Italia* (2d ed.; Bari, 1946), *Problemi di estetica* (4th ed.; Bari, 1949), *Saggi sulla letteratura italiana del seicento* (2d ed.; Bari, 1924), and *Nuovi saggi sulla letteratura italiana del seicento* (Bari, 1931); Mario Praz, *Seicentismo e marinismo in Inghilterra: John Donne—Richard Crashaw* (Firenze, 1925). The studies of these two poets were reprinted separately in 1945. See also Praz, *Studies in Seventeenth-Century Imagery* (London, 1939), an Italian version of which last appeared as *Studi sul concettismo* (Firenze, 1946). A companion volume to the English version of this book consisting of a bibliography of emblem books appeared in London in 1947 as vol. II of the same title. Also see Marcellino Menéndez y Pelayo, *Historia de las ideas esteticas en España* (4th ed.; Madrid, 1928–1933), vol. II, pt. II.

18. Praz, *John Donne,* 7. Other works in support of the emblem theory are Rosemary Freeman, *English Emblem Books* (London, 1948); Austin Warren, *Richard Crashaw: A Study in Baroque Sensibility* (University, La., 1939); Ruth Wallerstein, *Studies in Seven-*

teenth-Century Poetic (Madison, 1950). Miss Wallerstein also agrees with Miss Tuve on the influence of Ramist logic.

19. Praz, *Richard Crashaw*, 114 ff. This desire to force "influences" leads Praz to find it strange that metaphysical poetry should have flourished in English, although the emblem did not have a very wide vogue there (cf. *Studi sul concettismo* [Firenze], 202).

20. Emmanuele Tesauro, *Il cannochiale aristotelico* (2d ed.; Venezia, 1663), chs. xiv–xv. In these two chapters Tesauro sketched the outline of his generalized theory of wit. Cf. Croce, *Problemi di estetica*, 313 ff.

21. Warren, *op. cit.*, 73–74.

22. *Ibid.*, 177.

23. *Ibid.*

24. *The Hieroglyphics of Horapollo*, trans. George Boas (New York, 1950). Mr. Boas' introduction is quite valuable. The standard work on the emblem movement is by Ludwig Volkmann, *Bilderschriften der Renaissance: Hieroglyphik und Emblematik in ihren Beziehungen und Fortwirkungen* (Leipzig, 1923). A typical late Renaissance edition of Horapollo is the work of Nicolao Caussino, *Symbolica Aegyptiorum sapientia*, together with a *Polyhistor symbolicus* (Paris, 1647). These two works, consisting of the text and translation of Horapollo, an anthology of classical remarks on symbols and hieroglyphics, and a hieroglyphic bestiary, constitute a kind of encyclopedia. The hieroglyphic-emblem movement seems to have been in part a continuation of the tradition of medieval exemplarism, especially zoological exemplarism. It is in this enriched form that the emblem movement reached Quarles: "Before the knowledge of letters, God was known by *Hieroglyphicks;* and, indeed, what are the Heaven, and Earth, nay every Creature, but *Hieroglyphicks* and *Emblems* of his glory" (see Francis Quarles, *Emblemes* [London, 1635], "To the Reader").

25. Praz, *Studi sul concettismo*, 49–50 n., 199–200.

26. Michael Maier, *Atalanta fugiens* (Oppenheim, 1618). See also John Read, *Prelude to Chemistry* (New York, 1937), ch. vi, which is on Maier; some samples of his music in modern notation are appended to the work. For spiritual alchemy see Henri Bremond, *Historie littéraire du sentiment religieux en France* (Paris, 1925), vol. VII, pt. II, ch. v, and Evelyn Underhill, *Mysticism* (16th ed.; New York, 1948), 140 ff.

27. Warren, *op. cit.*, 75.

28. *Ibid.*, 173.

29. Etienne Gilson, *The Spirit of Medieval Philosophy* (New York, 1940), esp. chs. iv and v.

30. For example, St. Thomas Aquinas, *Summa contra gentiles* II, 21 ("Creatio est propria dei actio, et quod eius solius est creare"); cf. St. Augustine, *De civ. Dei* XI, 21, where he describes Creation as the Art of the Wisdom of God.

31. Cf. the remarks of St. Ambrose, *L'Esamerone*, ed. and trans. E. Pasteris in *Corona Patrum Salesiana, Series Latina*, IV (Turin, 1937), n. 1, 384–385; "Les gloses de Guillaume de Conches sur la Consolation de Boèce," ed. J. M. Parent in *La doctrine de la création dans l'école de Chartres* (Paris, 1938), 128 ("At dicit aliquis: nonne hoc est opus creatoris quod homo ex homine nascatur? Ad quod respondeo: nichil detraho Deo; omnia que in mundo sunt Deus fecit preter malum sed alia facit operante natura rerum que est instrumentum divine operationis et ea dicuntur opera nature que a Deo fiunt natura subserviente").

32. The first major attempt to use the *Timaeus* to elucidate Genesis is St. Augustine's. See Etienne Gilson, *Introduction à l'étude de Saint Augustin* (2d ed.; Paris, 1943), 246 ff. On the idea of creation as sharply separating Greek from Christian thought see J. Chevalier, *La notion du nécessaire chez Aristote et chez ses prédécesseurs* (Paris, 1915).

33. Edgar De Bruyne, *Etudes d'esthétique médiévale* (3 v.; Bruges, 1946), II, 256 ff. My discussion of the school of Chartres is based on De Bruyne, Parent, *op. cit.*, and Pierre Duhem, *Le système du monde: Histoire des doctrines cosmologiques de Platon à Copernic* (5 v.; Paris, 1913–1917), vol. III.

34. De Bruyne, *op. cit.*, II, 279.

35. *Ibid.*, 265. The Chartrian formula of *natura parens illa ac divina rerum artifex* can be traced to the younger Pliny (*ibid.*, 277).

36. *Ibid.*, 266 ff.; "Les gloses de Guillaume de Conches sur la Consolation de Boèce," in Parent, *op. cit.*, 127–128 ("Omne enim opus est vel opus creatoris vel opus naturae vel artificis imitantis naturam . . . ea dicuntur opera nature que a Deo fiunt natura subserviente"). Cf. Hugh of St. Victor, *Erudit, Didascal.; P.L.*, 176, cols. 747–748.

37. "Les gloses de Guillaume de Conches sur le Timée," in Parent, *op. cit.*, 154.

38. *Ibid.*, 147: Et est opus creatoris prima creatio sine prejacente materia ut creatio elementorum vel spirituum vel ea que vidimus fieri contra consuetum cursum nature ut partus virginis, etc. Opus nature est quod similia nascantur ex similibus ex semine vel ex germane, quia est natura vis rebus insita similia de similibus operans. Opus artificis est opus hominis quod propter indigentiam operatur.

39. De Bruyne, *op. cit.*, II, 267.

40. "Les gloses de Guillaume de Conches sur le Timée," in Parent, *op. cit.*, 148: Opus enim creatoris perpetuum est carens dissolutione: neque enim mundus neque spiritus dissolvuntur. Opus vero nature etsi in se esse desinet tamen in semine remanet. Opus vero artificis imitantis naturam nec in se remanet nec aliquid ex se gignit.

41. On true creation as the presupposition of the work of nature and man see St. Thomas Aquinas, *Summa theologiae* 1, q. 45 a. 8: Creatio non admiscetur in operibus naturae, nec artis sed praesupponitur.

42. Erwin Panofsky, *Idea: Ein Beitrag zur Begriffsgeschichte der älteren Kunsttheorie* (Leipzig, 1924), ch. ii. The Italian translation (Firenze, 1952) includes a new preface by the author and one by the translator, Edmundo Cione. The following analysis draws heavily on Panofsky's classic study.

43. Panofsky, *op. cit.*, ch. iv; cf., for example, St. Thomas Aquinas' use of the metaphor in *Summa theologiae* 1, q. 65 a. 3, and 2 *Contra gentiles* I, 3, c. 99.

44. Rudolf Bultmann, *Primitive Christianity* (New York, 1956), 128 ff., and, for example, the passages in Aristotle's *Metaphysics*, 1032a and b, 1034a, 1070a.

45. That creation analogies between God the Creator and the Artist have by no means lost their theologically persuasive powers for some is attested by D. L. Sayer's *The Mind of the Maker* (New York, 1941), a work entirely based on parallels between divine and artistic creativity.

46. *Par.* VII, 64–75:

La divina bontà, che de sè sperne
  ogni livore, ardendo in sè, sfavilla
  sì che dispiega le bellezze etterne.
Ciò che de lei sanza mezzo distilla

non ha poi fine, perchè non si move
la sua imprenta quand'ella sigilla.
Ciò che da essa sanza mezzo piove
libero è tutto, perchè non soggiace
alla virtute delle cose nove
Più l'è conforme, e però più le piace;
chè l'ardor santo ch'ogni cosa raggia,
nella più somigliante è più vivace.

47. *Par.* VII, 124–148:

Tu dici: "Io veggio l'acqua, io veggio il foco,
l'aere e la terra e tutte lor misture
venire a corruzione, e durar poco;
e queste cose pur furon creature;
per che, se ciò ch'è detto è stato vero,
esser dovrièn da corruzion sicure."
Li angeli, frate, e 'l paese sincero
nel qual tu se', dir si posson creati,
sì come sono, in loro essere intero;
ma li elementi che tu hai nomati
e quelle cose che di lor si fanno
da creata virtù sono informati.
Creata fu la materia ch'elli hanno;
creata fu la virtù informante
in queste stelle che 'ntorno a lor vanno.
L'anima d'ogne bruto e delle piante
di complession potenziata tira
lo raggio e 'l moto delle luci sante;
ma vostra vita sanza mezzo spira
la somma beninanza, e la innamora
di sè sì che poi sempre la disira.
E quinci puoi argomentare ancora
vostra resurrezion, se tu ripensi
come l'umana carne fessi allora
che li primi parenti intrambo fensi.

The conception of divine creation as an act of benevolence, "free of envy," goes back, of course, to the *Timaeus* (29D), but it became a commonplace of medieval speculation, for example, Boethius, *Cons.* III, metr. 9, 4–6. Whether the primal matter was coeternal with God was a great problem in medieval thought, and Dante had wondered about it at the time of the *Convivio* (IV, i, 8–9).

48. *Par.* XXIX, 13–36:

Non per avere a sè di bene acquisto,
ch'esser non può, ma perchè suo splendore
potesse, risplendendo, dir "Subsisto,"
in sua etternità di tempo fore,
fuor d'ogni altro comprender, come i piaque,
s'aperse in nuovi amor l'etterno amore.
Nè prima quasi torpente si giacque;
chè nè prima nè poscia procedette
lo discorrer di Dio sovra quest'acque.
Forma e materia, congiunte e purette,
usciro ad esser che non avia fallo,
come d'arco tricordo tre saette.
E come in vetro, in ambra od in cristallo
raggio risplende sì, che dal venire
all'esser tutto non è intervallo,
così 'l triforme effetto del suo sire
nell'esser suo raggiò insieme tutto
sanza distinzione in esordire.
Concreato fu ordine e costrutto
alle sustanze; e quelle furon cima
nel mondo in che puro atto fu produtto;
pura potenza tenne la parte ima;
nel mezzo strinse potenza con atto
tal vime, che già mai non si divima.

Cf. *Convivio* III, xiv, 2–8.

49. Clemens Baeumker, *Witelo: Ein Philosoph und Naturforscher des XIII Jahrhunderts*, in *Beiträge zur Geschichte der Philosophie des Mittelalters* (Munster, 1908), 541–542. Busnelli and Vandelli, as usual, argue that Dante is a Thomist (*Il Convivio* [2 v., 2d ed.; 1953–1954], Appendix V, vol. I, 464 ff.). But see Bruno Nardi, "Dante e Pietro d'Abano," in *Saggi di filosofia dantesca* (Milano, 1930), 41–65, and "Note al 'Convivio'" and "appendice: il tomismo di Dante ecc.," in *Nel mondo di Dante* (Roma, 1944); also Martin Baumgartner, "Dante's Stellung zur Philosophie," in *Zweite Vereinschrift d. Görresgesellschaft* (1921), 57–71.

50. St. Thomas denies to the angels any creative role in the making of either corporeal things or souls, but this is not necessarily identical with the orthodoxy of Dante's time. See *Summa theologiae* 1, q. 65 a. 3 and 4; 1, q. 90 a. 3; 1, q. 45 a. 5.

51. On the four coevals see Etienne Gilson, *The History of Christian Philosophy in the Middle Ages* (New York, 1955), 279 ff. Cf. St. Thomas Aquinas, *Summa theologiae* 1, q. 61 a. 2 and 3.

52. *Pur.* XXV, 61 ff. I cite always the translation of J. D. Sinclair (3 v.; New York, 1948) and the text of the Società Dantesca Italiana (Firenze, 1921).

Ma come d'animal divenga fante,
  non vedi tu ancor: quest'è tal punto,
  che più savio di te fè già errante,
sì che per sua dottrina fè disgiunto
  dall'anima il possibile intelletto,
  perchè da lui non vide organo assunto.
Apri alla verità che viene il petto;
  e sappi che, sì tosto come al feto
  l'articular del cerebro è perfetto,
lo motor primo a lui si volge lieto
  sovra tant'arte di natura, e spira
  spirito novo di vertù repleto,
che ciò che trova attivo quivi, tira
  in sua sustanzia, e fassi un'alma sola,
  che vive e sente e sè in sè rigira.

On Averroës' theory see Duhem, *op. cit.*, IV (Paris, 1916), 559 ff. Averroës' possible intellect (or *intellectus materialis*) is frequently confused with the passive intellect of the medieval Aristotelians. It was universally agreed that the latter was mortal and personal, being little more than the *vis aestimativa,* the sensory faculty, which even animals have, of judging danger and the like.

53. *Conv.* IV, xxi, 4–5 (trans. Philip Wicksteed [London, 1903], 330–331, and the text of Busnelli and Vandelli): E però dico che quando l'umano seme cade nel suo recettaculo, cioè ne la matrice, esso porta seco la vertù de l'anima generativa e la vertù del cielo e la vertù de li elementi legati, cioè la complessione; e matura e dispone la materia a la vertù formativa, la quale diede l'anima del generante; e la vertù formativa prepara li organi a la vertù celestiale, che produce de la potenza del seme l'anima in vita. La quale, incontanente produtta, riceve de la

vertù del motore del cielo lo intelletto possibile; lo quale potenzialmente in sè adduce tutte le forme universali secondo che sono nel suo produttore, e tanto meno quanto piu dilungato da la prima Intelligenza è.

54. *Op. cit.*, Appendix X, vol. II, 391 ff.

55. Bruno Nardi, "Sull'origine dell'anima umana," in *Dante e cultura la medievale* (2d ed.; Bari, 1949), 261–283.

56. Nancy Lenkeith, *Dante and the Legend of Rome* (London, 1952), 139.

57. *Summa theologiae* 1, q. 118 a. 3 ad 2.

58. Cf. Gilson, *History*, 224.

59. *Dante e la cultura*, "La conoscenza umana," 116–216, esp. 186 ff.

60. The expression *vertù formativa* is, according to Albertus Magnus, comparable to the image which guides the hand of artists and is impressed on the external matter. It is simply the agent which shapes the embryo and prepares it for the emergence of the vegetative and sensitive souls through the actualizing power of the heavens (cited in Nardi, *Dante e la cultura*, 264–265, with reference to Albertus' *De animal.* XVI, tr. 1, chs. iv, vi–vii, x–xii, xvi; *De anima* I, tr. 2 c. 15; *Meteor* IV, tr. 1 c. 13). Whether *prima intelligenza* could refer to the mover of the lunar sphere is debatable. Among the emanationists such as Alfarabi, Avicenna, and Averroës, the "first intelligence" would move the outermost sphere while the last of the intelligences would be the one responsible for the intellectual soul; cf. Duhem, *op. cit.*, IV, 440–441.

61. *Par.* XIII, 52 ff.:

Ciò che non more e ciò che può morire
non è se non splendor di quella idea
che partorisce, amando, il nostro sire:
chè quella viva luce che sì mea
dal suo lucente, che non si disuna
da lui nè dall'amor ch'a lor s'intrea,
per sua bontate il suo raggiare aduna,
quasi specchiato, in nove sussistenze,
etternalmente rimanendosi una.
Quindi discende all'ultime potenze
giù d'atto, tanto divenendo,
che più non fa che brevi contingenze;
e queste contingenze essere intendo
le cose generate, che produce

con seme e sanza seme il ciel movendo.
La cera di costoro e chi la duce
non sta d'un modo; e però sotto 'l segno
ideale poi più e men traluce. . . .
Se fosse a punto la cera dedutta
e fosse il cielo in sua virtù suprema
la luce del suggel parrebbe tutta;
ma la natura la dà sempre scema,
similmente operando all'artista
c'ha l'abito dell'arte e man che trema.

62. Cf. *De monarchia* II, 2, ll. 11 ff., ed. Edward Moore and Paget Toynbee, *Le opere di Dante Alighieri* (4th ed.; Oxford, 1924): "Sciendum est igitur, quod quemadmodum ars in triplici gradu invenitur, in mente scilicet artificis, in organo, et in materia formata per artem, sic et naturam in triplici gradu possumus intueri. Est enim natura in mente primi motoris, qui Deus est, deinde in coelo tanquam in organo, quo mediante similitudo bonitatis aeternae in fluitantem materiam explicatur." All of nature might be considered God's instrument, or, seen as an autonomous process, the heavenly bodies are the instruments of the intelligences who contemplate and "transmit" the divine archetypes. In a hierarchical universe of this kind what you see depends on which rung of the ladder you are on, that is, an effect may be simultaneously a cause.

63. *Par.* XIII, 79–81:

Però se 'l caldo amor la chiara vista
della prima virtù dispone e segna,
tutta la perfezion quivi s'acquista.

For the created universe as a defective rendering of its archetype cf. Dionysius Areopagita, *De divinis nominibus* II, 5–7; *P.G.*, 3, cols. 644A ff.

64. *Conv.* II, iv, 1–6: Poi ch'è mostrato nel precedente capitolo quale è questo terzo cielo e come in se medesimo è disposto, resta di dimostrare chi sono questi che 'l muovono. E adunque da sapere primamente che li movitori di quelli sono sustanze separate da materia, cioè intelligenze, le quali la volgare gente chiamano Angeli. E di queste creature, sì come de li cieli, diversi diversamente hanno sentito, avvegna che la veritade sia trovata. Furono certi filosofi, de'quali pare essere Aristotile ne la sua Metafisica (avvegna che nel primo di Cielo incidentemente

paia sentire altrimenti) che credettero solamente essere tante queste, quante circulazioni fossero ne li cieli, e non più, dicendo che l'altre sarebbero state etternalmente indarno, sanza operazione; ch'era impossibile, con ciò sia cosa che loro essere sia loro operazione. Altri furono, sì come Plato, uomo eccellentissimo, che puosero non solamente tante Intelligenze quanti sono li movimenti del cielo, ma eziandio quante sono le spezie de le cose (cioè le maniere de le cose): sì come è una spezie tutti li uomini, e un'altra tutto l'oro, e un'altra tutte le larghezze, e così di tutte. E volsero che sì come le Intelligenze de li cieli sono generatrici di quelli, ciascuna del suo, così queste fossero generatrici de l'altre cose ed essempli, ciascuna de la sua spezie; e chiamale Plato "idee" che tanto è a dire quanto forme e nature universali. Li gentili le chiamano Dei e Dee, avvegna che non così filosoficamente intendessero quelle come Plato.

65. Panofsky, *op. cit.*, ch. i.

66. *Inf.* XI, 97 ff.:

"Filosofia," mi disse, "a chi la'ntende
  nota non pur in una sola parte
  come natura lo suo corso prende
da divino intelletto e da sua arte;
  e se tu ben la tua Fisica note,
  tu troverai, non dopo molte carte,
che l'arte vostra quella, quanto pote,
  segue, come 'l maestro fa il discente:
  sì che vostr'arte a Dio quasi e nepote.
Da queste due, se tu rechi a mente
  lo Genesi dal principio, convene
  prender sua vita ed avanzar la gente."

67. *Pur.* XI, 94–99:

Credette Cimabue nella pintura
  tener lo campo, e ora ha Giotto il grido,
  sì che la fama di colui è scura:
così ha tolto l'uno all'altro Guido
  la gloria della lingua; e forse è nato
  chi l'uno e l'altro caccerà del nido.

As Barbi pointed out, the *Purgatorio* is a recreation of the world of art. There are many artists present—Casella, Belaqua, Sordello, Oderisi, Statius, Bonagiunta, Guinizelli, Arnaut Daniel—and there are many discourses on art with Virgil. It is here that Dante gets "an intellectual understanding of poetry" (Michele Barbi, *Life of Dante*, trans. G. P. Ruggiers [Berkeley, 1954], 78)

68. Creation metaphor applied to poetry seems first to appear in Ficino's circle. See M. H. Abrams, *The Mirror and the Lamp* (New York, 1953), 272 ff.

69. De Bruyne, *op. cit.*, II, 298 and *passim.* So thinks Alain de Lille on the theory, but for evidence that his practice implies a quite different poetic see R. H. Green, "Alan of Lille's *De Planctu Naturae*," *Speculum*, XXXI (1956), 649–674.

70. De Bruyne, *op. cit.*, 278 ff.

71. *Par.* X, 1 ff.:

> Guardando nel suo Figlio con l'Amore
> che l'uno e l'altro etternalmente spira,
> lo primo ed ineffabile Valore,
> quanto per mente e per loco si gira
> con tant' ordine fè, ch'esser non puote
> sanza gustar di lui chi ciò rimira.
> Leva dunque, lettore, all'alte ruote
> meco la vista, dritto a quella parte
> dove l'un moto e l'altro si percuote;
> e lì comincia a vagheggiar nell'arte
> di quel maestro che dentro a sè l'ama,
> tanto che mai da lei occhio non parte.

72. *Par.* XXVII, 88 ff.:

> La mente innamorata, che donnea
> con la mia donna sempre, di ridure
> ad essa li occhi più che mai ardea:
> e se natura o arte fè pasture
> da pigliare occhi, per aver la mente,
> in carne umana o nelle sue pitture,
> tutte adunate, parebber niente
> ver lo piacer divin che mi refulse,
> quando mi volsi al suo viso ridente.

Cf. *Paradiso* XXVIII, 11: "riguardando ne'belli occhi onde a pigliarmi fece Amor la corda" (gazing into the fair eyes of which love made the noose to capture me). Even the architecture of Hell, specifically Malebolge, reveals the art of the supreme wisdom, *Inferno* XIX, 10 ff.

Notes to Chapter V

V: Dante and Epicurus: The Making of a Type

1. See H. A. Wolfson, *The Philosophy of the Church Fathers*, I (Cambridge, Mass., 1956), ch. ii, 24 ff., for a study of rabbinical, Philonic, and patristic allegory, and Beryl Smalley, *The Study of the Bible in the Middle Ages* (2d ed.; Oxford, 1952).

2. Erich Auerbach, "Figura," *Archivum Romanicum*, XXII (1938), 436–489, reprinted with minor changes in *Neue Dantestudien* (Istanbul, 1944). See also his "Typological Symbolism in Medieval Literature," *Yale French Studies*, IX (1952), 3–10, and the more extensive treatment in *Typologische Motive in der Mittelalterlichen Literatur* (Krefeld, 1953). My description of figuralism draws heavily on these works of Auerbach's.

3. Auerbach, "Figura," 454 ff.

4. See Auerbach, "Figura," 466–468, and Rudolf Bultmann, *History and Eschatology* (Edinburgh, 1957), for a survey of the whole field of Christian historiography.

5. For a brief survey of the kinds of scriptural and secular allegory in the Middle Ages, see Mazzeo, "Dante's Conception of Poetic Expression," in *Structure and Thought in the Paradiso* (Ithaca, N.Y., 1958).

6. *De civitate Dei* XV, 27; X, 6, and XVIII, 11; XVII, 6; XVI, 31, and XVII, 3. Cf. Auerbach, "Figura," 456 ff.

7. *De doctrina Christiana* III, 12, 20; *P.L.*, 34, col. 73.

8. *De doc. Ch.* III, 12, 20; *P.L.*, 34, col. 73: non solum historice et proprie, sed etiam figurate et prophetice.

9. Bultmann, *History and Eschatology*, 148.

10. *Ibid.*, 147–149; also the theses of the opening chapter of Auerbach's great book, *Mimesis*, trans. W. R. Trask (Princeton, 1953).

11. Auerbach, "Figura," 479 ff.

12. *Ibid.*, 482 ff.

13. See Auerbach, "Figurative Texts Illustrating Certain Passages of Dante's *Commedia*," *Speculum*, XXI (1946), 474–489. Cf. also L. R. Rossi, "Dante and the Poetic Tradition of Benvenuto da Imola," *Italica*, XXXII (1955), 215–223, esp. p. 223 where the author refers to passages from Benvenuto in which he makes typological correspondences between Dante and Jason, Glaucus, Aeneas, and Elisha.

14. See Bruno Nardi, *Saggi di filosofia dantesca* (Milano, 1930), ch. i, "La dottrina delle macchie lunari del secondo canto del Paradiso."

15. Nardi, *Dante e la cultura medievale* (2d ed.; Bari, 1949), ch. vi, "Il linguaggio."

16. See C. S. Singleton, *Dante Studies I—Commedia: Elements of Structure* (Cambridge, Mass., 1954), Appendix, "The Two Kinds of Allegory," and Mazzeo, as cited in note 5 above.

17. See, for example, Nardi's essay in *Saggi*, ch. x, "Tre pretese fasi del pensiero politico di Dante."

18. I refer the reader for guidance on this problem to Umberto Cosmo's *Handbook to Dante Studies*, trans. David Moore (New York, n.d.).

19. *Il Convivio*, ed. Busnelli and Vandelli (2 v., 2d ed.; Firenze, 1953–1954), Appendix VI, vol. I, 466 ff., "Sopra la tolleranza dottrinale di Dante"; *Inf*. X, 14–16 ("Suo cimitero da questa parte hanno / con Epicuro tutt' i suoi seguaci, / che l'anima col corpo morto fanno"). All citations from the *Comedy* are from the text of the Società Dantesca Italiana, *Le opere di Dante Alighieri* (Firenze, 1921).

20. In addition to Nardi's works already cited see *Nel mondo di Dante* (Roma, 1944).

21. Etienne Gilson, *Dante et la philosophie* (Paris, 1939); Nancy Lenkeith, *Dante and the Legend of Rome* (London, 1952).

22. See G. Fraccaroli, *Il cerchio degli eresiarchi* (Modena, 1891); Felice Tocco, *Quel che non c'è nella Divina Commedia o Dante e l'eresia* (Bologna, 1899); G. Volpe, *Movimenti religiosi e sette ereticali nella società medievale italiana* (Firenze, 1926); Edward Moore, *Studies in Dante* (2d ser.; Oxford, 1899). A more recent work which briefly summarizes the literature on this question is A. De Salvio, *Dante and Heresy* (Boston, 1936).

23. *Conv.* III, xiv, 14–15: Onde, sì come per lei molto di quello si vede per ragione, e par consequente essere per ragione, che sanza lei pare maraviglia, così per lei si crede [ch'] ogni miracolo in più alto intelletto puote avere ragione, e per consequente può essere. Onde la nostra buona fede ha sua origine; da la quale viene la speranza, de lo proveduto desiderare; e per quella nasce l'operazione de la caritade. Per le quali tre virtudi si sale a filosofare a quelle Atene celestiali, dove gli Stoici e Peripatetici e Epicurii, per la l[u]ce de la veritade etterna, in uno volere concordevolemente concorrono.

All references to the *Convivio* are to the Busnelli-Vandelli edition already cited. I also always cite the translation of Philip H. Wickstead,

The Convivio of Dante Alighieri (Temple Classics; London, 1903). The passage here quoted is on p. 214.

24. Busnelli and Vandelli, *op. cit.*, commentary on 430–431; Lenkeith, *op. cit.*, 143 ff.

25. In the *Convivio*, Dante both distinguished and identified philosophy and theology. The Wisdom which loved Solomon also loved the true philosopher (III, xiv, 12). God sees this most noble of all things, philosophy, both here below and in Himself who has it perfectly (III, xii, esp. 11 ff.). The various heavens, however, correspond to the various sciences—for example, the starry sphere to both physics and metaphysics, the *primum mobile* to ethics, and the empyrean to theology (II, xii and xiv)—and philosophy fixes its vision most firmly on metaphysics or the "starry sphere" (III, xi, 10). Cf. Nardi, *Dante e la cultura,* 204 ff., and Lenkeith, *op. cit.*, 148 ff. Lenkeith argues that Dante maintains that divine grace is innate in human nature, a product of natural conditions, and that eternal beatitude is simply the culmination of earthly happiness.

26. *Conv.* IV, vi, 9–13: Furono dunque filosofi molto antichi, de li quali primo e principe fu Zenone, che videro e credettero questo fine de la vita umana essere solamente la rigida onestade; cioè rigidamente, sanza respetto alcuno, la verità e la giustizia seguire, di nulla mostrare dolore, di nulla mostrare allegrezza, di nulla passione avere sentore. E diffiniro così questo onesto: "quello che, sanza utilitade e sanza frutto, per se di ragione è da laudare." E costoro e la loro setta chiamati furono Stoici, e fu di loro quello glorioso Catone di cui non fui di sopra oso di parlare. Altri filosofi furono, che videro e credettero altro che costoro; e di questi fu primo e principe uno filosofo che fu chiamato Epicuro; chè, veggendo che ciascuno animale, tosto che nato è, quasi da natura dirizzato nel debito fine, che fugge dolore e domanda allegrezza, quelli disse questo nostro fine essere voluptade (non dico "voluntade," ma scrivola per P), cioè diletto sanza dolore. E però [che] tra 'l diletto e lo dolore non ponea mezzo alcuno, dicea che "voluptade" non era altro che "non dolore," si come pare Tullio recitare nel primo di *Fine di Bene*. E di questi, che da Epicuro sono Epicurei nominati, fu Torquato, nobile romano, disceso del sangue del glorioso Torquato del quale feci menzione di sopra. (Wicksteed, *op. cit.*, 254, for the translation.)

27. *Conv.* IV, xxii, 4–5: Lasciando dunque stare l'oppinione che di

quello [i.e., the final good] ebbe Epicuro filosofo, e di quello ebbe Zenone, venire intendo sommariamente a la verace oppinione d'Aristotile e de li altri Peripatetici. Sì come detto è di sopra, de la divina bontade, in noi seminata e infusa dal principio de la nostra generazione, nasce un rampollo, che li Greci chiamono "hormen," cioè appetito d'animo naturale. (Cf. *De finibus*, V, vi, 17; Wicksteed, *op. cit.*, 355, for the translation.)

28. Dante was thoroughly acquainted with Boethius' *Consolation of Philosophy* at the time of writing the *Convivio*, but he does not seem to have shared Boethius' contempt for the Stoic and Epicurean herd (*Cons.* I, 3).

29. "Tanto discenderebbe in quella de la deitade, che quasi sarebbe un altro Iddio incarnato. E quasi questo è tutto ciò che per via naturale dicere si puote." On the phrase *quasi sarebbe un altro Iddio incarnato* Busnelli and Vandelli report a passage from Albertus Magnus (*De somno et vigilia* 3 tr. 1 c. 6) in an appendix "Avicenna, Algazel, Platone e Pittagora: loro opinioni intorno alla nobilità delle anime" (*op. cit.*, II, 388 ff.). The passage in question paraphrases the opinions of Avicenna and Algazel on the degree of nobility of souls, a nobility that is higher according to the degree in which such souls participate in the universal, impersonal active intellect. The souls that participate in the highest degree in the active intellect are conformed to pure intelligence and receive knowledge from it directly, even knowledge of things which are about to happen. Such a kind of soul which knows all things through itself (*omnia scit per seipsum*) is, in the view of Avicenna and Algazel, *quasi Deus incarnatus.*

Dante may well have been inspired by the passage. However, the use of the phrase is in a different context, for Dante is not expounding a theory of psychology, but is describing those natural conditions which must obtain for the conception of a human being who is so perfect that he is almost another incarnate God. The influence of Avicenna and Algazel on Dante, through Albertus Magnus, and perhaps independently, remains to be investigated. In view of the presumed Neopelagian character of the *Convivio*, Gilson's remark on Avicenna is instructive: "Avicenna was destined to remain for the Christian theologians of the middle ages, both a great help and a perilous temptation. His whole system was a striking example of the possibility of a *natural* and philosophical explanation of the world crowned by a no less natural and philosophical doctrine of salvation" (*History of Christian Philosophy in the Middle Ages* [New York, 1955], 188). I believe that a study of Avicenna and Dante's *Convivio* would have important results for our understanding of the latter. Cf., for example, Gilson's remark (*op. cit.*, 215) on Avicenna's conception of the continuity between philosophy in this life and in the hereafter: "Those who begin to philosophize during the present life do not cease to seek for knowledge after the death of their bodies. They then continue to do what they have done up to then, only they do it much better than was possible for them while they were still in their bodies." Does this perhaps provide a better gloss than any we now have on the passage in which Dante speaks of the three great schools of antiquity rising to philosophize in "that celestial Athens"?

30. *Conv.* IV, xxii, 12: Per molta corr[e]zione e cultura; chè là dove questo seme dal principio non cade, si puote inducere [n]el suo processo, sì che perviene a questo frutto; ed è uno modo quasi insetare l'altrui natura sopra diversa radice. E però nullo e che possa essere scusato; che se da sua naturale radice uomo non ha questa sementa, ben la puote avere per via d'insetazione. (Wicksteed, *op. cit.*, 337–338, for the translation.)

31. *Conv.* IV, xxii, 13–17: Veramente di questi usi l'uno è più pieno di beatitudine che l'altro; sì come è speculativo, lo quale sanza mistura alcuna è uso de la nostra nobilissima parte, la quale, per lo radicale amore che detto è, massimamente è amabile, sì com' è lo 'ntelletto. E questa parte in questa vita perfettamente lo suo uso avere non puote— lo quale [è ved]ere [in s]è Iddio, ch'è sommo intelligibile—, se non in quanto considera lui e mira lui per li suoi effetti. E che noi domandiamo questa beatitudine per somma, e non altra, cioè quella de la vita attiva, n'ammaestra lo Vangelio di Marco, se bene quello volemo guardare. Dice Marco che Maria Maddelena e Maria Iacobi e Maria Salomè andaro per trovare lo Salvatore al monimento, e quello non trovaro; ma trovaro uno giovane vestito di bianco che disse loro: "Voi domandate lo Salvatore, e io vi dico che non è qui; e però non abbiate temenza, ma ite, e dite a li discepoli suoi e a Piero che elli li precederà in Galilea; e quivi lo vedrete, sì come vi disse." Per queste tre donne si possono intendere le tre sette de la vita attiva, cioè li Epicurei, li Stoici e li Peripatetici, che vanno al monimento, cioè al mondo presente che è recettaculo di corruttibili cose, e domandono lo Salvatore,

cioè la beatitudine, e non la truovano; ma uno giovane in bianchi vestimenti, lo quale, secondo la testimonianza di Matteo e anche de li altri, era angelo di Dio. E però Matteo disse: "L'angelo di Dio discesse di cielo, e vegnendo volse la pietra e sedea sopra essa. E 'l suo aspetto era come fulgore, e le sue vestimenta erano come neve." (Wicksteed, *op. cit.*, 338–339, for the translation.)

32. *Conv.* II, viii, 8: Dico che intra tutte le bestialitadi quella è stoltissima, vilissima e dannosissima, chi crede dopo questa vita non essere altra vita.

33. Cicero, *Tusculan Disputations*, ed. and trans. J. E. King (Loeb Classical Library; London, 1927), I, xxxi, 77.

34. Cicero's opinion that the Peripatetics taught that moral virtue is superior to intellectual excellence and that virtue is the perfection of reason—the exact opposite of what Aristotle said—was imposed on the Peripatetics of his time by Antiochus under Stoic influence. See *De finibus bonorum et malorum*, ed. and trans. H. Rackham (Loeb Classical Library; London, 1914), V, xiii, 38; cf. V, xiv, 38.

35. *De finibus* V, ix, 24 ff. Cicero tends in his discussion of the chief good to equate the academic and Peripatetic views and even to argue that the Stoics really agree with both these schools (*De finibus* V, viii, 21 ff.).

36. *De finibus* V, ix, 24.

37. *De finibus* II, xxv, 80–81.

38. *De finibus* II, ix, 28.

39. *De finibus* II, X, 32.

40. *De finibus* II, xxxi, 100.

41. J. Philippe, "Lucrèce dans la théologie chrétienne du IIIe au XIIIe siècle et spécialement dans les écoles carolingiennes," *Revue de l'histoire des religions* (Annales du musée Guimet; Paris, 1895 and 1896), XXXII (1895), 284–302; XXXIII (1896), 19–36 and 125–162.

42. Philippe, *op. cit.*, XXXIII, 154 ff. Among those "who make the soul die with the body" Dante places the Ghibellines Farinata, Frederick II, and Cardinal Ottaviano degli Ubaldini and also the Guelf Cavalcante (*Inf.* X).

43. Isidori Hispalensis episcopi, *Etymologiarum sive originum, libri XX*, ed. W. M. Lindsay (2 v.; Oxford, 1911), Lib. VIII, vi, "De philosophis gentium," 6–8.

44. *Etymol.* VIII, vi, 8–11.

45. *Etymol.* VIII, vi, 15–17. The Peripatetics believed in the immortality of part of the soul, although most of it, in their view, perished (*ibid.*, 13).

46. *Etymol.* VIII, vi, 18, 19–20.

47. *Etymol.* VIII, vi, 20–23.

48. *Etymol.* VIII, iii, 1–3. The same arguments are repeated in Rabanus Maurus, *De universo*, Lib. XV, i, "De philosophis"; *P.L.*, 3, cols. 415 ff.

49. De Salvio, *op. cit.*, 3 ff., who reviews the literature on the question.

50. There is one other reference to Epicurus in Dante's work. In *De monarchia* (II, 5, 83 ff., ed. Edward Moore and Paget Toynbee in *Le opere di Dante Alighieri* [4th ed.; Oxford, 1924]), he gives Cincinnatus as an example of the public spirit of the Romans and cites a passage from *De finibus* about him, locating it by saying that it occurs where Cicero argues against Epicurus. The *De monarchia* leans heavily on Cicero, especially *De officiis* and *De finibus.* It is possible that a careful study of Ciceronian references and citations in the works of Dante and of his attitude toward them would reveal a pattern of changing thought which would help us to fix a more accurate date for *De monarchia*, concerning which there has been such wide disagreement.

51. The central passage from this canto is the following:

Se fosse a punto la cera dedutta,
   e fosse il cielo in sua virtù suprema,
   la luce del suggel parebbe tutta;
ma la natura la dà sempre scema,
   similmente operando all'artista,
   ch'ha l'abito dell'arte e man che trema.
Però se 'l caldo amor [the Holy Ghost] la chiara vista
   della prima virtù dispone e segna,
   tutta la perfezion quivi s'acquista.
Così fu fatta già la terra degna
   di tutta l'animal perfezione;
   così fu fatta la Vergine pregna.

Notes to Appendix

Appendix: The "Sirens" of Purgatorio *XXXI, 45*

1. *Pur.* XXXI, 43–60. I cite the translation of J. D. Sinclair, *The Divine Comedy* (3 v.; New York, 1948), and the text of the Società Dantesca Italiana (Firenze, 1921).

2. The reader must be referred to the studies of C. S. Singleton for the validation of this approach. See *An Essay on the Vita Nuova* (Cambridge, Mass., 1949), *Dante Studies I* (Cambridge, 1954), and "Virgil Recognizes Beatrice," *Seventy-fourth Report of the Dante Society* (Cambridge, 1956), 29–38.

3. *Dante's Divina Commedia*, ed. C. H. Grandgent (rev. ed.; New York, 1933), 613–614.

4. See Nancy Lenkeith, *Dante and the Legend of Rome* (London, 1952), ch. iv, and Umberto Cosmo, *Handbook to Dante Studies*, trans. David Moore (New York, n.d.), for a guide to the literature on this subject, especially the studies of Bruno Nardi.

5. Grandgent, *op. cit.*, 612. *Consolatio philosophiae* I, pr. 1, 11, 26 ff., esp. 39–41: Sed abite potius, Sirenes usque in exilium dulces, meisque eum Musis curandum relinquite.

6. Isidori, *Etymologiarum*, ed. W. M. Lindsay (2 v.; Oxford, 1911), Liber XI, xiv, 30–31: Sirenas tres fingunt fuisse ex parte virgines, ex parte volucres, habentes alas et ungulas: quarum una voce, alterea tibiis, tertia lyra canebant. Quae inlectos navigantes sub cantu in naufragium trahebant. Secundum veritatem autem meretrices fuerunt, quae transeuntes quoniam deducebant ad egestatem, his fictae sunt inferre naufragia.

7. See the index references in *Il Convivio*, ed. G. Busnelli and G. Vandelli (2 v., 2d ed.; Firenze, 1953–1954).

8. Bruno Nardi, *Dante e la cultura medievale* (Bari, 1949), ch. iv, "La tragedia d'Ulisse," 153–164.

9. Cicero, *De finibus bonorum et malorum*, ed. and trans. H. Rackham (Loeb Classical Library; London, 1914), V, xviii–xix, 48–50.

10. In this chapter Dante seems to identify the wisdom available to the pagan philosophers with the Christian logos. On this interpretation and its bearings on a Neopelagian interpretation of the *Convivio* see Lenkeith, *op. cit.*, esp. 142–143.

Index

Index

Index

Index

Index